CONGRESS AND THE POLITICS OF EMERGING RIGHTS

edited by

COLTON C. CAMPBELL
and
JOHN F. STACK, JR.

ROWMAN & LITTLEFIELD PUBLISHERS, INC.
Lanham • Boulder • New York • Oxford

ROWMAN & LITTLEFIELD PUBLISHERS, INC.

Published in the United States of America
by Rowman & Littlefield Publishers, Inc.
4720 Boston Way, Lanham, Maryland 20706
www.rowmanlittlefield.com

12 Hid's Copse Road, Cumnor Hill, Oxford OX2 9JJ, England

British Library Cataloguing in Publication Information Available

Library of Congress Cataloging-in-Publication Data

Congress and the politics of emerging rights/edited by Colton C. Campbell and John F.
Stack, Jr.
   p. cm.
   Includes bibliographical references and index.
   ISBN 0-7425-1646-6 (alk. paper) —ISBN 0-7425-1647-4 (pbk.: alk. paper)
   1. Civil rights—United States. 2. United States Congress. 3. Political questions and
judicial power—United States. 4. Law and politics. I. Campbell, Colton C., 1965- II.
Stack, John F.

KF4749 .C644 2002
323'.0973—dc21

                                                                    2001041929
Printed in the United States of America

⊗™ The paper used in this publication meets the minimum requirements of
American National Standard for Information Sciences—Permanence of Paper for
Printed Library Materials, ANSI/NISO Z39.48-1992.

Congress and the Politics of Emerging Rights

Contents

vii

Tables

Tables

Introduction

COLTON C. CAMPBELL AND JOHN F. STACK, JR.

The language of rights has formed much of the moral, legal, institutional, and political vocabulary of our nation (Jones 1994). But what are *rights* and how do we conceive them? Are they something inherently enjoyed, held in virtue (White 1984) or are they legally given by someone or some institution with the right, authority, or power to bestow them (Wellman 1985; Lomasky 1987)? Are rights accorded when, for some reason, a collective goal is not sufficient justification for denial or not ample justification for imposing loss or injury (Dworkin 1977)? One could enter here into a long and protracted discussion of all the issues involved in a theory of rights, such as origins, conditions, limits, and so on. But for the purpose of this work, how are rights, especially the emergence of new rights, recognized and protected by the branch of government closest to the people, Congress?

When average Americans think of rights, they generally conceive written guarantees (Lowi and Ginsberg 2000), like the Bill of Rights, the first ten amendments to the Constitution that provide a framework for the defense and protection of the individual. But the drafters of the Bill of Rights were not thinking about issues such as reproductive rights, gay rights, the right to die, or many other emerging rights. The transformation of American society in terms of technology from cars (police searches), to telephones (wiretaps), to e-mail (privacy) has created new rights issues. The Internet, for example, is a powerful new medium creating revolutionary challenges and claims for our political system, drawing strong comparisons to the Guttenberg Press as a prodigious tool for the dissemination of information (*Senate Committee on Rules and Administration*

1

2000). Changing marriage patterns, urban violence, and gender equality also have produced a panoply of rights never envisioned by the Framers. In short, provisions of the Constitution and the Bill of Rights have been interpreted over time to protect a variety of rights not explicitly stated (O'Connor and Sabato 2000).

Rights issues present complex problems for Congress and its members. While lawmakers are frequently called on to balance competing interests, it generally falls to the judiciary to balance those interests. Depending on the composition of the Supreme Court and the political wants and needs of the times, the fulcrum may move away or toward the power of Congress to limit or expand rights. The principal aim of this volume is to explore the various dimensions of emerging rights not explicitly contained in the Constitution and the Bill of Rights from both congressional and judicial perspectives. Such selected rights illustrate both personal and institutional challenges, especially under conditions of divided government and increased levels of partisanship. As the Supreme Court demonstrated in *Bush v. Gore* (2000), even apparently settled ways of examining voting rights, deference to state sovereignty, and judicial restraint may result in unexpected interpretations with significant political consequences.

As the 1879 cartoon cover of this volume suggests, the assertion of rights is never a static process. How rights are defined and who defines them are the ongoing products of history, conflict, and culture. Certainly, the institutional setting of American politics, be it the great federal divide (between states and the national government) or the struggle for authority in lawmaking between Congress and the judiciary, gives particular meaning to how these rights are conceptualized.

CONGRESS AND RIGHTS

As it is the primary function of the legislative branch to act on behalf of the very majority from which the individual may need protection, congressional action and personal rights often clash. Congress often approaches emerging rights problems in a way not much different from the general public's struggle to understand and embrace the same issues. Members might be wary of public opinion, or do not see the concern as particularly pressing, leaving it to sympathetic advocates to take the lead legislatively. Measures initially addressing these issues tend to be introduced toward the end of a legislative session to enable Congress to adjourn without passing or even debating them, or in nonelection years to minimize expected voter backlash. When Congress does respond, it might engage in symbolic acts—that is, expressing an attitude of toleration but endorsing no proactive policies, or prescribing policy goals but neglecting to follow through on them (Campbell and Davidson 2000). Eventually, as rights become more widely and openly discussed, the issues move toward a more conspicuous place in the legislative session, and a majority in Congress concedes the legitimacy of the claims. Lyndon B. Johnson likened this slow-to-respond aspect of the legislative process to a bottle of bourbon: "If you take a glass at a time, it's fine," he said. "But if you drink the whole bottle in one evening, you have troubles" (quoted in Cassata 1995).

Congressional rights policymaking has experienced many different facets. Historically, rights were first extended to a minority of white propertied males. By the early part of the twentieth century legislative action turned to minor-minority rights (Nye 1995). Of particular significance was the congressional extension of statutory rights from the traditional New Deal constituencies of interest-group pluralism (farmers, veterans, organized labor, homeowners, and pensioners) to the politically mobilized new constituencies making civil rights claims (Graham 1994). Such rights included equal freedom to vote and to participate in the political process; equal access to the courts and to the guardianship of the judicial process, to schools and other public facilities and accommodations; and equal opportunities for employment and advancement and fair housing.

By the 1970s, congressional attention to traditional civil rights concern waned, the focus shifting to rights-based legislative programs for groups other than racial minorities. In response to the political mobilization of youthful Americans, for example, Congress lowered the voting age to eighteen by statute, and in 1972 it constitutionalized the eighteen-year-old franchise by approving the Twenty-sixth Amendment. Legislators also created a right to special assistance for people with disabilities, especially those with physical disabilities, requiring large expenditures by state and local governments, employers, and educational institutions to provide more equal access for persons with disabilities in education, jobs, transportation, and housing. During this period Congress in its regular authorizations and appropriations for federal departments and programs outlined detailed requirements for policies concerning race, sex, disability, and selected ethnicity. Members of the 93d Congress (1973–75), for example, increased appropriations for an Expanded Office of Bilingual Education and Minority Language Affairs (OBEMLA) (Graham 1994). Congress also created the minority set-aside program in the Public Works Employment Act of 1977, requiring that 10 percent of the Commerce Department grants be allocated to business enterprises controlled by African Americans, Hispanics, Asian Americans, Native Americans, and Aleuts. And, circumventing the committee system, lawmakers enacted the first statute creating a racial classification (Graham 1994).

As Congress enters its third century, and as rights are more broadly conceived, new policy areas are transforming rights in the legislative arena. Problems of endemic violence against women, expanded privacy concerns based on technological innovation, changing societal institutions like same-sex marriage, the reinvigorated rights of states, and the rights of lawmakers themselves are all part of the shifting landscape of American politics.

Politically, decades of entrenched partisan division have cultivated a propensity for Democrats and Republicans in Congress to align themselves with their own interest group claimants (Ginsberg, Mebane, and Shefter 1995), to form distinct issue networks (Heclo 1978; Thurber 1991), and to protect and advance their interests and rights. Forty successive years of Democratic direction of Congress laid the foundation for increasingly expansive and liberal interpretations of rights.

But the Republican takeover of Congress, beginning with the 104th Congress (1995–97) constituted a not-so-quiet reversal of rights policy favored under Democratic rule (Campbell and Davidson 1998), dramatically altering which policy issues were pushed to the top and how such issues were processed (Thurber 1995). Issues once hidden or subordinated suddenly tumbled from the closet.

Like the Democrats who preceded them, the Republican leadership embraced organizations consistent with and committed to common objectives, adopting rules and practices that had the effect of enhancing the fortunes of certain special interests and issues and weakening the influence of others (Campbell and Davidson 1998). These special interests—some of which were previously excluded from the policymaking process or relegated to working politically with Democratic leaders whose policy interests they did not share—were among the prime political beneficiaries of the GOP revolution of 1994. Early on, they were privy to the deliberations of the Republican leadership; they worked with member and staff task forces drafting and developing legislation; and they were invited to testify and participate in the markup of legislation. Reciprocally, these interest groups acknowledged that their work for the Republicans was prompted by their commitment to the party's conservative agenda.

Concurrently, the Supreme Court has exceeded Congress in safekeeping various individual rights. In requiring states to respect individual rights such as free speech, personal privacy, and various principles of fairness, for example, the Court has relied on the Fourteenth Amendment's due process clause. In prohibiting nearly all forms of race discrimination and most forms of sex discrimination, the Court has relied on the Equal Protection Clause. Ironically, when the Fourteenth Amendment was enacted in 1868, it was expected that Congress, not the Supreme Court, would play the principal enforcement role. Barely a decade earlier, in 1856, the Court, in *Dred Scott v. Sandford*, invalidated the Missouri Compromise on the ground that Congress lacked constitutional authority to confer citizenship on African Americans. With this experience in mind, the

Reconstruction-era Republicans who proposed the Fourteenth Amendment did not trust the judiciary to protect the rights of then-newly freed slaves. In the past decade, however, the Rehnquist bare majority has mandated its own narrow conception of the rights protected by the Fourteenth Amendment, rejecting Congress's broader one.

THE ORGANIZATION OF THE BOOK

The contributing authors consider the emergence of new rights from both congressional and judicial viewpoints. The first chapter explores the consequences of the Supreme Court's decision in *United States v. Morrison* (2000), which declared the federal Violence Against Women Act of 1994 unconstitutional on the grounds that Congress had exceeded its authority under the Commerce Clause to exercise its police power. *Morrison* continued a pattern that began in *United States v. Lopez* (1995), in which the Court invalidated a federal gun possession law for similar reasons. In between, the Court, in *Printz v. United States (1997)*, struck down the 1993 Brady Bill, another gun-control measure, ruling that Congress had exceeded its limits under the Tenth Amendment to regulate matters properly belonging to the states. Together, these three decisions suggest that the current Court is serious about limiting the ability of Congress to regulate various social matters under its police power. Since the late 1930s, when the Supreme Court endorsed the New Deal legislative agenda of President Franklin D. Roosevelt, Congress had enjoyed nearly unchecked authority to use the commerce clause as an instrument of social reform. Perhaps the most far-reaching use of congressional police power came in 1964, when Congress, relying on the commerce clause, enacted the nation's most extensive civil rights law since Reconstruction. In enacting both the gun possession law invalidated in *Lopez* and the Violence Against Women Act (VAWA), Congress believed it was following the example of the Civil Rights Act of 1964. Gregg Ivers and David Kaib ask whether or not *Morrison* calls into question the power of Congress to regulate social policy under the Commerce Clause, or simply represents new limits on the reach of congressional authority in this area.

In chapter 2, David O'Brien suggests that legislation frequently has unanticipated consequences because statutes generally authorize interpretation and implementation by federal agencies, which in turn invites litigation and judicial rulings that may expand or contract the application of the law in ways unforeseen by Congress. Title VII of the Civil Rights Act of 1964 is a case in point, illustrating the unanticipated and occasionally ironic consequences of Congress legislating on rights. The title forbids discrimination in employment on the basis of race, color, national origin, religion, and sex. It also authorizes the Equal

Employment Opportunity Commission (EEOC) to enforce its provisions. During the following decades, however, Title VII was incrementally interpreted to apply not only to discrimination in the hiring, promoting, and firing of employees, but also to sexual harassment, including same-sex harassment in the workplace. That expansion of Title VII was not merely unanticipated but deeply ironic, because sex was included, along with race, national origin, and religion, as an amendment, introduced by Representative Howard Smith (D-Va.) in order to defeat the passage of the Civil Rights Act of 1964. In its first section, this chapter examines the legislative history and congressional politics of the enactment of Title VII. The second section of the chapter turns to the incremental expansion of the scope of Title VII by the EEOC and the lower federal courts in the 1970s and early 1980s, which led to the U.S. Supreme Court's rulings on sexual harassment in the late 1980s and 1990s.

There is no mention of a right to privacy in either the main body of the Constitution or the Bill of Rights. This right is a judicially created right, carved from the implications of several amendments, including the First, Third, Fifth, and Fourteenth Amendments. Beginning in the 1960s public and congressional concerns about the collection and uses of personal information were defined in terms of privacy invasions, and policy solutions were framed in terms of giving individuals "rights" with respect to that information. This definition elicited debates about balancing individual rights against competing governmental interests, including efficiency and law enforcement. Although the "privacy invasion" definition of the problem proved quite compelling, the "rights"-based solution did not provide a substantial platform on which Congress could easily fashion safeguards. Today, Congress and the Court are grappling with the scope of privacy and the Internet. According to Priscilla Regan in chapter 3, as Congress considers policy solutions for online privacy problems, solutions are being framed both in terms of rights (e.g., Electronic Privacy Bill of Rights Act), and in terms of consumer protection (e.g., Consumer Internet Privacy Protection Act). Chapter 3 compares the "rights" solutions and the "consumer protection" solutions to determine how this informs an understanding of Congress's ability to define and accommodate protections for citizens that are not covered by the Constitution.

Chapter 4 looks at how in the waning days of the 104th Congress (1995–97), the House of Representatives was filled with heated exchanges over an unusual foray into an area of domestic law typically left to the states. The issue of same-sex marriages came to Capitol Hill following a legal challenge in Hawaii brought by three gay couples suing for the right to marry. Fearing that actions of one state ruling could effectively force all states to recognize same-sex marriages, Republican lawmakers crafted the Defense of Marriage Act (DOMA) legislation to thwart that possibility. During the debate on the defense of marriage, a second measure—the Employment Non-Discrimination Act (ENDA)—was work-ing its way through the Senate. ENDA was aimed at banning most bias against gays and lesbians on the job. Nicol Rae illustrates how the new institutional arrangements on Capitol Hill forced gay rights organizations to bargain more centrally with party leadership and to build new relationships, because many tra-ditional allies were deposed as heads of relevant committees or subcommittees.

Chapter 5 examines how the new judicial activism of the High Bench under-scores the fluidity of rights in the legislative arena. In recent years the Supreme Court has defined new, unexpected rights for states. In a series of landmark deci-sions, reinvigorating the Tenth Amendment and substantially defining the Eleventh Amendment, the Rehnquist majority is in the process of redefining tra-ditional federal-state relations as well as redefining long-established rights created under the Fourteenth Amendment's Equal Protection Clause and voting rights. The Supreme Court has personified states, drawing strong analogies between state sovereign immunity and individual rights. Thus, not only do states seem to have rights, they also apparently have human emotions.

Within Congress, rights are equated to the minority's use of restrictive pro-cedures to divide, thwart, or obstruct majoritarian rule (Binder 1997; Dion 1997). But what of the institution's rights? In chapter 6 Rebecca Mae Salokar explores the role of lawyers assigned to defend the interests of Congress in court. Established in the late 1970s, the General Counsel of the House of Representatives and the Senate Legal Counsel are responsible for providing advice to representatives and senators in connection with their legislative roles; for protecting the special rights afforded to members of Congress under Article I of the U.S. Constitution; and for defending the interests of Congress as an institution in litigation where the executive branch cannot or will not provide representation. That the offices have survived the various transitions in leader-ship in both the House and the Senate speaks to the success of these lawyers in negotiating the partisan halls and committee rooms of Capitol Hill. Their focus on the institution's interests when defending members' rights and their vigorous defense of the constitutional powers delegated to the legislative branch have made these attorneys an important fixture in the congressional support structure.

The concluding chapter looks at the rights protected by the U.S. Constitution, including those that have been judicially and legislatively created, in contrast to those recognized in the larger world. The U.S. Constitution is an eighteenth-century creation, Mary Volcansek argues, and reflects the liberal val-ues of that era, but has been modernized, particularly during the last half of the twentieth century, by Congress and the Supreme Court. Its vintage and the American culture mark the U.S. perspective as distinct from that of many other parts of the globe. Volcansek begins with the post–World War II UN statement of universal human rights as a template and then contrasts them to those rights enshrined and judicially protected in Europe, Africa, and Latin America. The so-called American exceptionalism can be viewed more clearly through a comparative lens.

ACKNOWLEDGMENTS

As with any collaborative enterprise, this volume would not be possible without the cooperation and generosity of so many individuals, in this case, at Florida International University. Once again, the Jack D. Gordon Institute for Public Policy and Citizenship Studies made enormous contributions. The steady support and encouragement by Provost Mark B. Rosenberg is especially appreciated. We gratefully acknowledge the contributions of Thomas Breslin, vice president for research; Arthur W. Herriott, dean of the College of Arts and Sciences; Ivelaw L. Griffith, associate dean of the College of Arts and Sciences; and Joyce Shaw Peterson, associate dean of the Biscayne Bay Campus. A special acknowledgment is extended to Nicol C. Rae, chair of the Department of Political Science, for his intellectual contribution and his insightful understanding of the role of Congress, therein. We appreciate Timothy J. Power, director of the graduate program in political science at FIU, for facilitating the interest of our graduate students. And we would in particular like to thank Elaine Dillashaw of the Gordon Institute for providing invaluable support, assistance, and, above all, unwavering patience in the production of this volume.

Jennifer Knerr of Rowman & Littlefield made a number of constructive suggestions that greatly improved both the book's conceptualization and organization. And Brigitte Scott and Julie E. Kirsch shepherded the book through the production process.

Last, but not least, we are thankful to our families—old and new—who continue to make life a joy and whose love is not contingent on this volume's success.

To the reader, we hope our efforts and those of the contributing authors will advance your understanding and appreciation for an institution that is never short of excitement, the United States Congress.

PART ONE

Evolving Socioeconomic Rights

CHAPTER ONE

Congressional Power to Establish and Enforce Social Rights after *United States v. Morrison:* Limits and Possibilities

GREGG IVERS AND DAVID KAIB

In August 1994, Christy Brzonkala left her Fairfax County, Virginia, home in suburban Washington, D.C., to begin her freshman year at the Virginia Polytechnic Institute, better known as Virginia Tech. In early September, shortly after the beginning of the fall semester, Brzonkala met varsity football players Antonio Morrison and James Crawford at a party. Brzonkala later alleged that Morrison and Crawford gang-raped her sometime that evening and told school officials that Morrison's final words to her had been, "You better not have any fucking diseases." Other witnesses later told school officials that in campus dining facilities, they had heard Morrison boasting of his various sexual conquests. In one instance, Morrison allegedly announced that he "like[d] to get girls drunk and fuck the shit out of them" (*Brzonkala v. Virginia Polytechnic Institute* 1997, 953).

Brzonkala filed a complaint with Virginia Tech authorities under the university's Sexual Assault Policy. Morrison admitted that he had, in fact, had sex with Brzonkala, but insisted that it was consensual, although he also acknowledged that she had twice told him "no." After an investigation, the university's Judicial Committee found insufficient evidence to sustain Brzonkala's charges against Crawford. But Morrison was found guilty of sexual assault and was suspended for two semesters. As permitted under the university's Abusive Conduct Policy, which had been in place prior to the Sexual Assault Policy, Morrison requested a second hearing to review his guilty verdict. The panel affirmed Morrison's guilt, but dropped the charge from sexual assault to "using abusive language." Continuing to deny Brzonkala's account of their encounter, Morrison appealed the verdict under the Abusive Conduct Policy directly to the university provost.

11

In August 1995, Provost Peggy Meszaros stated that "there was sufficient evidence to support the decision that Morrison violated the University's Abusive Conduct Policy." However, the provost concluded that the two-semester sanction imposed on Morrison was "excessive when compared with other cases where there has been a finding of violation of the Abusive Conduct Policy." Provost Meszaros sent Morrison a letter dated August 21, 1995, informing him that his suspension had been lifted and he would be permitted to return to Virginia Tech for the 1995–96 academic year on a full athletic scholarship (*Brzonkala v. Virginia Polytechnic Institute* 1997, 955).

The next day, Brzonkala learned of the university's action from reading an article in the *Washington Post*. After Morrison and Crawford allegedly raped her, Brzonkala had stopped attending classes, had become disheveled in appearance, and had fallen into clinical depression. Stunned that Morrison would be returning to campus, Brzonkala decided not to return to Virginia Tech for the 1995 fall semester. She applied for and received a retroactive request for a formal withdrawal from the university. In November 1995, Brzonkala learned from another newspaper report that the university had changed its Judicial Committee's original sexual assault verdict against Morrison. The following month, Brzonkala, convinced that the university's actions were intended to discredit her rape allegations and preserve the reputation of the university's football program, filed an $8.3 million civil suit against Morrison, Crawford, and Virginia Tech in federal district court. Brzonkala was represented by the National Organization for Women Legal Defense and Education Fund (NOW LDEF), which had closely followed her case. On behalf of Christy Brzonkala, NOW LDEF invoked the Civil Rights Remedy provision of the federal Violence Against Women Act (VAWA), which was passed as Title IV of the Violent Crime Control and Law Enforcement Act of 1994, after four years of congressional hearings. In August 1994, the House had passed the law by a vote of 235 to 195 and by a vote of 61 to 38 in the Senate. The VAWA included numerous programs designed to aid women who had been victims of domestic violence, stalking, sexual assault, and other gender-motivated criminal conduct. The law also included money for transitional housing assistance for battered women and children, counseling programs for offenders and victims, law enforcement programs intended to encourage the arrest of abusers, rape-awareness workshops, and many other programs related to domestic and sexual violence. Signed into law by President Bill Clinton in September 1994, the VAWA authorized more than $1.6 billion in funds for these various programs over a five-year period (*Brzonkala v. Virginia Polytechnic Institute* 1997).

The Civil Rights Remedy provision of the VAWA authorized victims of gender-motivated violence to sue their attackers for compensatory and punitive damages in federal court. A separate provision in the VAWA permitted federal prosecutors to seek criminal penalties against any person who crossed a state line to assault a spouse or domestic partner. These penalties were, on the whole, much more stringent than those available for similar offenses under state law. In 1995, the Department of Justice brought the first successful domestic violence case under the new criminal penalties section of the VAWA. In that case, Christopher Bailey had beaten his wife unconscious, locked her in the trunk of his car, and then had driven back and forth between West Virginia and Kentucky for six days before seeking medical attention for her. By then, Sonia Bailey had lapsed into a coma. Under West Virginia law, Christopher Bailey would only have been eligible for a ten-year sentence. Under the VAWA, federal prosecutors were authorized to ask for life imprisonment on kidnapping charges and twenty years for disfiguring his wife. In August 1995, Bailey received the maximum sentence on both charges.

In July 1996, a federal district court dismissed Brzonkala's argument under the VAWA, holding that Congress had exceeded its authority under the Commerce Clause of the Constitution by permitting domestic violence victims to file civil lawsuits in federal court (*Brzonkala v. Virginia Polytechnic and State University* 1996). In December 1997, the Fourth Circuit Court of Appeals, one of the nation's most conservative, reversed the lower court, holding that Congress was within its authority under the Commerce Clause to enact the VAWA. Judge Dianna Motz, writing for a 2 to 1 majority, concluded that the VAWA was a fair and constitutional reaction by Congress to a social problem of great magnitude. Judge Motz noted that Congress, over a four-year period, had offered voluminous evidence on the "substantial effects" of domestic violence on interstate commerce (*Brzonkala v. Virginia Polytechnic Institute* 1997). But in March 1999, the Fourth Circuit, after hearing the case en banc, ruled, by a 7 to 4 majority, that while Brzonkala had properly stated a civil rights claim under the VAWA, the law was nonetheless an unconstitutional exercise of congressional power under the Commerce Clause. Judge Michael Luttig, perhaps the most conservative member of the Fourth Circuit, reasoned that any impact on interstate commerce resulting from violence against women was too remote to justify the establishment of a federal civil rights remedy (*Brzonkala v. Virginia Polytechnic Institute and State University* 1999).

In May 2000, the U.S. Supreme Court affirmed the en banc Fourth Circuit's decision. By a slim 5 to 4 majority, the Court, in *United States v. Morrison* (2000), decided along with *Brzonkala v. Morrison* (2000), ruled that the Civil Rights Remedy provision of the VAWA was not properly grounded in the Commerce Clause authority of Congress. We will discuss the basis for the Court's ruling later in this chapter. For now, it is important to note how the Court's decision in *Morrison* has called substantial attention to the power of Congress to establish and protect civil and constitutional rights. *United States v. Morrison* (2000) came on the heels of two important decisions in the mid- to late

1990s that limited the power of Congress to enact legislation affecting gun control, *United States v. Lopez* (1995) and *Printz v. United States* (1997), and another
one, *City of Boerne v. Flores* (1997), which curtailed Congress's authority under
Section 5 of the Fourteenth Amendment to expand the Court's interpretation of
existing constitutional guarantees.

   Lopez was, in particular, a watershed moment for the Court in the modern
constitutional era. Not since 1937, when the Court transformed the constitutional structure of the American governmental system by upholding several key
pieces of New Deal legislation, had the Court invalidated a federal law enacted by
Congress under its Commerce Clause power. On only two occasions had the
Court struck down a federal law as unconstitutional under the Tenth
Amendment. The first came in *National League of Cities v. Usery* (1976), when the
Court struck down a provision of the Fair Labor Standards Act, which required
state and local governments to meet federal minimum wage and overtime mandates for their employees. That decision, however, was overturned less than ten
years later in *Garcia v. San Antonio Metropolitan Transit Authority* (1985). In *New
York v. United States* (1992), the Court invalidated several provisions of the Low-
Level Radioactive Waste Policy Amendments Act of 1985, which authorized
states with radioactive waste disposal sites to impose surcharges on states using
their facilities. Beyond these two cases, the Court's emerging conservative majority, while expressing a desire to return power to the states, had done little to alter
the distribution of federal and state power in place since the New Deal outside the
area of criminal procedure (Ackerman 2000).

   In this chapter, we will address the consequences of *United States v. Morrison*
on the power of Congress to establish and enforce rights under the Commerce
Clause. Before we reach that question, we will examine the fluid transfer of the
legislative dynamics behind the VAWA into the judicial arena and describe how
many of the same groups that supported the law's passage went to the courts to
defend its constitutionality. But first we will turn to the political dynamics that
resulted in the passage of the VAWA of 1994.

THE VIOLENCE AGAINST WOMEN ACT OF 1994: POLITICAL AND CONGRESSIONAL DYNAMICS

Encouraged by women's rights and victims' rights advocates, Senator Joseph R.
Biden (D-Del.) introduced the VAWA in June 1990 (Siskin 2001). As chairman
of the Senate Judiciary Committee, which deals with the constitutionality of federal legislation, Biden was in a favorable position to shepherd the bill through
Congress. However, what the VAWA sought to accomplish and how it sought to
do so made its passage far from certain.

One problem that came up soon after the VAWA had been introduced was defining the very nature of violence against women. Racial discrimination, including bias-motivated violence, is seen as a quintessential public problem. Some gender-based discrimination, particularly in employment and education, is also seen as a public problem. But gender-motivated violence, which often takes place within an environment in which the abuser and victim are usually acquainted, and frequently in an established relationship, is often viewed as a private matter beyond regulatory authority (Nourse 1996). In *Morrison*, for example, the defendants argued that Christy Brzonkala had agreed to have sex with them, thus disputing the alleged victim's account. A scenario involving racially motivated conduct rarely, if ever, suggests that the victim granted consent. Rather, such cases usually involve disputes over whether or not the perpetrators of racially motivated "hate crimes" are being unfairly punished for their prejudicial beliefs (see, for example, *Wisconsin v. Mitchell* [1990], upholding a state law enhancing penalties for racially motivated criminal conduct).

The Civil Rights Remedy in the VAWA provided the first federal cause of action for a victim of gender-motivated violence, complementing other provisions in the law declaring that all persons had a federal right to be free from domestic violence. By defining freedom from domestic violence as a statutory right, the VAWA followed the model set out by other federal civil rights laws that made, for example, freedom from workplace discrimination on the basis of race, color, national origin, or sex a legal right. Still, the notion of freedom from domestic violence as a civil right struck some opponents of the legislation as a novel legal innovation ungrounded in any federal constitutional authority. Other concerns over the VAWA included its potential impact on the caseload of the federal judiciary, whether the Civil Rights Remedy was an effective weapon to redress and deter gender-motivated violence, and whether Congress was usurping a law enforcement function of the states.

The initial Biden-sponsored VAWA included six cosponsors, three Democrats and three Republicans; by October 1990, the measure had attracted twenty-five cosponsors, twenty-two of whom were Democrats. President George H. W. Bush opposed the VAWA as unconstitutional, claiming that Congress had no authority under the Commerce Clause to establish a federal cause of action for victims of domestic violence. When the Senate Judiciary Committee opened hearings on the VAWA in the fall of 1990, the initial focus was on the barriers to justice faced by victims of gender-motivated violence. Numerous witnesses, including rape victims and other survivors of domestic violence, physicians, law professors, and state and local law enforcement groups, offered their testimony on the inadequacy of current legal remedies (*United States v. Morrison* 2000, 629). But the 101st Congress (1989–91) adjourned before additional action could be taken on the VAWA.

On January 14, 1991, the first day of the 102d Congress (1991–93), Senator Biden reintroduced the VAWA. Shortly after Senate hearings began on the Biden bill, then-Representative Barbara Boxer (D-Calif.) introduced a similar bill in the House. The Boxer measure soon attracted opposition from the Bush administration, which had been busy lobbying senators behind the scenes that the Civil Rights Remedy of the VAWA was unconstitutional. The Department of Justice had submitted a letter to the House and Senate Judiciary Committees urging them not to approve the legislation (Nourse 1996). The Judicial Conference of the United States, which represents federal judges, passed a resolution opposing the VAWA, claiming that the Civil Rights Remedy would lead to the proliferation of lawsuits in the federal courts, which were unequipped to handle such a burden. The Conference on Chief Justices, which represents state supreme court chief justices, also lodged its opposition, arguing that the VAWA impeded the responsibility of state courts to deal with a matter that was properly a function of state law. U.S. Supreme Court Chief Justice William H. Rehnquist subsequently echoed the concerns of his colleagues in the lower courts, criticizing the Civil Rights Remedy in his 1991 year-end report on the status of the federal judiciary. The chief justice specifically pointed to the increased workload that he believed the Civil Rights Remedy would pose for what he believed was an already overburdened federal judiciary (*Congressional Record* 1992, S443).

While opponents of the VAWA continued their campaign to defeat the legislation in the House and Senate, supporters for the Biden and Boxer bills fought back. The National Association of Attorneys General adopted a resolution supporting passage of the VAWA, including the Civil Rights Remedy. The state attorneys general group claimed that the VAWA would not threaten the proper balance between the states and the federal government on law enforcement matters. Senator Strom J. Thurmond (R-S.C.), the ranking minority member on the Senate Judiciary Committee, and Senator Orrin G. Hatch (R-Utah), one of the Senate's more conservative members, withdrew their earlier objections to the Civil Rights Remedy after hearings on the legislation convinced them of the constitutionality of the Civil Rights Remedy. These hearings focused more specifically on the nationwide problem of gender violence and its effects on interstate commerce. By this time, nearly two dozen state task forces on gender bias had provided data to Congress on the extent of domestic violence and on the inadequacy of state and local law enforcements' ability to address the problem. VAWA sponsors claimed that gender-motivated violence had just as pernicious an effect on interstate commerce as racial discrimination and noted that the Supreme Court had upheld the landmark Civil Rights Act of 1964 as a valid exercise of congressional commerce power (Nourse 1996). By October 1991, fifty-six senators—forty-six Democrats and ten Republicans—had signed on as sponsors of the VAWA.

In October 1991, the Senate Judiciary Committee favorably reported the VAWA, including the controversial Civil Rights Remedy. In the House, however, Representative Boxer was unable to clear the VAWA out of the Judiciary Committee because of objections to the Civil Rights Remedy. The legislation subsequently languished for more than a year until Biden and Boxer (who had won election to the Senate in November 1992) reintroduced the VAWA under their sponsorship in the first days of the 103d Congress (1993–95). Senator Hatch, who had replaced Senator Thurmond as the ranking minority member, introduced an alternative bill that did not include the Civil Rights Remedy.

After holding field hearings on the issue of domestic violence in Salt Lake City in the spring of 1993, Hatch agreed to negotiate a mutually acceptable bill with Biden. The modified VAWA was based substantially on Biden's earlier version, but it included an important change that required that some element of gender "animus" must motivate domestic violence or sexual assault (Nourse 1996). By October 1993, the Biden-Boxer-Hatch compromise bill had garnered sixty-seven cosponsors: forty-nine Democrats and eighteen Republicans.

Biden subsequently added the VAWA as an amendment to the Violent Crime Control and Law Enforcement Act (VCCLEA), which he had also cosponsored. The VCCLEA dealt with issues as wide-ranging as prison regulation, death penalty eligibility, mandatory minimums sentences, drug offenses, drunk driving, controlling domestic gang warfare, domestic and international terrorism, firearms, and child pornography.[1] The House, by a 421 to 0 vote, passed a version of the VAWA that did not include the Civil Rights Remedy. By the end of the 1993, forty-one state attorneys general had sent letters to House members urging passage of the VAWA with the Civil Rights Remedy. The National Association of Women Judges also expressed their support. President Clinton, a vocal supporter of the VAWA during his successful 1992 presidential campaign, urged Congress to go forward with the legislation. Separately, the Justice Department reversed the Bush administration's position on the VAWA and sent a letter to the House and Senate judiciary committees defending the constitutionality of the Civil Rights Remedy. Encouraged by a changed political environment, women's rights organizations, victims' rights advocates, and other civil rights groups stepped up their pressure on Congress to enact the VAWA. Although the Judicial Conference of the United States had withdrawn its objection after the changes from Senator Hatch's bill were incorporated into the VAWA, it refused to support the VAWA. Moreover, the Conference of Chief Justices continued to oppose it.

In the spring of 1994, the House passed its version of the VCCLEA, which included a version of the VAWA without the Civil Rights Remedy. After the House and Senate failed to reconcile their differences, the VAWA was brought to a joint conference committee in the summer of 1994. Senators Hatch and Biden supported VAWA as a whole, while the House conferees objected to the Civil Rights Remedy, arguing that it was unnecessary and that it would undercut existing civil rights law (Nourse 1996). The joint committee finally agreed to include the Civil Rights Remedy. By September, the House and Senate passed the conference VAWA as part of the VCCLEA of 1994 and President Clinton signed the bill into law almost immediately thereafter.

LITIGATION POLITICS AND THE VAWA

The Supreme Court accepted *Brzonkala v. Morrison* and *United States v. Morrison* for review during its 1999–2000 term. The Department of Justice had intervened to defend the constitutionality of the VAWA when the case was argued before the original three-judge panel of the Fourth Circuit Court of Appeals. On behalf of Virginia Tech football players Antonio Morrison and James Crawford, the Center for Individual Rights (CIR), a conservative public interest law group, had entered *Morrison* to sharpen the attack on the constitutionality of the Civil Rights Remedy of the VAWA. Beginning in the early 1990s, the CIR had achieved several notable victories in the courts, including limiting affirmative action in university admissions and the reach of congressional power under the Tenth Amendment and expanding the right under the First Amendment of religious organizations to receive state funding for their publications.[2] The NOW LDEF, supported by the National Women's Law Center, continued to represent Christy Brzonkala in her separate suit against Virginia Tech, Morrison, and Crawford.

The VAWA's constitutionality was supported by a number of liberal groups that had lobbied for its passage in Congress, such as the National Network to End Domestic Violence, the Lawyers Committee for Civil Rights Under Law, and a coalition of law professors that had previously testified on behalf of its passage during Senate and House hearings on the legislation. Senator Biden, the sponsor of the original VAWA in 1990, filed an amicus brief in support of the Civil Rights Remedy's constitutionality, the only member of Congress to do so.[3] Biden argued that the congressional hearings had demonstrated how widespread the problem of gender-motivated violence was nationwide and how it affected interstate commerce. He stressed the overwhelming bipartisan support the VAWA had received in the House and Senate and took great care to distinguish *Morrison* from *Lopez*, noting that Congress had built an extensive record to document the impact of domestic violence on interstate commerce. Unlike the Gun Free School Zones Act, struck down in *Lopez*, the VAWA did not fail to offer a legislative record that demonstrated a "substantial effect" of the relationship between interstate commerce and domestic violence. Separately, thirty-six states and Puerto Rico filed amicus briefs arguing that the VAWA was crucial to joint federal and state efforts to combat domestic violence. The National Association of Attorneys General also filed a brief in support of the VAWA, arguing that its Civil Rights Remedy did not usurp a traditional function of the states.

On the other side, Morrison was defended by a number of conservative groups, such as the Independent Women's Forum, the Center for the Original Intent of the Constitution, the Eagle Forum, a conservative women's group, and the Institute for Justice. In addition, the National Association of Criminal Defense Lawyers (NACDL), which normally takes very liberal positions on criminal justice issues and is anti-death penalty, filed an amicus brief opposing the Civil Rights Remedy provision of the VAWA. The NACDL had opposed the provision while the law was still before Congress as unfair to criminal defendants and ineffective in solving the problem, a position it set forth in its amicus brief. It is fair to say that both sides, attuned to the Court's decisions in *Lopez* and *Printz*, understood the considerable stakes in *Morrison* for the power of Congress to create rights and remedies under the Commerce Clause.

THE COMMERCE CLAUSE AS AN INSTRUMENT OF SOCIAL REFORM

Police power, or the power of government to promote health and social welfare objectives through legislation, is most often considered the constitutional responsibility of the states. Beginning in the late 1830s, the Supreme Court recognized a need for states to regulate the social consequences of the changes brought about by the nation's ever-shifting industrial and economic base. By then, the nation was mired in a severe economic depression, and the social disorder and political dissatisfaction that brought about this turn of events had emerged to a greater degree than ever before. Legislative responses by the states to address these concerns had become more common. Rather than set aside such efforts as an impediment to the economic and property rights of individuals and corporations, as the Court under Chief Justice John Marshall (1801–35) had done to promote the Federalist vision of America as a large commercial republic, the Court, under Chief Justice Roger Taney (1836–64), was now prepared to extend greater lawmaking power to the states. Consistent with the principles promoted by President Andrew Jackson (1829–37), the Court believed that the states were better tuned to the health and welfare needs of their people than was the federal government.

The Taney Court's vision was of a carefully delineated federalism in which the national government, on the one hand, and state and local authorities, on the other hand, remained within their particular orbits. Even after the Civil War, most Americans still viewed the national government as distant and remote in its relationship to everyday matters of governance. This constitutional arrangement left the states in a position of considerable discretion to respond to social and economic problems largely free from federal mandate (Curtis 1990, 179). But the Court's understanding of legislative power to regulate in the public interest also meant that states were often free *not* to respond to some of the most severe problems of the time. By the late 1800s, the arrival of the Industrial Revolution had visited substantial changes on the social and economic infrastructure of the United States. Rapid urbanization, environmental decay, the spread of disease, domestic violence, and rising crime rates were just some of the problems that began to confront states and localities as never before.

Congress, however, was largely inattentive to these problems. In 1887, Congress enacted the Interstate Commerce Act in an effort to bring order and greater competition to the most powerful new social and economic creation of the Industrial Revolution: the concentration of disproportionate power in a small number of large corporate "trusts" that dominated such critical areas of the economy as transportation, agricultural production, energy, and manufacturing. Three years later, Congress passed the Sherman Antitrust Act, the federal government's first major effort to break up the large monopolistic corporations that restrained trade through unfair business practices. In passing the 1887 and 1890 laws, Congress was not motivated by a desire to deal with the harsh consequences of the Industrial Revolution. Rather, congressional concern was to promote fair and equitable competition in the nation's new economy. But in two key decisions, *United States v. E. C. Knight Co.*, (1895) and *Interstate Commerce Commission v. Cincinnati, New Orleans, and Texas Pacific Railway Co.* (1897), the Court interpreted the power of Congress to regulate the economy narrowly. Favorably disposed to laissez-faire economic theories, the Court was extremely reluctant to extend the regulatory power of Congress to manage the economy, even if there was a demonstrated public interest (Horwitz 1992, 9–21).

Moreover, the Court had also entered an era when it was largely unwilling to uphold state and local efforts to deal with the social and economic changes brought about by the Industrial Revolution. In *Lochner v. New York* (1905), the Supreme Court captured this spirit at its most robust when it ruled that the Due Process Clause of the Fourteenth Amendment protected a "liberty of contract" that largely precluded any power by states and localities to promote police power objectives through legislation. At issue in *Lochner* had been the New York Bakeshop Law of 1895, which placed maximum hours on the workweek of bakers. Despite an extensive legislative record that documented the health hazards of the commercial baking trade, the Court viewed the law as an unconstitutional abridgement of the right of employers and employees to enter into a contractual agreement (Kens 1990; Gillman 1993). The Court's narrow construction of congressional commerce power combined with its equally cramped interpretation of state police power meant that governmental bodies at all levels were largely incapacitated from promoting redistributive economic policies or social welfare objectives through legislation (Irons 1999, 233–64).

Ironically, the Court had formally recognized a police power for Congress shortly before it decided *Lochner*. In *Champion v. Ames* (1903), the Court held that Congress could use its commerce power in expansive terms to guard the "people of the United States against the 'widespread pestilence of lotteries'" (*Champion v. Ames* 1903, 356). In *Stone v. Mississippi* (1880), the Court ruled that the Contract Clause (Article I, Section 10) did not act as a barrier to a *state* decision to rescind a charter it had granted to a local business to own and operate a lottery. *Ames* offered a similar line of reasoning to justify permitting Congress to regulate the social consequences of commercial activity. This decision came as a surprise considering the narrow interpretation the Court was giving to congressional commerce power in cases that dealt more explicitly with "pure" commercial activities.

By and large, however, the Supreme Court continued to curb congressional power to regulate the economic and social effects of commercial activity until well into the 1930s. By then, the Court, still committed to a laissez-faire conception of the economic marketplace, had entered into a very public and often nasty confrontation with Congress and Democratic President Franklin D. Roosevelt. In 1932, Roosevelt had been elected by a wide margin based on his promise to offer Americans a "New Deal" from the federal government, one that placed congressional power at the front and center of the effort to address the social and economic dislocation brought about by the Great Depression. In the first one hundred days of his presidency, President Roosevelt signed over fifteen laws that vastly increased the power of the federal government to regulate economic affairs, including the National Industrial Relations Act, the Agricultural Adjustment Act, and numerous laws to provide benefits to the long-term unemployed. Over the next two years, Congress enacted one revolutionary measure after another, including the National Labor Relations Act and the Social Security Act, only to have the Court strike them down. Congress and the president knew full well that the ambitious legislative agenda of the New Deal amounted to nothing less than a frontal assault on the established constitutional order. By embracing an experimental, pragmatic approach to law that emphasized its dynamic qualities, the architects of the New Deal openly rejected the legal formalism of their laissez-faire adversaries (Shamir 1995).

This clash of legal cultures all but invited the constitutional crisis that reached its peak when Roosevelt announced his plan in February 1937 to expand the number of justices currently sitting on the Court from nine to fifteen by appointing a new justice for each justice more than seventy years old (Nelson 1988). Whether Roosevelt's Court-packing plan intimidated the justices to reverse course on the New Deal has been a subject of considerable scholarly speculation since then, for in March 1937 the Court announced two key decisions, *West Coast Hotel v. Parrish* (1937) and *National Labor Relations Board v. Jones and Laughlin Steel Corp.* (1937), that greatly expanded both congressional and state legislative power to regulate the economy. Several decisions followed that further broadened congressional power under the Commerce Clause to promote the public welfare aspects of commercial activity (*United States v. Darby* [1941] and *Wickard v. Filburn* [1942]). By 1943, President Roosevelt had appointed all nine justices of the Supreme Court, all of whom were firmly committed to the expansive administrative state created by the New Deal (Ivers 2001, 321–22).

The Constitutional Revolution of 1937, as the Court's decision to embrace the New Deal has sometimes been called, enabled Congress to extend its police power on behalf of social and economic reform as never before. Congress's subsequent use of the Commerce Clause to eradicate racial discrimination provides perhaps the most striking example of the degree to which the Court, until only recently, was willing to defer to the legislative branch on matters designed to promote the public welfare. In *Heart of Atlanta Motel v. United States* (1964) and *Katzenbach v. McClung* (1964), the Court upheld the Civil Rights Act of 1964, which barred discrimination in public accommodations, by employers of fifteen persons or more and by institutions receiving federal funds. Justices ruled that the law was a valid exercise of congressional commerce power, concluding that racial discrimination posed a "substantial and harmful effect" upon interstate commerce.

Justice William O. Douglas, concurring in *Heart of Atlanta* and *Katzenbach*, suggested that Congress should have relied on its power under Section 5 of the Fourteenth Amendment to enforce the nondiscrimination guarantee of the 1964 law rather than the Commerce Clause. Douglas wrote that his reluctance to join the Court's opinion "was not due to any conviction that Congress lacks power to regulate commerce in the interest of human rights. It is rather my belief that the right of people to be free of state action that discriminates against them because of race . . . occupies a more protected position in our constitutional system than does the movement of cattle, fruit, steel and coal across state lines" (*Heart of Atlanta Motel, Inc. v. United States*, 1964, 279). Congress, however, was hamstrung by one of the Court's early post-Reconstruction decisions, *The Civil Rights Cases of 1883*, from using its amendment-enforcing power under Section 5 of the Fourteenth Amendment.[4]

There, an 8 to 1 Court invalidated an 1875 civil rights law that sought to guarantee African Americans full and equal rights in public accommodations. The Court ruled that "civil rights, such as are guaranteed by the Constitution, against State aggression, cannot be impaired by the wrongful acts of individuals, unsupported by State authority in the shape of laws, customs, or judicial or executive proceedings. The wrongful act of an individual, unsupported by any such authority, is simply a private wrong," one that Congress is powerless to prohibit under Section 5 of the Fourteenth Amendment. Justice Joseph Bradley, who wrote the Court's opinion, did suggest in dicta that "Congress, in the exercise of its power to regulate commerce amongst the several states, might or might not pass a law regulating rights in public conveyances passing from one state to another." But even if Congress had demonstrated any interest in pursuing an aggressive civil rights agenda on behalf of African Americans, the Court's pre–New Deal approach to the Commerce Clause would have rendered such legislation meaningless.

After the Constitutional Revolution of 1937, the Court rejected the notion advanced in earlier Commerce Clause decisions that carved out formal boundaries between those activities having a "direct" and an "indirect" effect on interstate commerce. For almost fifty years, this pattern went undisturbed until the Supreme Court's decision in *Lopez* to revive the "substantial effects" test as the measure by which to determine whether Congress had acted within its Commerce Clause authority. *Lopez* surprised students of the Court and constitutional law, as there was nothing to indicate that Congress, in making it a federal offense to possess a firearm on or within one thousand feet of a public, private, or parochial school, had exceeded its commerce power beyond that defined in *Wickard, Heart of Atlanta Motel,* or *McClung.* It also encouraged a more receptive environment for the Commerce Clause challenge in *Morrison.*

CONCLUSION

What does *Morrison* mean for the power of Congress to establish and enforce social rights? It is important to note what the Supreme Court's decision in *Morrison* did not do as much as what it did do. Without a doubt, the 5 to 4 majority in *Morrison* (consisting of Chief Justice Rehnquist, Sandra Day O'Connor, Antonin Scalia, Anthony Kennedy, and Clarence Thomas) that had successfully reigned in congressional power in *Lopez, Printz,* and *Boerne* achieved another important victory for the power and autonomy of states in the federal system. In holding that victims of gender-motivated violence had no right to sue their attackers in federal court, the *Morrison* majority reinforced a lesson drawn from several earlier decisions limiting the right of criminal defendants to sue for federal habeas corpus relief to contest convictions under state law (Harriger 1997). *Morrison* also made clear the Court's belief that it was the responsibility of the states, not the federal government, to use their police power to combat what it believed were the noneconomic consequences of private behavior. Wrote Chief Justice Rehnquist in his majority opinion:

> The regulation and punishment of intrastate violence that is not directed at the instrumentalities, channels, or goods involved in interstate commerce has always been the province of the States. Indeed, we can think of no better example of the police power, which the Founders denied the National Government and reposed in the States, than the suppression of violent crime and vindication of its victims. (*United States v. Morrison* 2000, 618)

But *Morrison* did not hold that Congress lacked the constitutional authority to create and fund the programs that formed the core of the VAWA. Nor was there any suggestion that the criminal penalties imposed by the VAWA for gender-motivated violence were unconstitutional. Indeed, no other provision of the law was challenged as unconstitutional in *Morrison* except for the Civil Rights Remedy. In October 2000, President Clinton signed a five-year reauthorization of the appropriations for the VAWA, and included "targeted improvements" to the law. These improvements included computerized tracking of protection orders issued to protect the victims of gender-motivated violence, expanding grant programs to cover violence arising in dating relationships, and better protections for battered immigrant women. An important sign that Congress was not prepared to give in to the Court on the possibility of establishing a federal cause of action for the victims of gender-motivated violence came in January 2001, when a bipartisan coalition of Representatives in the House introduced the Violence Against Women Civil Rights Restoration Act (VAWCRA). The VAWCRA noted that the Court did not foreclose Congress's authority to establish a federal remedy for gender-motivated violence, if that remedy is properly drafted. An early version of the law restores the Civil Rights Remedy when there is a connection to interstate commerce and authorizes the attorney general to bring lawsuits against state actors when a pattern of discrimination exists in the prosecution of gender-motivated crimes.

Lopez, Printz, and *Morrison* all dealt with issues that posed a more tenuous link to interstate commerce than other areas, such as racial discrimination, in which Congress had used its power under the Commerce Clause to create and enforce rights. Moreover, the Court's majority opinions in these cases have, so far, been rather narrowly drawn. Although Justice Clarence Thomas has suggested in *Lopez* and *Morrison* that the Court should revisit its entire understanding of congressional power under the Commerce Clause, that view has not commanded a majority of the Court. So far, the Court seems willing to distinguish between the noneconomic and economic "effects" of private behavior on interstate commerce and has not cast doubt on the broader power of Congress to regulate the economy. Still, *Morrison* is another important step away from the Court's deferential approach toward the power of Congress to exercise its police power under the Commerce Clause in the post–New Deal era. How far the Court is prepared to go in challenging the foundation of the Constitutional Revolution of 1937 is very much an open question, one that, only a short time ago, was considered settled.

Notes

1. The Violent Crime Control and Law Enforcement Act, Public Law 103–322.

2. See, for example, *Hopwood v. Texas*, 78 F.3d 932 (1996) (striking down the admissions policy of the University of Texas Law School as unconstitutional) and *Rosenberger v. Virginia*, 515 U.S. 819 (1995) (holding that the University of Virginia could not withhold funds from a student-operated religious magazine on free speech grounds).

3. Senator Biden represented only himself. No other member of the Senate signed the brief.

4. 109 U.S. 3 (1883).

CHAPTER TWO

Ironies and Unanticipated Consequences of Legislation: Title VII of the 1964 Civil Rights Act and Sexual Harassment

DAVID M. O'BRIEN

The Supreme Court handed down three rather remarkable statutory rulings at the end of its October 1997–98 term. Together, they extended the protection of Title VII of the Civil Rights Act of 1964 to make employers liable for same-sex harassment of workers and for tolerating "hostile-workplace sexual harassment."[1] These rulings not only were sweeping and significant in their impact on employers' liability but also serve to illustrate how congressional legislation frequently has unanticipated (and occasionally even ironic) consequences. That is, of course, in part because when enacting statutes, Congress cannot foresee all possible future applications. Statutory language typically has an "open texture" and is ambiguous. Moreover, judges and legal scholars disagree about whether congressional statutes should be interpreted according to their "plain meaning" or in light of their legislative history (see and compare Scalia 1997; and Eskridge 1994). Statutes, thus, generally require interpretation and implementation by federal agencies, which in turn invites litigation and judicial rulings that may expand or contract their application in ways unforeseen or contemplated by Congress (Grofman 2000; Halpern 1995; Bullock and Lamb 1984; and Melnick 1983).

Notably, writing for a unanimous Court in *Oncale v. Sundowner Offshore Services* (1998), one of the most conservative justices—Justice Antonin Scalia—held that Title VII applies to same-sex harassment of workers by coworkers no less than to the harassment of employees by supervisors of different sexes or sexual orientations in the workplace. In *Faragher v. City of Boca Raton* (1998), the Court reaffirmed that employers are subject to liability for hostile-environment or workplace sexual harassment created by supervisors. Furthermore, in his opinion for the Court, Justice David H. Souter ruled that employees need not show that employers knew or should have known about the sexual harassment and failed to stop it. Even if employees do not suffer the loss of promotion or employment, suits may be brought if the harassment or abuse was severe or pervasive, although employers may offer as defenses that they took reasonable care to prevent or correct the sexually harassing behavior and that employees unreasonably failed to take advantage of corrective opportunities offered by the employer. Here, Justice Souter concluded that Boca Raton, Florida, failed to exercise reasonable care in protecting its female lifeguards from a hostile environment of sexual harassment. In that case only Justices Scalia and Clarence Thomas dissented, as they did in the third ruling. Delivering the opinion for the Court in the third decision, *Burlington Industries v. Ellerth* (1998), Justice Anthony Kennedy ruled that employers are liable under Title VII for hostile-environment sexual harassment by supervisors unless they demonstrate (a) reasonable care to prevent or correct promptly the harassing behavior and (b) that the allegedly harassed employee unreasonably failed to take advantage of grievance procedures offered by the employer in order to avoid harm.

These rulings, to be sure, extended two other significant prior high court decisions in *Harris v. Forklift Systems, Inc.* (1993) and *Meritor Savings Bank, FBD v. Vinson* (1986). In *Harris v. Forklift Systems*, the Court addressed an important issue left unresolved by *Meritor Savings Bank*. In *Meritor Savings Bank* Justice William H. Rehnquist had held for a unanimous Court—for the first time—that Title VII of the Civil Rights Act bars sexual harassment in the workplace and not just gender discrimination in the hiring and firing of employees. *Harris v. Forklift Systems*, then, extended *Meritor Savings Bank* in holding that victims of sexual harassment in the workplace need not meet the high standard of proving actual psychological injury. Instead, in her opinion for the Court, Justice Sandra Day O'Connor ruled that judges and juries have substantial leeway in deciding whether sexual advances, insults, or other offensive conduct, and not just physical assaults, constitute harassment within the workplace environment.

The trio of 1998 decisions, along with *Harris v. Forklift Systems* and *Meritor Savings Bank*, nonetheless, underscore the unanticipated and occasionally ironic consequences of Congress legislating on rights. In this regard, Title VII of the Civil Rights Act of 1964 provides, perhaps, a classic case in point. Title VII forbids discrimination in employment on the basis of race, color, national origin, religion, and sex. Section 706 of the Civil Rights Act also authorizes the Equal Employment Opportunity Commission (EEOC) to enforce its provisions. During the decades following the passage of the Civil Rights Act, however, Title VII was incrementally interpreted to apply not only to discrimination in the hiring, promoting, and firing of employees, but also to sexual harassment in the workplace. Moreover, the expansion of the application of Title VII to sexual harassment was not merely unanticipated but also deeply ironic, for "sex" was included as a category of prohibited discrimination, along with race, national origin, and religion, as an amendment introduced by Virginia's Democratic Representative Howard Smith in order to defeat the passage of the Civil Rights Act of 1964.

This chapter first reexamines the legislative history and congressional politics of the enactment of Title VII of the Civil Rights Act. It then turns to the incremental expansion of the scope of Title VII by the EEOC and, finally, to the federal judiciary's rulings on sexual harassment in the 1970s and early 1980s, which led to the EEOC's expanded regulations on sexual harassment and to the Supreme Court's decisions on sexual harassment under Title VII of the Civil Rights Act.

PURPOSES AND PARADOXES OF THE CIVIL RIGHTS ACT

Looking back almost forty years after the passage of the Civil Rights Act of 1964 gives one pause when considering how much law and politics has changed in the country. The Civil Rights Act of 1964 remains the most significant and comprehensive civil rights legislation since the Reconstruction era after the Civil War. It was the product of the long, bitter, and occasionally violent struggles of the civil rights movement. More specifically, in 1963 the "sit-in" movement to dramatize segregation in the South resulted in a change in the national political climate as a consequence of televised coverage of the ugly use of police dogs and fire hoses against peaceful protesters in Birmingham, Alabama. That violent episode moved the administration of Democratic President John F. Kennedy (JFK) to make a commitment to the advancement of civil rights. Congress, though, remained unmoved until after JFK's assassination. His successor, and notably a former very powerful Senate leader, President Lyndon B. Johnson (LBJ) and his Democratic supporters pushed the act through Congress as a kind of memorial to JFK (Graham 1990).

In short, in historical perspective there is no gainsaying that the primary purpose of the Civil Rights Act was to combat the persistence of racial discrimination. The most important and controversial provision was deemed to be contained in Title II, barring racial discrimination in all public accommodations if their operations affect interstate commerce, including hotels and other lodging of more than five rooms, restaurants, theaters, and other places of entertainment. That provision was immediately challenged for its constitutionality and upheld by the Supreme Court in *Heart of Atlanta Motel, Inc. v. United States* (1964) and *Katzenbach v. McClung* (1964).

From LBJ's special message to Congress on June 19, 1963, proposing the legislation throughout the acrimonious debates in Congress, attention was almost
exclusively given to the problem of racial discrimination. Indeed, LBJ's message
focused solely on discrimination based on "race, color, religion, or national origin" (reprinted in Schwartz 1970, 1055). Likewise, the congressional debates and
committee reports of both the House of Representatives and the Senate focused
overwhelmingly on the problems of racial segregation and discrimination
(reprinted in Schwartz 1970, 1017–1466).

Ironies abound in the legislative history and politics of how "sex" came to be
included in Title VII and other provisions of the Civil Rights Act. Not until the
bill that would become the Civil Rights Act was finally debated on the floor of
the House was the "sex amendment" introduced by Virginia's Democratic
Representative Howard W. Smith. Smith was an eighty-year-old segregationist
and former judge who had served in the House for almost three decades. As the
powerful chair of the House Rules Committee, he was known for manipulating
procedures to obstruct the passage of civil rights legislation.

When introducing the "sex amendment" on the floor, Representative Smith
explained:

> This amendment is offered to prevent discrimination against another minority
> group, the women, but a very essential minority group, in the absence of which
> the majority group would not be here today. . . . I do not think it can do any
> harm to this legislation; maybe it can do some good. I think it will do some good
> for the minority sex. I think we all recognize and it is indisputable fact that all
> throughout industry women are discriminated against in that just generally
> speaking they do not get as high compensation for their work as do the majority
> sex. (quoted in Bird 1970, 3)

In a perversely dishonest defense of what he wryly called his "little amendment," Smith read a letter from a woman who complained about the "imbal-
ance" between the sexes and asserted that:

> The census of 1960 shows that we had 88,331,000 males living in this country,
> and 90,992,000 females, which leaves the country with an "imbalance" of
> 2,661,000 females.
>   Just why the Creator would set up such an imbalance of spinsters, shutting off
> the "right" of every female to have a husband of her own, is, of course, known
> only to nature.
>   But I am sure you will agree that this is a grave injustice to womankind and
> something the Congress and President Johnson should take immediate steps to
> correct, especially in this election year.
>   Would you have any suggestions as to what course our Government might
> pursue to protect our spinster friends in their "right" to a nice husband and fam-
> ily? (quoted in Vass 1966, 441)

Representative Smith's reading of that letter literally brought the proverbial "house down" (recall, too, that the House of Representatives at the time was dominated by white males). Quickly playing to the laughter in the House, Smith reminded the House of the seriousness of the matter since, as he claimed again with tongue in cheek, half of the voters in the country were female. "I am serious about this thing," he concluded disingenuously, "What harm can you do this bill that was so perfect yesterday?" (quoted in Bird 1970, 4–5).

The "pandemonium" on the floor, as Charles and Barbara Whalen nicely recount in their book *The Longest Debate: A Legislative History of the 1964 Civil Rights Act*, was eventually broken by the Democratic House leadership. New York's liberal Democratic Representative Emanuel Celler and Oregon's Democratic Representative Edith S. Green, who was also a member of the president's Commission on the Status of Women, both spoke out against adoption of the amendment. They feared, exactly as Smith hoped, that the amendment would defeat passage of the entire bill.

Remarkably, at the time most other liberal Democrats and women's organizations opposed the amendment as well. However, a bipartisan coalition of five female representatives—Frances P. Bolton (R-Ohio), Martha W. Griffiths (D-Mich.), Catherine D. May (R-Wash.), Edna F. Kelly (D-N.Y.), and Katherine P. St. George (R-N.Y.)—did break ranks and came out in support of Smith's amendment.

Ultimately, Smith's amendment was approved by a vote of 168 to 133. Two days later the act passed the House on a 290 to 130 vote. Subsequently, the Senate eventually concluded an incredible five-hundred-hour-long filibuster and passed the bill on a vote of 73 to 27. Throughout the debate in the Senate, which also focused almost exclusively on the problem of racial discrimination and federalism concerns, there was virtually no attention paid to the Smith amendment.

Outside of Congress, even the press and media gave Smith's amendment scant attention. It was largely portrayed for what it was—a tactical move to derail the strongest civil rights legislation since the Reconstruction Amendments (the Thirteenth, Fourteenth, and Fifteenth Amendments) to the U.S. Constitution, not as a major step forward in the struggle for women's rights.

PUTTING TITLE VII INTO PRACTICE

In light of the terse legislative history and the fact that the Title VII prohibition against gender discrimination in employment originated as a kind of mischievous joke aimed at derailing the enactment of the Civil Rights Act, perhaps inevitably the Equal Employment Opportunity Commission (EEOC), which was entrusted with its enforcement, initially treated it as a joke as well. The

EEOC's first executive director, Herman Edelsberg, for instance, publicly called it a "fluke," "conceived out of wedlock" (quoted in Bird 1970, 15). "EEOC commissioners and staff," in the words of historian Cynthia Harrison, "expressed a general belief that the addition of *sex* into the law [Title VII] had been illegitimate—merely a ploy to kill the bill—and that it did not therefore constitute a mandate to equalize women's employment opportunities" (Harrison 1988, 187).

Not surprisingly, then, when the EEOC in November 1965 issued its first guidelines for employers it took a very narrow view of "bona-fide sex qualifications": In hiring, promoting, and firing employees, employers could not prefer one sex or another in order to please customers or coworkers, or on the basis of stereotypes and generalizations about males and females.

Given its inauspicious origins and in spite of its potential legal and political significance, the prohibition on gender discrimination in Title VII continued to invite jokes in the press. It did, though, spark a controversy that many likewise thought was a laughing matter in late 1965. The controversy centered on whether newspapers had to stop their traditional gender discrimination in the placement of classified advertisements. The mere suggestion that gender-classified ads might be discriminatory moved, for instance, a 1965 *Wall Street Journal* article to ask "its readers to picture, if they could, 'a shapeless, knobby-kneed male bunny' serving drinks to a group of stunned businessmen in a Playboy Club' or a 'matronly vice-president' chasing a male secretary around her desk" (quoted in Harrison 1988, 188–89).

Remember that forty years ago it was common for "Help Wanted" advertisements to be separate for males and females. Admittedly, a few newspapers had begun to integrate their ads even before Title VII went into effect. But others, including the *New York Times*, declined to do so. They sought to protect themselves by citing the First Amendment's guarantee for freedom of the press and, as permitted by the EEOC at the time, with the disclaimer that separate columns for male and female positions was for "the convenience of readers and not intended as an unlawful limitation or discrimination based on sex" (quoted in Bird 1970, 16).

In retrospect it seems remarkable that in the mid-1960s one of the first controversies ignited by Title VII revolved around the use of gender-segregated classified ads. Moreover, the EEOC initially tried to duck that controversy by announcing in April 1966 that it would judge only the advertising by employers, not the headings used by newspapers. The EEOC's position that it could not force newspapers to stop using gender-segregated ads, though it could stop them from using racially segregated ads, angered Representative Griffiths and some other leaders of women's organizations. They countered that such discrimination was just as objectionable and illegal as classified ads based on race—"Help

Wanted White," for instance, and "Help Wanted Negro"—which also had once been common but now was illegal.

Nonetheless, not until December 1, 1968, did the EEOC finally move to bar gender-based classified advertisements. Some newspapers still resolutely refused to comply. And they did not comply until after the Supreme Court handed down its 1973 ruling in *Pittsburgh Press v. Pittsburgh Commission on Human Rights.* There, over the dissent of conservative Chief Justice Warren E. Burger and the Court's leading liberal, Justice William O. Douglas, the high bench laid to rest claims by newspapers to First Amendment protection for gender-segregated advertisements. Writing for the majority in *Pittsburgh Press,* Justice Lewis F. Powell Jr. found no impairment of editorial freedom. And he emphasized what should have been clear and noncontroversial from the outset, namely: "The advertisements, as embroidered by their placement, signal that the advertisers were likely to show an illegal sex preference in their hiring decisions."

In fairness, admittedly the EEOC initially had very weak enforcement authority. That was the result of compromises and deals struck in the halls of Congress during the passage of the Civil Rights Act. Provisions that would have authorized the EEOC to bring litigation on behalf of employees and to enforce Title VII were eliminated in the final act. Hence, the EEOC had no independent enforcement authority to bring litigation. When responding to complaints of employment discrimination, the EEOC could investigate them. But, if the EEOC determined that they were well grounded, it only had the power to try to persuade employers to abandon their discriminatory practices. If that failed, the EEOC was in a position only to refer cases for litigation to the Civil Rights Division of the Department of Justice (DOJ).

By 1970, however, the EEOC confronted a growing backlog of complaints. Congress gave some consideration in 1971 to empowering the EEOC to issue cease and desist orders to employers with discriminatory employment policies. Yet, the proposal was defeated by the combined opposition of some Republicans and Southern Democrats. Instead, a year later Congress passed the Equal Employment Opportunity Act of 1972. Under that legislation the EEOC was authorized to bring suits against employers who refused to abandon discriminatory practices. Subsequently, a full decade after the passage of the Civil Rights Act, in 1974 the authority to file "pattern and practice" lawsuits— lawsuits challenging systemic discrimination on a company-wide or industry-wide basis—was transferred from the DOJ's Civil Rights Division to the EEOC. Besides thereby reinforcing and expanding the EEOC's power, the commission's jurisdiction was broadened to include federal, state, county, and municipal employees within the scope of Title VII. Nonetheless, the EEOC continued drawing criticism from some women's groups for failing to sue more offending employers.

The EEOC's power was yet again broadened under Democratic President Jimmy Carter's Reorganization Plan Number 1. As of July 1, 1979, the EEOC was reorganized as the "lead agency" in enforcing employment discrimination law (Rose 1989, 1136). The EEOC's authority and the statutory basis for bringing gender-discrimination employment lawsuits was also gradually reinforced by lower federal court and Supreme Court rulings in the 1970s and early 1980s (*Griggs v. Duke Power Company* [1971], *McDonnell Douglas v. Green* [1973], *Albemarle Paper Company v. Moody* [1975], *Dothard v. Rawlison* [1977], and *Texas Department of Community Affairs v. Burdine* [1981]).

But, following the 1980 election of Republican President Ronald Reagan, the direction of the EEOC changed in 1982 under Clarence Thomas, Reagan's EEOC chairman, who was later named by President George H. W. Bush to the Court of Appeals for the District of Columbia Circuit and, then, to the Supreme Court in 1991. Under Thomas, the EEOC abandoned its policy of bringing class action lawsuits and shifted to concentrating on cases of individualized discrimination. Although drawing sharp criticisms from women's groups and others, Thomas defended his approach as "more methodical, more cautious and certainly less noisy" than that of his predecessors (Thomas 1985, 35, and compare Norton 1988, 681; and Days 1989, 1005). Still, by the 1980s the EEOC's authority concerning gender-discrimination in employment litigation, as noted above, was finally firmly established.

FROM DISCRIMINATION TO SEXUAL HARASSMENT IN EMPLOYMENT

Given the controversial origins and the tenuous initial status of both the Title VII prohibition on gender-based discrimination in employment and the EEOC itself, perhaps not surprisingly, over a decade passed before claims of sexual harassment in the workplace were filed under Title VII, initially without much success. Furthermore, the EEOC did not issue guidelines on sexual harassment until 1980. Indeed, it seems fair to say that such claims were virtually unimaginable when the Civil Rights Act of 1964 was enacted.

Recall that not until the 1970s and 1980s was there a political and legal movement, as an outgrowth of the "women's movement," to recognize claims of "sexual harassment" in employment—or, in other words, to develop categories and a legal basis for reconstructing the social reality of the workplace. The battles waged over acknowledging sexual harassment in the workplace culminated, improbably, in a kind of dramatic way, played out with no little irony, during the 1991 nationally televised hearings before the Senate Judiciary Committee on Clarence Thomas's nomination to the Supreme Court.

The Senate's confirmation of Justice Thomas was almost defeated by the allegations of law school professor Anita Hill that, almost a decade earlier, when she served as an assistant to the then chair of the EEOC, Thomas had sexually harassed her. Hill testified that Thomas had repeatedly asked for dates, frequently talked about pornographic movies, and created a hostile work environment. Thomas in turn categorically denied the accusations and angrily protested that the confirmation process had become "a circus" and "a high tech lynching for uppity blacks."

The nasty drama of "she said, he said" failed to resolve the immediate questions about the veracity of either Hill or Thomas; nor could it have resolved their and others' conflicting perceptions of sexual harassment in the workplace. Still, the episode served to underscore how much public perception of sexual harassment in the workplace had changed (and was continuing to change) as a result of the legal and political battles of the preceding two decades (Morrison 1992; Chrisman and Allen 1992; and O'Brien 2000d, 70–82).

Before the mid-1970s there was virtually no reliable empirical data on sexual harassment in the workplace. But that changed with a series of surveys documenting complaints by women about sexual harassment (Association of American Colleges 1978; Hill and Behrens 1981). In addition, by the mid-1970s individual women and women's groups began filing sexual harassment lawsuits, and feminist legal scholars were advancing arguments and theories for recognizing legal claims to sexual harassment.

In her pioneering 1979 book, *Sexual Harassment of Working Women,* law professor and leading feminist theorist Catherine MacKinnon distinguished between two kinds of sexual harassment claims in advocating their legal recognition: Quid pro quo harassment, on the one hand, involves an employer or supervisor demanding sexual favors in exchange for employment advantages, such as a promotion or simply not being laid off. On the other hand, MacKinnon distinguished "condition of work harassment," or what the EEOC and the courts eventually came to term "hostile workplace harassment" and "hostile-environment sexual harassment." That arises when employees are subjected to sexual comments, insults, or demands for favors, but there are not adverse employment consequences. In MacKinnon's words:

> [U]nwanted sexual advances, made simply because she has a woman's body, can be a daily part of a woman's work life. She may be constantly felt or pinched, visually undressed and stared at, surreptitiously kissed, commented upon, manipulated into being found alone, and generally taken advantage of at—but never promised or denied anything explicitly connected with her job. (MacKinnon 1979, 40)

As a feminist theorist, MacKinnon viewed sexual harassment principally as the expression of male dominance over females. Yet, on a different theoretical basis, as courts in the 1990s eventually acknowledged, both categories of sexual harassment—quid pro quo and hostile environment harassment—would apply (and now do apply) to females harassing males and to same-sex harassment (*Oncale v. Sundowner Offshore Services* [1998]).

Initially, courts neither distinguished between quid pro quo and hostile environment harassment, nor were they very receptive to claims of sexual harassment. The first workplace harassment suit was brought successfully by a Hispanic worker, in *Rogers v. EEOC* (1971). Other harassment claims based on race, religion, and national origins followed (*Gray v. Greyhound Lines, East* [1976], *Compston v. Borden, Inc.* [1976], *Cariddi v. Kansas City Chiefs Football Club* [1977], and *Firefighters Institute for Racial Equality v. St. Louis* [1977]). By contrast, although federal courts proved willing to uphold claims to quid pro quo sexual harassment in the late 1970s, it was not until 1981 that a claim to workplace sexual harassment proved successful (*Bundy v. Jackson* [1981]).

Lower federal courts were generally unreceptive to sexual harassment claims for a number of reasons, including simply that either sex could engage in harassing behavior and that sexual advances or comments were not deemed to be employment related or a condition of employment. Moreover, since Title VII forbids discrimination by employers, some courts were reluctant to impose liability on them for sexual harassment by supervisors and coworkers, especially in large companies.

One measure of the difficulty of successfully bringing early sexual harassment suits is that between 1974 and 1977 just five such suits in federal district courts were decided. Not only was the number small, reflecting the novelty of the claims, but three courts held that Title VII did not apply to sexual harassment (*Barnes v. Costle* [1977], *Corne v. Bausch and Lomb* [1975], and *Tomkins v. Public Service Electric and Gas* [1977]).

Another court ruled that, while Title VII did not apply in the case before it, the statute might apply in other cases and circumstances. Moreover, that court also warned of the potential for widespread and abusive Title VII sexual harassment litigation, observing that "it would not be difficult to foresee a federal challenge based on alleged sex motivated considerations of the complainant's superior in every case of a lost promotion, transfer, demotion or dismissal" (*Miller v. Bank of America* [1976]).

In only one suit, *Williams v. Saxbe* (1976), was a sexual harassment claim successful; indeed, it was the first to succeed in a federal district court. Diane Williams, a Department of Justice public information officer, sued when she was fired less than two weeks after refusing her supervisor's sexual advances. In holding that Title VII's prohibition did apply, the district court rejected as a defense that sexual demands could be made to both sexes and, thus, fell outside of the scope of the statute. And it concluded that the actions of supervisors "created an artificial barrier to employment which was placed before one gender and not the other."[2]

Nevertheless, each of the three district court decisions that had expressly rejected Title VII sexual harassment claims were subsequently reversed by federal appellate courts (*Barnes v. Costle* [1977], *Tomkins v. Public Service Electric and Gas* [1977], and *Miller v. Bank of America* [1979]). Notably, the Court of Appeals for the Third Circuit held squarely that Title VII is violated when a supervisor "makes sexual advances or demands towards a subordinate employee . . . and the employer does not take prompt and appropriate remedial action" (*Tomkins v. Public Service Electric and Gas* [1977]).

The Court of Appeals for the Ninth Circuit in *Miller v. Bank of America* (1979), likewise, affirmed employers' liability under Title VII for its supervisory employees' harassment of coworkers, reasoning by analogy that:

> It would be shocking to most of us if a court should hold, for example, that a taxi company is not liable to a pedestrian caused by the negligence of one of its drivers because the company has a safety training program and strictly forbids negligent driving. Nor would the taxi company be exonerated even if the taxi driver, in the course of his employment, became enraged at a jaywalking pedestrian and intentionally ran him down. (215)

On the basis of that analogy the Ninth Circuit concluded, as had the Third Circuit and some other appellate courts, that Congress did not intend in Title VII to exempt employers from standard rules for employer liability.

In light of the lower federal appellate court rulings interpreting Title VII to extend to sexual harassment claims and to impose liability on employers for their employees' harassing behavior, the Carter administration's controversial and outspoken EEOC chair, Eleanor Holmes Norton, moved in 1980 to issue guidelines, based on the emerging Title VII federal case law, as amendments to EEOC Guidelines on Discrimination Based on Sex. After a sixty-day public comment period, the guidelines were released on November 10, 1980.

The EEOC's 1980 guidelines built on and in some respects further extended and refined the developing Title VII case law. In particular, they provided a comprehensive definition of "sexual harassment," distinguishing between quid pro quo and hostile workplace harassment, as well as expanded employer liability. The guidelines specified provided that,

> Unwelcome sexual advances, requests for sexual favors, and other verbal or physical conduct of a sexual nature constitute sexual harassment when (1) submission to such conduct is made either explicitly or implicitly a term or condition of an individual's employment (2) submission to or rejection of such conduct by an individual is used as a basis for employment decisions affecting such individual, or (3) such conduct has the purpose or effect of unreasonably interfering with an

individual's work performance or creating an intimidating hostile, or offensive working environment. (5)

In addition, the guidelines recommended holding companies strictly liable—that is, always liable—and made no distinction in this regard between quid pro quo and hostile workplace harassment when supervisors are involved. However, when coworkers harass coworkers, the guidelines did recommend holding employers liable only if they knew or should have known about the harassing behavior and failed to do anything about it.

Needless to say, perhaps, the EEOC's guidelines on sexual harassment claims invited an increasing number of complaints and litigation. Indeed, the number of complaints rose rather dramatically thereafter, rising to 7,273 complaints filed at the EEOC in 1985 alone (Machlowitz and Machlowitz 1987, 78). The courts in turn became even more receptive to Title VII sexual harassment claims, though initially more responsive to quid pro quo claims than to claims of hostile workplace harassment.

Still, within a year the influential Court of Appeals for the District of Columbia Circuit upheld a hostile workplace sexual harassment claim in light of the EEOC's new guidelines, in *Bundy v. Jackson* (1981). It did so when reversing a 1979 district court decision that had, prior to the EEOC's guidelines, dismissed the claim.

Sandra Bundy, a Department of Corrections employee, charged that her supervisor's sexual advances constituted workplace harassment and a hostile environment, even though she was neither fired nor denied benefits for refusing the advances. The district court, which in retrospect appears "out of tune with the times," dismissed her claim upon concluding that, in its words, "the making of improper sexual advances to female employees [was] standard operating procedure, a fact of life, a normal condition of employment in the office" (*Bundy v. Jackson* [1979], 831).

The district court's language and reasoning appears antiquated in light of the developing Title VII case law and the EEOC's 1980 guidelines, and accordingly the Court of Appeals for the District of Columbia Circuit reversed the decision. On appeal, in *Bundy v. Jackson* (1981) the appellate court emphasized that developing case law had found "Title VII violations where an employer created or condoned a substantially discriminatory work *environment*, regardless of whether the complaining employees lost any tangible job benefits as a result of the discrimination." Moreover, in no uncertain terms the appellate court made clear that to hold otherwise would amount to subjecting female employees to:

> a "cruel trilemma" [in that] she can endure the harassment. [Alternatively,] she can attempt to oppose it, with little hope of success, either legal or practical, but

with every prospect of making the job even less tolerable for her. Or she can leave her job, with little hope of legal relief and the likely prospect of another job where she will face harassment anew. (*Bundy v. Jackson* [1981], 946)

While *Bundy v. Jackson* was pending in the lower federal courts, another lawsuit was moving up through the federal judiciary and would eventually result in the Supreme Court's watershed ruling on Title VII sexual harassment claims in *Meritor Savings Bank, FBD v. Vinson* (1986). After four years of working as a bank teller-trainee, teller, and finally as an assistant manager, Mechelle Vinson filed a lawsuit against her supervisor, Sidney Taylor, and her employer, at the time Capital City Federal Savings and Loan Association, but later known as Meritor Savings Bank, FBD. Vinson did so after notifying Taylor in September 1978 that she was taking indefinite sick leave and, then, the bank discharged her for taking excessive leave. In her suit, Vinson claimed that during the preceding four years she had "constantly been subject to sexual harassment" by Taylor in violation of Title VII.

At an eleven-day trial, Vinson testified that Taylor was initially "fatherly" but soon asked her out to dinner, whereupon he suggested going to a motel for sex. While Vinson at first refused, she ultimately agreed out of fear of losing her job. After that Taylor allegedly repeatedly made demands for sexual favors and Vinson testified to having intercourse with him some forty to fifty times over the next several years. For his part, Taylor denied all of Vinson's allegations and countered that her accusations stemmed from a business dispute.

The federal district court ruled that Vinson had failed to substantiate a Title VII claim and, furthermore, held that, since the bank had a policy against gender discrimination and Vinson had failed to complain, the bank was not liable for Taylor's behavior, even if true (*Vinson v. Taylor* [1985]).

On appeal, the Court of Appeals for the District of Columbia Circuit reversed. Relying on its own decision in *Bundy*, the appellate court asserted that it was now established that quid pro quo harassment was impermissible under Title VII. In addition, the appellate court ruled that the EEOC's 1980 guidelines also made a "persuasive" argument for applying Title VII to the second category of "hostile workplace harassment." And the circuit court remanded the case to the district court in order to determine whether Taylor's behavior had created a hostile environment in violation of Title VII.

The circuit court rejected as well the district court's view of employer liability, which the lower court had set aside because Vinson had not filed a grievance with her supervisor, Taylor. The appellate court deemed that arrangement unacceptable and impractical under the circumstances, as well as reasoned that Title VII applies to both the employer *and* its agents. Furthermore, on a theory of vicarious liability, the court concluded that Taylor's violation of Title VII was also attributable to the bank, regardless of its knowledge of the behavior (*Vinson v. Taylor* [1985]).

Meritor Savings Bank appealed the District of Columbia Circuit's decision to the Supreme Court. And the justices unanimously affirmed the appellate court's decision to remand the case back to the district court on Vinson's complaint of hostile workplace harassment in violation of Title VII. Besides legitimating the basis for claims of hostile workplace harassment under Title VII, no less importantly the Court rejected the contention of Meritor Savings Bank that Title VII applied only to gender discrimination that imposes "tangible, economic barriers."

Notably, in so ruling in his opinion for the Court in *Meritor Savings Bank*, Justice Rehnquist relied on, and affirmed, the EEOC's 1980 guidelines that extended Title VII to complaints of a hostile workplace environment. Justice Rehnquist did so because, as he noted in summarizing the origins of the "sex amendment," there "was little legislative history to guide [the Court] in interpreting the [Civil Rights] Act's prohibition against discrimination based on 'sex.'" Although affirming the EEOC's interpretation of Title VII, Justice Rehnquist cautioned that "not all workplace conduct that may be described as 'harassment' affects a 'term, condition, or privilege' of employment within the meaning of Title VII." And he stressed that, "For sexual harassment to be actionable, it must be sufficiently severe or pervasive 'to alter the condition of [the alleged victim's] employment and create an abusive working environment.'"

In *Meritor Savings Bank*, however, the Court did reject the appellate court's holding on employers' vicarious liability. At the same time, the Court declined "to issue a definite rule on employer liability." On the one hand, the Court refused to impose strict liability on employers for a hostile workplace environment, like that for quid pro quo harassment. On the other hand, the Court acknowledged that employers may not escape liability in such cases by claiming that they lacked notice or knowledge of their agents' or supervisors' sexually harassing behavior. Instead, Justice Rehnquist emphasized that lower courts should look to the EEOC's guidelines when imposing liability under Title VII and, although notably only a bare majority of the justices agreed to this point,[3] to developing case law and "common law principles."

In other words, in *Meritor Savings Bank*, as with decisions in other areas of law, the Court concluded that the issue of employer liability should percolate for a while in the lower courts before the Supreme Court weighed in on the matter. Hence, the Court waited more than a decade before squarely ruling on that issue in two of its 1998 decisions, *Faragher v. City of Boca Raton* and *Burlington Industries v. Ellerth*, as well as left other unresolved matters in *Meritor Savings*

Bank for subsequent decisions, as noted at the outset here, in *Harris v. Forklift Systems*, for instance, and *Oncale v. Sundowner Offshore Services*.

CONCLUSION

There is no need here to go into greater detail on the developing law of sexual harassment under Title VII, or the related law on sexual discrimination and harassment in education under Title IX (*Gebser v. Lago Vista Independent School District* [1998]; and Mezey 1992, 180–83). For, the aim here has been simply to illustrate some of the ways in which congressional legislation on rights may have unanticipated, even ironic, consequences. The ways in which the prohibition in Title VII on gender discrimination came to be enforced remains doubly ironic, given both the origins of its inclusion in the Civil Rights Act of 1964 in the first place and the subsequent extension to claims—claims not merely unanticipated but virtually unimaginable—of same-sex harassment.

Statutory language, of course, is rarely unambiguous, and this case study serves to underscore the enormous influence that federal agencies and courts may have on the application of civil rights legislation. Beyond that, though, the development of Title VII sexual harassment law demonstrates the power of ideas and social forces in pressuring Congress to enact legislation and, then, pushing federal agencies and courts to enforce that legislation, at times in directions completely unforeseen by Congress.

NOTES

1. In a fourth decision, *Gebser v. Lago Vista Independent School District* (1998), a bare majority of the Court held that damages may not be recovered for teacher-student sexual harassment in an implied private right-of-action suit under Title IX, which forbids sex discrimination by schools that receive federal funding. Writing for the Court, Justice Sandra Day O'Connor ruled that schools are not liable for such misconduct unless school officials with authority to institute corrective measures are "deliberately indifferent" to a teacher's misconduct. In her opinion, Justice O'Connor emphasized that Title IX is unlike Title VII of the Civil Rights Act because it provides for the loss of federal funding when school officials know of and fail to respond to misconduct, and Congress, therefore, did not contemplate private cause of action suits for sexual harassment. The dissenting justices—Justices John Paul Stevens, David H. Souter, Ruth Bader Ginsburg, and Stephen Breyer—countered that school districts should be liable for teachers' misconduct on the theory that teachers are acting on behalf of the school. In *Franklin v. Gwinnett County Public Schools* (1992), the Court had held that students in public schools that receive federal funds may sue and win damages for sexual harassment under Title IX of the Educational Amendments of 1972.

2. *Williams v. Saxbe* (1976). The district court's decision, however, was reversed on appeal on other grounds, in *Williams v. Bell* (1978). But, on remand the district court nonetheless, again, concluded that "submission to the sexual advances of the plaintiff's supervisor was a term and condition of employment in violation of Title VII" (*Williams v. Civiletti* [1980], 1389).

3. Although concurring in the judgment in *Meritor Savings Banks, FBD v. Vinson*, Justice Thurgood Marshall, joined by Justices William J. Brennan Jr., Harry Blackmun, and John Paul Stevens, rejected the majority's treatment of the issue of employer liability. They would have upheld the imposition of strict liability of employers for both quid pro quo and hostile workplace harassment.

PART TWO

Expanding Privacy at Work and at Home

From Privacy Rights to Privacy Protection: Congressional Formulation of Online Privacy Policy

PRISCILLA M. REGAN

"Rights talk" (Glendon 1991) has long been entangled in the political rhetoric, policy debates, and policy solutions surrounding information privacy issues. In large part this construction of the issue dates back to 1890 when Samuel Warren and Louis Brandeis penned "The Right to Privacy," a *Harvard Law Review* article that has become a seminal piece analyzing privacy invasions and suggesting solutions. Their article, and subsequent debate about a right to privacy, was provoked by a technological change—specifically instantaneous photographs and mechanical devices that pick up conversations from a distance. They argued that the common law protected a "right to privacy" and that "now the right to life has come to mean the right to enjoy life, the right to be let alone" (Warren and Brandeis 1890, 193). The language of rights dominated the 1960s and 1970s congressional and public discussions regarding computers and privacy. But as the twenty-first century approached and Congress considered online privacy issues, the language of rights became less prominent in policy discussions, both in terms of a rights-based definition of the problem and also in terms of rights-based solutions.

In many instances involving rights-based disputes the judicial branch provides the primary forum for policy discussion and resolution. But for the issue of information privacy, including online privacy, Congress has been called on to act, generally without judicial guidance or intervention. With the introduction of computerized record systems, the dialogue about privacy rights involved Congress and federal agencies, especially the Department of Health, Education and Welfare and later the Office of Management and Budget. During the debate about online privacy a dialogue between Congress and agencies such as the

Federal Trade Commission and Department of Commerce was instrumental in determining the contours of and protection offered by privacy rights.

This chapter compares the two eras of congressional policy formulation regarding information privacy, with particular attention given to congressional ideas about problem definition and viable solutions. Although the core concern—giving individuals some control over the uses and disclosures of their personal information—has not deviated, there have been significant modifications in the cause of the concern, with the activities of the private sector becoming of more concern than government agencies, and in the scope of the impact, with emphasis on the online environment as a whole rather than on specific sectors. These modifications have led, in part, to a rethinking of the ability of singular individuals to exercise control. As these changes have been recognized, they have been accompanied by alterations in problem definition and in formulation of solutions. Whereas the early era of the 1960s and 1970s emphasized ideas about fundamental rights and liberties with solutions framed in terms of individual legal remedies, the current era emphasizes consumer protection with solutions framed in terms of preventing "unfair and deceptive trade practices." The change is not a complete one, however, with the roots of the consumer protection emphasis existing in the earlier era and the rights tradition persisting into the online era. But the shift is an interesting one in terms of understanding the congressional politics of rights-based issues and the limitations of framing policy problems and policy solutions in terms of rights.

The chapter proceeds as follows: first, the initial congressional debates about privacy and computers are briefly reviewed with special attention given to the definition of the problem and the range of policy options; second, the recent (104th to 107th) congressional debates about online privacy are investigated with attention given to the same features of policymaking; and, finally, explanations for the similarities and differences in these two periods of congressional policy formulation are examined and the implications of these similarities and differences on Congress's ability to define and accommodate new protections for citizens are explored.

THE ERA OF COMPUTERS AND PRIVACY

Computer Privacy Issues

Beginning in the mid-1960s, the computerization of personal record systems served as a catalyst to focus congressional and public attention on the potential abuses and misuses of such systems (Brenton 1964; Packard 1964; Wheeler 1969). It was widely recognized that computers allowed for the collection and storage of more personal information, easier manipulation of that information, quicker retrieval of items of personal information, and broader disclosure and exchanges of information. The problems that resulted could be defined as ones of organizational accountability, control of technology, or threats to personal privacy rights. The latter definition is the one that resonated most strongly in the United States, although in Europe the definition of organizational accountability was more dominant (Bennett 1992 and Flaherty 1989).

As computerization spread throughout public and private organizations, the policy problem was framed in philosophical and legal terms. Policy thinking derived in part from philosophical analyses of the importance of individual privacy and how collection of personal information violated an individual's right to privacy (Regan 1995). These remarks of Representative Cornelius E. Gallagher (D-N.J.), who in the mid-1960s chaired the House's Special Subcommittee on Invasion of Privacy, well illustrate this perspective: "'The Computerized Man,' as I see him, would be stripped of his individuality and privacy. Through the standardization ushered in by technological advance, his status in society would be measured by the computer, and he would lose his personal identity" (U.S. House 1966, 2). In these policy discussions, the fundamental nature of the right of privacy and its character as an element of autonomy and dignity were emphasized. The moral component of the issue was critical to policy formulation. Privacy, as reflected by the title of Alan Westin's book *Privacy and Freedom*, was intrinsically linked to freedom. Westin stated that the core of the "right of individual privacy" was "the right of the individual to decide for himself, with only extraordinary exceptions in the interest of society, when and on what terms his acts should be revealed to the general public" (Westin 1967, 42). In the philosophical writing at that time (Bloustein 1964; Fried 1968; Pennock and Chapman 1971), the importance of privacy was rooted firmly in liberal thinking—privacy inhered in the individual as individual and was important to the individual for self-development and the establishment of intimate or human relationships.

From a more concrete policy perspective, the question became whether existing constitutional or common law protections for the "right to privacy" could be easily extended to protect information privacy. For example, in an important article, William Prosser (1960) considered whether tort law protections against privacy invasions—intrusion, disclosure, false light, and appropriation—could provide a basis for protection. Arthur Miller (1971) raised the possibility that property law might provide protection for personal information. And others weighed whether the Fourth Amendment or the "reproductive privacy" decisions might furnish a basis for a right to information privacy. For a variety of reasons, both constitutional and common law protections were seen as inadequate or inappropriate in dealing with the information privacy issues raised by computers. The Supreme Court's ruling in *Whalen v. Roe* (1977), which involved a 1972 New York statute that required identification, as well as retention of information in a computer for a five-year period, of patients for whom were prescribed the most dangerous legitimate drugs, clearly illustrates the difficulty of finding constitutional protection. The New York provision was challenged on the grounds that it invaded the constitutionally protected zone of privacy surrounding the doctor-patient relationship. Relying on both the security protections afforded the records and the state's reasonable exercise of its police powers, the Court ruled that New York's statutory scheme reflected a proper protection of the individual's interest in privacy. The Court recognized two kinds of privacy interests—an interest in nondisclosure of private information and an interest in making important decisions independently (*Whalen v. Roe* 1977, 600)—but held that the New York program did not "pose a sufficiently grievous threat to either interest to establish a constitutional violation" (*Whalen v. Roe* 1977, 600). The Court acknowledged that the duty to avoid unwarranted disclosures "arguably has its roots in the Constitution" (*Whalen v. Roe* 1977, 605) but noted that its ruling only affected those systems with security protections similar to those in New York. Following *Whalen* lower courts have deferred to state arguments about accountability and bureaucratic needs and have been reluctant to extend constitutional safeguards to personal information (Schwartz 2000).

Congressional Formulation

Policy deliberations about how to give concrete meaning to the idea of a "right to privacy" focused attention on the goal of giving an individual the means to "control" the collection, use, and disclosure of personal information. A "code of fair information practices," first developed in 1973 by an advisory committee in the Department of Health, Education and Welfare (HEW), provided the core statement of principles for how such control could be achieved. The principles emphasized the rights of individuals to know about record-keeping systems and the uses of personal information in those systems, to access their records, to prevent information collected for one purpose to be used for another purpose without consent, and to correct or amend information. In addition to these rights of individuals, the code also spoke to the responsibility of organizations to publicize the existence of the record system, to ensure the reliability of data, and to prevent misuse of data (HEW 1973). The HEW Code of Fair Information Practices provided both the meaning for the idea of a right to information privacy and the framework for a policy solution that would give individuals the legal basis to take action to protect their privacy.

Following revelations about the abuses of government records that occurred during Watergate and combined with growing congressional concern about the potential abuses from computerization, hearings on a number of privacy bills were held in both the House and Senate in 1974. In the Senate, the Committee on Government Operations, through its Ad Hoc Subcommittee on Privacy and Information Systems, and the Judiciary Committee, through its Subcommittee on Constitutional Rights, held joint hearings on five privacy bills. All five bills— S. 3418, S. 3633, S. 3116, S. 2810, and S. 2542—were framed in terms of a "right to privacy." In introducing S. 3418, Senator Samuel J. Ervin Jr. (D-N.C.) stated that "the appetite of government and private organizations for information about individuals threatens to usurp the right to privacy which I have long felt to be among the most basic of our civil liberties as a free people" (Senate Ad Hoc Subcommittee on Privacy and Information Systems 1974, 352). The centerpiece of Senator Ervin's measure was a code of fair information practices giving individuals the rights to see and amend files, and to be informed of disclosures of information. The bill covered all personal information systems, whether public or private, computerized or manual. It also provided for a Federal Privacy Board with some regulatory power. Similarly, S. 2542 incorporated a statutory basis for the code of fair information practices and a legal basis for individual action. In introducing S. 2542, Senator Birch E. Bayh (D-Ind.) emphasized "the average citizen's right to be free from the unreasonable invasion of his privacy by the Federal Government" (Senate Ad Hoc Subcommittee on Privacy and Information Systems 1974, 407).

In congressional floor debates, Warren's and Brandeis's definition of privacy as the "right to be let alone" was used repeatedly. Senator Ervin, for example, introduced his bill by saying that it was "an important first step in the protection of our individual right to be left alone." Senator Barry Goldwater Jr. (R-Ariz.) stated: "By privacy I mean the right 'to be let alone'—from intrusions by Big Brother in all his guises." Similarly, Representative Richard H. Ichord (D-Mo.) defined the right to privacy as the "right to be left alone . . . without a doubt a right inherent in our libertarian system" (quoted in Regan 1995, 80). Throughout the floor debates in both the House and Senate, the images of *1984* and Watergate were repeatedly evoked. Representative William S. Moorhead (D-Pa.), the House bill manager, noted that the proposed Privacy Act would "make it legally impossible for the Federal Government in the future to put together anything resembling a '1984' personal dossier on a citizen." Senator Ervin also pointed out that many witnesses had "said that the disclosures of Watergate highlighted the need for this bill" (quoted in Regan 1995, 81).

The congressional hearings provoked opposition from the organized interests that were threatened by proposals to give individuals rights to protect their privacy. Members of Congress recognized that this privacy right was not absolute and needed to be balanced against other interests such as law enforcement, investigative concerns, administrative efficiency, and national security. Although support for the idea or value of privacy was unwavering, when Congress had to balance privacy against competing interests, these interests generally prevailed. For example, in House votes, numerous types of information were exempted from restrictions in the Privacy Act, including testing materials for federal employment, evaluation materials supporting promotion, and "routine uses" that were compatible with the purpose for which information was collected.

On November 21, 1974, the House adopted its version of the Privacy Act by a vote of 353 to 1, and the Senate adopted its version by a vote of 74 to 9. Differences between the two versions were reconciled by staff from both chambers, and the compromise conference bill passed with minimal opposition. The final version only covered personal record systems maintained by federal agencies; gave individuals rights of access, correction, and knowledge about personal records; subjected agencies to standards of fair information handling; charged the Office of Management and Budget (OMB) with implementation and oversight; and established a study commission to investigate the private sector and questions about the need for additional oversight.

THE ERA OF ONLINE PRIVACY

Online Privacy Issues

When people "surf" the Internet for commercial, social, or research purposes, there are few visual cues as to when and how personally identifiable information is being captured, but there are a number of ways in which "clickstream data" or "mouse droppings" leave "electronic footprints." First, each site that a user visits obtains the user's Internet Protocol (IP) address. The IP address is the unique address that a user has when connected to the Internet. It locates that computer on the Internet. Although the IP address may not yield personally identifiable information, it does allow tracking of Internet movements from a particular computer. Second, "cookies" can be placed on the user's hard drive so that a web site can determine a user's prior activities at that web site when the user returns. This transactional information reveals not only what pages the user viewed but also the route by which the user arrived at the web site and where the user went on departure. Although there are ways of disabling cookies, few Internet users do this, in part because they do not know about cookies or this option or because disabling cookies slows online movements. A new online tracking device, known as "web bugs," is increasingly being used by Internet marketing companies and others. A web bug is a graphic embedded in a web page or e-mail message that monitors who is reading the page or message. Pharmatrak, a Boston technology firm tracking Internet use for pharmaceutical companies, used web bugs to track consumers' activity at web sites of eleven pharmaceutical companies. This tracking occurred without any notice to consumers, and future plans indicated that information gleaned from the web bugs may be used to identify individuals (O'Harrow 2000). In a statement to the Congressional Privacy Caucus, a computer security expert stated that in January 2000, about 2,000 "web bugs" were in use on the web and that five months later the number had increased to 27,000 (Smith 2000).

Despite this tracking, the online world does provide options for anonymity and pseudonymity. For example, one can use "anonymous remailers" to send messages, or one can open multiple accounts with Internet service providers and use different identities to mask cyberspace movements. Opportunities for anonymity and pseudonymity may be more possible in cyberspace than physical space, but only if one takes the time to find out how to use the necessary technology and organizational practices and makes the effort to implement what is necessary either automatically or for certain information or communications. As with disabling or monitoring cookies, there are costs in terms of time and effort that the individual must bear. At this time, anonymity and pseudonymity are legally protected in cyberspace. In *ACLU v. Miller* (1997) a federal district court struck down a Georgia statute that prohibited anonymous or pseudonymous electronic communications and instead required that the true identity of the sender be revealed. There are a number of "John Doe" cases under litigation where plaintiffs, usually businesses, are challenging anonymous or pseudonymous online comments that they allege are defaming their company (Lidsky 2000). The courts will decide the extent of First Amendment protections over online criticism of this type.

Although options for anonymity and pseudonymity exist technically and legally, most commercial web sites and many noncommercial web sites ask individuals for personally identifiable information such as e-mail address, name, and credit card number. In some instances this information is merely requested; in other instances providing some registration information, an e-mail address for example, is required before one can browse at that web site. If one wishes to make a purchase online, one is required to give a credit card number and mailing information. If individuals are surfing the web with no intention of returning to a web site, they may well misrepresent themselves in the information they provide. Concerns about the automatic capture of information about people surfing online and about requests for personally identifiable information become even more contentious when, without obvious clues as to the age of the web surfer, personal information about children's online activities are also being captured and exchanged.

The information gained through automatic tracking of Internet activities via cookies, web bugs or other devices, and individual revelations provides a detailed profile of an individual's demographic characteristics, entertainment and research interests, preferences, transactions, and purchasing habits. Web sites argue that "online profiles" allow them to better understand and serve their online visitors, but the profiles are generally compiled without the knowledge or review of individuals leading to possible manipulation or discrimination. Online profiles can also be created by network advertisers, often referred to as third-party web sites because they have no direct relationship with the individuals they profile. Network advertisers are able to track Internet behavior at a variety of web sites, allowing the development of a more complex and detailed online profile. DoubleClick and Engage are network advertisers who together have reportedly compiled an estimated 170 million profiles (Electronic Privacy Information Center [EPIC] and Junkbusters 2000).

Public opinion surveys indicate that more than 80 percent of respondents are concerned about threats to their privacy online. Although only 6 percent of Internet users reported that they were victims of an online privacy invasion, a 1998 *Privacy and American Business* survey revealed that almost three-quarters of Internet users regard fairly typical online privacy issues as very serious. For example, 70 percent of respondents regarded it as a "very serious" privacy invasion if web sites were "collecting email addresses of Web site visitors without their knowledge or consent to compile email marketing lists" (Harris and Westin 1998, 8). Industry-sponsored research confirms these findings. A 1999 Forrester Technographics report found that two-thirds of online shoppers are insecure about exchanging personal information over the Internet (Forrester Research, Inc. 1999).

Although large numbers of people express concern about online privacy invasions, people do reveal information online and are most comfortable doing so when they are told about the uses of that information. Surveys also reveal that people differentiate among the kinds of information that web sites request. An AT&T survey, conducted in November 1998, asked Internet users about how comfortable they generally feel providing specific types of information to web sites; people were more comfortable revealing general information, such as their favorite TV show, and less comfortable releasing their phone number and credit card number (Cranor et al. 1999, 9). The survey also found that 96 percent of respondents believed the most important factor affecting the release of information was whether or not the information would be shared with other companies and organizations. Knowledge about how personal data will be used is also important to people in making revelations in exchange for survey "freebies"— such as free e-mail, discounts, sweepstakes, and notices of how the information will be used. A 1999 *Privacy and American Business* survey found that, depending on the circumstances, about 75 percent of respondents believed that it was fair to require disclosure of personal information in exchange for a benefit if a web site offered a "valuable benefit" and "fully" informed individuals about what would be done with personal information. Only 14 percent responded that they were not concerned about privacy policies as long as they got the benefit (Opinion Research Corporation and Alan F. Westin 1999).

The Pew Internet and American Life Project surveyed more than 2,000 respondents to gauge public concern about online privacy (Fox 2000). The analysts of the survey results reached two conclusions: Americans want the presumption of privacy online, and a great many Internet users are not knowledgeable about the basics of how their online activities are being observed and what they can do to protect themselves. Specifically, 54 percent thought that it would be "harmful, because it invades your privacy" if an Internet company tracked the pages you went to online, while 27 percent thought that it would be "helpful, because the company can provide you with information that matches your interests." Sixty-three percent thought that Internet companies should not be allowed to track activities of people who visit their web sites, while 22 percent thought they should be allowed to do so. But, only 5 percent of respondents had "used software that hides your computer identity from Web sites you visit," and 9 percent had "sent an encrypted email that has been scrambled to keep other people from reading it." From a policy perspective, 86 percent favored an "opt-in" privacy policy, where information cannot be collected unless an individual gives prior permission.

In the case of privacy, a recurring question has been whether these surveys are measuring a latent public concern that is belied by individual behavior. As discussed above, people do trade privacy for tangible benefits. But there are some concrete indications that online privacy does matter to people and that they do and will act on their privacy concerns. In several instances, the online public has been quickly and effectively mobilized to take grassroots action in response to privacy threats. The first instance was in 1990 when Lotus and Equifax developed Lotus MarketPlace: Households, a CD-ROM and software product containing personally identifiable information—including name, address, estimated household income, lifestyle, and shopping habits—that was designed to help small businesses in marketing their products. In response to criticisms of the privacy implications that arrived via phone, letters, and e-mail to Lotus's CEO, Lotus canceled the product (Gurak 1997). Similar online protests occurred in 1999 when Intel announced its Pentium III processor containing a Personal Serial Number (PSN). Privacy advocates were critical of the possibility that the PSN would function as a unique identifier. A boycott initiated by the Electronic Privacy Information Center (EPIC), Junkbusters, and Privacy International posted information about the controversy on their web sites and on a joint web site dedicated to this issue, bigbrotherinside.com. This generated media attention and provided people with information necessary to contact Intel directly. Intel made two modifications in response. When DoubleClick announced plans to combine its online profiles with personally identifiable information from the

Abacus direct database, a barrage of negative publicity and complaints to the Federal Trade Commission resulted. The Center for Democracy and Technology (CDT) offered at its web site the opportunity to "opt out" of DoubleClick's tracking, to send a message to DoubleClick's CEO, and to send messages to several companies using DoubleClick's services. In less than 72 hours, 13,000 people opted out, 6,000 sent messages to the CEO, and, in the first thirty-six hours, more than 4,400 messages were sent to affiliates. A *Wall Street Journal* article compared the public reaction to the DoubleClick/Abacus proposal to that of the "Colonials to the Stamp Act" (Bushkin 2000).

Congressional Policy Formulation

When online privacy began to receive policy attention in the early 1990s, the concept and principles of "fair information practices" provided the foundation for policy discussions, and the locus of policy formulation was primarily the executive branch. In their "Framework for Global Electronic Commerce," President Clinton and Vice President Gore recognized what public opinion polls and consumer behavior had indicated: "Commerce on the GII [Global Information Infrastructure] will thrive only if the *privacy rights* of individuals are balanced with the benefits associated with the free flow of information" (emphasis added, Clinton and Gore 1997, 10). This definition of the problem—balancing rights of individuals against benefits to organizations—was identical to the earlier definition from the era of paper files and computer records. However, this definition and the rhetoric of rights did not dominate for long. Instead the economic concerns of the online industries—including Internet Service Providers (ISPs), online retailers, and technology companies—took center stage. Online business models rely on the secondary use and compilation of personally identifiable information as a source of revenue. Businesses regard their collection and exchanges of information as a legitimate business interest. Personally identifiable information is seen both as valuable in generating revenue and as an asset itself. In this environment, the issue of online privacy was not defined as a rights issue but as a business and consumer issue.

The public concern about online privacy and the industry recognition of the importance of ensuring some privacy in order to lure consumers generated congressional initiatives. But the executive branch took the lead in policy formulation, and the threat of legislation brought private sector representatives to several government tables. In general the industry position, shared by the Clinton administration, was that industry self-regulation would be a more effective and efficient way of protecting consumer privacy than congressional legislation. The industry argument was that government regulation would unnecessarily hamper technological innovation and the natural development of protections responsive to consumer demand. It was in these executive venues that the political rhetoric and problem definition shifted from a "right of privacy" to "consumer protection," a policy construction with which industry was more comfortable.

Two executive branch study commissions, the Information Policy Committee of the White House's Information Infrastructure Task Force (IITF 1995) and the National Information Infrastructure Advisory Council (NIIAC 1995) crafted privacy principles that echoed many of the traditional "fair information" principles developed earlier. For example, notice, correction or amendment, security, and access were seen as important in the online environment as they had been in the paper and computer environments. But some of the core principles, such as consent and redress, were modified if not weakened. Consent became choice, which had its roots more in the consumer protection model where you inform consumers of risks and benefits and let them decide what to do—that is, "consumer beware."

As policy formulation focused on the feasibility of industry self-regulation as a policy solution, the Federal Trade Commission (FTC) came to play a more dominant role. Under Section 5 of the FTC Act, the FTC may enforce actions against "unfair and deceptive trade practices." Industry practices regarding the collection and use of personal information that are not clearly stated can fall under this jurisdiction and with leadership from Christine Varney, a commissioner appointed by President Clinton, the FTC began to explore online privacy. In April 1995 the FTC held its first public workshop on privacy, followed by a series of hearings in October and November 1995, and public workshops in June 1996, 1997, 1999, and 2000. It also brought several enforcement actions against deceptive online information practices. Two cases, one in 1998 against GeoCities and one in 1999 against Liberty Financial Companies, had to do with web sites misrepresenting the purposes for which they were collecting personal information and their practices for uses of such information.

While the executive branch and the FTC were beginning the process of defining the policy problem and considering alternatives, Congress remained relatively inactive. The first online privacy bill, the Consumer Internet Privacy Protection Act, was introduced by Representative Bruce F. Vento (D-Minn.) in September 1996. This bill adopted the definition of the problem that had been promoted by the FTC; the goal was to protect consumer privacy and the concern was targeted narrowly on an "interactive computer service," or Internet service provider (ISP). The bill prohibited an ISP from disclosing personally identifiable information without the subscriber's informed written consent and required the ISP to give subscribers access to the information, the ability to verify and correct the information, and the identity of third party recipients of information. Additionally, the bill gave the FTC the authority to investigate potential violations and to issue cease and desist orders if an interactive computer service was in violation. The bill received little interest, and no hearings were held. Representative Vento reintroduced this bill in the 105th and 106th Congresses (1997–99 to 1999–2001). In 1997, Representative Vento said, "the preservation of our privacy is one of our nation's most cherished freedoms, which unchecked technology must not be allowed to circumvent" (*Congressional Record* 1997, E8). In 1999 he reiterated that sentiment and noted that "privacy protections are good for consumers and good for business," a slogan that received much support from industry (Vento 1999).

The FTC continued to monitor the development of self-regulatory mechanisms, particularly the posting of privacy or information practice notices on commercial web sites. In 1998, the FTC surveyed a sample of 1,400 commercial web sites and found that more than 85 percent collected personal information from consumers, 14 percent provided some notice with respect to their personal information practices, and 2 percent provided a comprehensive privacy policy notice (FTC 1998). The FTC concluded that "substantially greater incentives are needed to spur self-regulation and ensure widespread implementation of basic privacy principles" (FTC 1998, iii). In its report, the FTC indicated that it would make more specific recommendations in the summer, thus putting industry on notice that some regulation or legislation was likely.

Largely in response to these results and the perceived likelihood of federal legislation, several large private sector companies formed the Online Privacy Alliance, which drafted privacy guidelines and encouraged online posting of such policies. Also in the summer of 1998, the Department of Commerce held a series of "privacy conversations" with privacy advocates, industry representatives, and government officials to evaluate the effectiveness of self-regulation and the possible need for government regulation. In July hearings before the Telecommunications, Trade and Consumer Protection Subcommittee of the House Commerce Committee, FTC Chairman Robert Pitofsky said that if industry efforts were not effective by the end of the year, Congress should intervene to protect consumers online (Gruenwald 1998). In general though, the Department of Commerce's activities had the effect of diverting attention from the FTC and Congress back to the executive branch where policy formulation occurred largely among the group that saw itself as most affected. The Department of Commerce's activities also provided the Online Privacy Alliance more time to develop principles, get support from other industries, and strengthen its case that self-regulation could work.

Legislative interest picked up in the 105th Congress (1997–99) when nine bills specifically addressing online privacy were introduced, one in the Senate and nine in the House. Several bills addressing use of the Social Security number and identity theft, such as H.R. 1813, S. 600, and S. 512, were also introduced and would have impacted online activities as well. The core definition of the online privacy problem was framed in terms of protecting consumer privacy or online privacy: Federal Internet Privacy Protection Act (H.R. 1367); Consumer Internet Privacy Protection Act (H.R. 98); and Data Privacy Act (H.R. 2368). Of the nine bills introduced in the 105th Congress, only one included "rights" in its short title—Electronic Privacy Bill of Rights (H.R. 4667). However, its official title—"A bill to enhance consumer privacy, prevent unfair and deceptive trade practices, and protect children's privacy"—did not convey any rights orientation but instead fully incorporated the consumer protection definition. Interestingly, this bill was introduced by Representative Edward J. Markey (D-Mass.), who also introduced the Communications Privacy and Consumer Empowerment Act (H.R. 1964). Representative Markey's remarks introducing H.R. 4667 illustrate the dual definitions of rights and consumer protection and an attempt to merge the two into a seamless whole:

> The bill I am introducing today is premised on the belief that regardless of the technology that consumers use, their privacy rights and expectations ought to remain a constant. Whether consumers are using a phone, a TV clicker, a satellite dish, or a modem, every consumer should enjoy a Privacy Bill of Rights for the Information Age. Those core rights are embodied in a proposal I have advocated for many years and I call it "Knowledge, Notice and No." (*Congressional Record* 1998, E1861)

The policy tradition of privacy rights focused on giving individuals rights, such as knowledge and notice, by which they could negotiate their relationships with information-gathering organizations. The consumer protection tradition focused on requiring organizations to inform consumers and on providing for legal action against them if they did not do so.

In the 105th Congress the primary concern regarding online privacy focused on children. The FTC in its June 1998 report had found that 89 percent of children's web sites collected personal information and that less than 10 percent provided any parental controls over that collection. The FTC report recommended that Congress develop legislation. "Such legislation would require web sites that collect personally identifying legislation from children to provide actual notice to parents and obtain parental consent" (FTC 1998, iii). In July 1998, Senators Richard H. Bryan (D-Nev.) and John S. McCain (R-Ariz.) introduced the Children's Online Privacy Protection Act of 1998 (S. 2326). In comments on the bill, Senator Bryan characterized the problem of online collection of information from children as "leaving them unwittingly vulnerable to exploitation and harm by deceptive marketers and criminals" and that in order to "protect privacy" Congress should pass "these commonsense proposals" (*Congressional Record* 1998, S8483). The bill required the FTC to come up with rules for notice, consent, access, and integrity, and gave both the FTC and states' attorneys general enforcement power. The bill received almost universal support from: children's groups, such as Center for Media Education (CME), Public Advocacy for Kids, American Academy of Child and Adolescent Psychiatry, and American Academy of Pediatrics; consumer groups, including the Consumer Federation of America (CFA) and National Consumers League; education groups, such as the National Association of Elementary School Principals and National Education Association; and privacy groups including Electronic Privacy Information Center and Center for Democracy and Technology. The strength of the advocacy coalition coupled with media attention and the report and recommendations of the FTC succeeded in garnering overwhelming support for the bill, which was passed as an amendment to the Internet Tax Freedom Act in October 1998.

A year later the FTC reviewed web site privacy policies and concluded that sufficient increase in the number, if not necessarily the quality, of web site notices had occurred to indicate that self-regulation was working and that legislation was not needed (FTC 1999). The FTC based its conclusion on a 1999 survey that was commissioned primarily by several large corporations and conducted through the Georgetown Business School. This survey sampled 361 commercial web sites drawn from 7,500 of the most-often visited web sites and found that more than 92 percent of the sites collected personal information, 66 percent posted a privacy notice or information practice statement, and more than 43 percent posted a privacy policy notice (Culnan 1999). Several groups criticized the FTC's interpretation of the survey results because few web sites actually posted the full set of fair information practices that the FTC and the Clinton administration had advocated (CDT 1999).

The 106th Congress (1999–2001) saw increased activity both in terms of bill introduction—eight in both chambers—and in the number of hearings—two in the Senate and two in the House. Of the sixteen bills introduced in the 106th Congress, only two included a focus on rights: Electronic Rights for the 21st Century Act (S. 854) and Electronic Privacy Bill of Rights Act of 1999 (H.R. 3321). The remaining fourteen bills emphasize protecting online privacy or protecting consumer information. In the 106th Congress, the four bills that received the most attention were the Online Privacy Protection Act (S. 809), the Internet Integrity and Critical Infrastructure Protection Act of 2000 (S. 2448), the Privacy Commission Act (H.R. 4049), and the Internet Growth and Development Act (H.R. 1685). Two of the four bills regarded protection of consumer privacy as integral to the Internet infrastructure and not as an afterthought. Except for the Privacy Commission Act, all three bills rather uniformly emphasized a similar framework. First, they required web sites to give notice of their information collection practices and to enable consumers to consent, usually through opt out but in some cases opt in, to the collection and disclosure of personally identifiable information. Second, they recognized the authority of the FTC to bring enforcement action against web sites and in some cases to pre-scribe further regulations about online privacy. Some bills also made it a crime to fraudulently access personal information. Other bills sought to create a pri-vate right of action.

In February and March 2000, FTC staff again conducted a web surf of online privacy policies. In its May 2000 report the FTC concluded, by a narrow 3 to 2 vote, that industry self-regulatory efforts had not been shown to be effec-tive alone in protecting privacy and recommended that legislation was necessary as well (FTC 2000). The FTC's conclusion was based in large part on the results of its 2000 web survey reporting both good news and bad news. The good news was that there was improvement in the number of web sites posting some infor-mation about their privacy disclosures. The bad news was more significant: most web sites were not complying with all of the fair information practices, most web sites were not disclosing third-party cookies, and very few web sites were using seal programs to verify enforcement of their policies. In response Senator McCain, joined by Senators Spencer Abraham (R-Mich.), Barbara Boxer (D-Calif.), and John F. Kerry (D-Mass.), introduced the Consumer Internet Privacy Enhancement Act (S. 2928). In remarks on the Senate floor, Senator McCain emphasized the need "to protect consumers and provide for the continued growth of e-commerce" (*Congressional Record* 2000, S7669). Senator Kerry spoke of both the importance of privacy in encouraging people to go online, and of "core privacy principles" and "the right to full disclosure and the right to not have their personally identifiable information sold or disclosed" (*Congressional Record* 2000, S7671). Senator Abraham, on the other hand, spoke directly from the rights tradition, noting that privacy "is enshrined in our Bill of Rights" (*Congressional Record*, 2000, S7672).

Although some privacy advocates had begun in the 106th Congress with optimism that legislation would pass, that optimism waned as time progressed. Resources and time were devoted largely to hearings and comments on the reg-ulations to implement the Children's Online Privacy Protection Act as well as on the medical privacy issues associated with the Health Insurance Portability Protection Act and with privacy protections in the Gramm-Leach–Bliley Financial Services Act. Even without these distractions from online privacy, chances of passage were still slim given that industry was largely opposed to leg-islation that required them to post notices and to give consumers choice and access and granted the FTC and state officials any enforcement and oversight authority. This industry opposition resonated with many Republican lawmakers, including House Majority Leader Richard K. (Dick) Armey (R-Tex.) and Senate Judiciary Committee Chair Orrin G. Hatch (R-Utah). Coupled with the preoc-cupation of a presidential election year, it was no great surprise that online pri-vacy legislation was not enacted.

The beginning of the 107th Congress (2001–3) elicited much of the same initial predictions that legislation would pass. Within the first few weeks, several bills directly related to online privacy were introduced, including the Online Privacy Protection Act of 2001 (H.R. 89), the Social Security Online Privacy Protection Act (H.R. 91), the Consumer Internet Privacy Enhancement Act (H.R. 237), and the Consumer Online Privacy and Disclosure Act (H.R. 347). All adopted a consumer protection rather than an individual rights orientation. The Subcommittee on Commerce, Trade and Consumer Protection in March 2001 held hearings on "Privacy in the Commercial World," the tenor of which in part was to question the value and possibility of consumer privacy. The Bush administration nominated to the FTC a new head for antitrust enforcement and Internet privacy policy and indicated that a new Republican majority on the FTC was likely to reverse FTC support for strong online privacy rules.

"RIGHTS" OR "PROTECTION"

Since the 1970s public opinion polls show consistently high agreement that privacy is an important value if not fundamental right, that Americans are concerned about threats to their personal privacy, and that consumers have lost all control over how personal information about them is circulated and used by companies. Despite this public concern, Congress has not been successful in legislating to address these privacy concerns. In 1974, Congress enacted legislation that was far weaker than the bills originally proposed. Rather than giving individuals rights with respect to the information practices of all public and private organizations, Congress legislated rights only for federal agencies. Rather than establishing a Federal Privacy Board to regulate and implement legislation, Congress gave implementation authority to OMB. And as we enter the twenty-first century, Congress has been no more successful in legislating to protect online privacy.

In the earlier era the problem was seen as an invasion of individual privacy by record-keeping organizations, and the solution was framed in terms of giving individuals rights so that they could control information about themselves. In the second era the problem is seen as a result of the system by which people browse online, and the solution is framed in terms of protecting people by informing them of when and how personally identifiable information is collected and exchanged. The emphasis has shifted from "rights" to "protection."

This shift in policy rhetoric and policy solution began in the late 1980s. Congress enacted two privacy laws in 1988 that emphasized "privacy protection" rather than "privacy rights": The Computer Matching and Privacy Protection Act and the Video Privacy Protection Act. The shift from rights to protection is also apparent in the Driver's Privacy Protection Act (DPPA) of 1994, which was the first legislation restricting access to public record information. A number of states challenged this statute on Tenth Amendment grounds and in *Reno v. Condon* (2000) a unanimous Supreme Court upheld the DPPA on the grounds that the DPPA regulates the states as "owners of databases" and not "in their sovereign capacity" (*Reno v. Condon* 2000, 9). Three aspects of that opinion are relevant to this discussion. First, the Court recognized that drivers' information is an "article of commerce" and that "its sale or release into the interstate stream of business is sufficient to support regulation" (*Reno v. Condon* 2000, 7). Second, the Court did not dispute the amended DPPA's requirement for affirmative consent, or opt in, before disclosure of driver's personal information for use in surveys, marketing, solicitations, and other purposes. The Court here allowed the legislature to establish a high standard for consent. Third, the Court permitted regulation not only on state Departments of Motor Vehicles (DMV) but also on those who had obtained drivers' personal information from a state DMV, noting that "the DPPA regulates the universe of entities that participate as suppliers to the market for motor vehicle information" (*Reno v. Condon* 2000, 10). It would appear that if Congress developed the political will to legislate more privacy protections, the Court would initially look favorably on the decision. There is, however, one issue that would raise further constitutional questions. No First Amendment claims were raised in this case, as may be likely in a suit involving a business litigant, and such claims may affect the Court's analysis (Volokh 2000).

The "privacy rights" and "privacy protections" orientations are not mutually exclusive; there are elements that are similar to both as well as those that are different. The implications of the similarities and differences are worth exploring in order to better understand congressional policymaking. In terms of similarities, the concept of "fairness" is common to both traditions. The privacy rights principle that individuals should be given notice of information practices has a natural counterpart in the consumer protection principle of truth in advertising or in lending. The privacy principle that individuals should have choices with respect to disclosures and exchanges of personally identifiable information is similar to product labeling so that individuals can make informed decisions. But this investigation of "fairness" also reveals policy-related differences in the "rights" and the "protection" traditions.

A key difference in how the concept of fairness plays out in the rights and protection traditions is revealed by the goals of prohibiting "unfair and deceptive trade practices" and the goal of providing "fair information principles." Prohibiting trade practices restricts the organization and requires it to comply with authorities that have enforcement power, while providing principles gives the individual the means to query the organization and ask for a redress of grievances. In the first, the organization is the target of legislation and is restricted in what it can do; in the second, the individual is the focus and is given the means to take action as an individual. Given the imbalances in bargaining power between an individual and an organization, restricting an organization would appear to be a more effective solution to privacy invasions than giving individuals rights. But such proposals will elicit opposition from the organizations. The question then becomes whether the opposition of organizations is likely to be more successful against "protection" solutions than against "rights" solutions.

In the privacy rights tradition, the focus is on giving individuals rights so that they can individually take action, whereas in the consumer protection tradition, the focus is on giving protections to a group. In the rights tradition the assumption is that individuals may have different preferences and sensitivities with respect to personal information practices. Individuals are regarded as uniquely situated. In the protection tradition, individuals are assumed to share some characteristics in common. For example, they are all "drivers" or "video renters" or, most broadly, "consumers." This group identification can strengthen their claim by increasing the number of people who are identified with the claim. From a congressional perspective, this clarification of the group to be protected may lend more legitimacy and visibility to policy proposals. Instead of a vague and amorphous concern with "individual privacy," the concern is now on protecting the privacy of a specified group. The group identification also affects the possibility of forming coalitions. When privacy invasions are viewed as individual rights problems, few natural coalitions emerge. But as a consumer protection problem, privacy advocates find a number of obvious allies with consumer, education, union, and family groups as occurred for the Children's Online Privacy Protection Act. The group definition may also provide incentives for organizations to compromise on proposed legislation rather than to oppose it.

CONCLUSION

Conversations between the rights-based privacy tradition and the consumer-protection privacy focus continue in many online policy discussions. Although the consumer focus may be more pragmatic in terms of garnering political support and in terms of fashioning legislation, for some people it lacks the moral and philosophical justifications for the importance of privacy. Stephanie Perrin, a former Canadian privacy official and currently the chief privacy officer at Zero-Knowledge, captures this sentiment well: "Privacy is not just good business. We are framing the information age, and it is important to take that job seriously. We really do look at privacy as a *human right*, and not just a luxury item for spoiled North Americans" (emphasis added, Schwartz 2001). Similarly, the language of "The Privacy Pledge," which was drafted by members of the Privacy Coalition, a nonpartisan group of consumer, civil liberties, educational, library, labor, and family groups, returns to these rights roots. It begins by stating, "Privacy is one of America's most *fundamental values*" and asks members of Congress and state legislatures to "support a privacy framework to safeguard the *rights* of Americans in this information age" (emphasis added, EPIC 2001).

Although consumer "protection" may be a more pragmatic and effective solution, may enhance congressional support, and may decrease organizational opposition, it does not seem to constitute an inherently superior approach. The primary weakness of the "protection" solution is that it is essentially instrumental. The individual is protected as a consumer or purchaser, not as a moral being. The mantra that "privacy is good for business" can be viewed as self-serving and narrow. Using the privacy rights tradition as a basis upon which to build a consumer-protection solution may provide a stronger rationale as it can draw support from both instrumental and moral premises. The instrumental basis can offer incentives and grounds for congressional coalition building, while the moral basis contributes political rhetoric and public support. The maxim that "privacy is good for a just society" fortifies the slogan that "privacy is good for business."

CHAPTER FOUR

A Right too Far? The Congressional Politics of DOMA and ENDA

NICOL C. RAE

In recent commentary on the state of American society it has become common-place to bemoan the erosion of "community," "civil society," or "social capital" (Putnam 2000; Etzioni 1994; Ehrenhalt 1996). Increasingly it seems Americans operate as individual beings outside traditional communitarian activities, or have reverted to new, and less intimate, "virtual communities" via the media or the internet. Contemporary political discourse in the United States has been defined in terms of individual "rights" yet is lacking in discussion of social responsibilities. One of the earliest and most eloquent statements of this position is by Mary Ann Glendon in her work *Rights Talk*:

> Our legal and political vocabularies deal handily with rights-bearing individuals, market actors, and the state, but they do not afford us a ready way of bringing into focus smaller groups and systems, where the values and practices that sustain our republic are shaped, practiced, transformed, and transmitted from one generation to the next. (Glendon 1991, 120)

The prevalence of "rights talk" at the expense of other political vocabularies is a fairly recent phenomenon, however. Glendon traces it to the triumph of the black civil rights movement in the 1950s and 1960s, primarily engendered by federal court decisions, civil disobedience, and the advent of the news media as the primary medium of political communication in American politics. Other disadvantaged groups have imitated this strategy with some success, although the price that has been paid, according to Glendon (1991, xi) is a tendency for opposing groups to become politically alienated and strident in opposition.

Rights talk thus fails to resolve issues but merely serves to perpetuate them in a dialogue of the deaf between polar opposites:

> This unique brand of rights talk often operates at cross-purposes with our venerable rights tradition. It fits perfectly within the ten-second formats currently preferred by the news media, but severely constricts opportunities for the sort of ongoing dialogue upon which a regime of ordered liberty ultimately depends. A rapidly expanding category of rights—extending to trees, animals, smokers, nonsmokers, consumers, and so on—not only multiplies the occasions for collision, but it risks trivializing core democratic values. A tendency to frame nearly every social controversy in terms of a clash of rights (a woman's right to her own body vs. a fetus's right to life) impedes compromise, mutual understanding, and the discovery of common ground. A penchant for absolute formulations ("I have the right to do what ever I want with my property") promotes unrealistic expectations and ignores both social costs and the rights of others. A near-aphasia concerning responsibility makes it seem legitimate to accept the benefits of living in a democratic social welfare republic without assuming the corresponding personal and civic obligations.

If rights talk makes accommodation and consensus harder, the fact that the major battleground for these rights disputes has been the courts rather than legislatures has also tended to raise frustration levels given that the judiciary is the least popularly accountable branch of government in the United States. According to Glendon (1991, 145–70) the language of contemporary American judicial opinions generally tends to ignore social or communitarian considerations, regarding these as totally secondary to individual rights.

Yet while legislative solutions to social problems might be preferable, disadvantaged minorities in American history have traditionally found the legislative branch largely unresponsive to their demands, unless judicial intervention has first paved the way. Congress like all popularly elected legislatures tends to follow majority opinion and is thus highly unsuited to the role of protector of minority rights. This is especially true of the House, the branch that has always been closer to the people, while the Senate on the other hand has developed an institutional tradition of concern for geographically concentrated minorities (Binder and Smith 1997).

According to the model of the civil rights revolution: disadvantaged groups petition the courts, the courts acknowledge their rights, and the legislative and executive branches follow as public opinion adjusts and accepts the granting of fundamental constitutional rights to the disadvantaged group. Unfortunately the civil rights precedent has not been borne out in many other cases of rights claims. While federal courts have recognized the constitutionally protected rights of women, pornographers, religious minorities, and atheists, public opinion has not accepted the courts' viewpoint so rapidly, and Congress, following public opinion, has dragged its feet. Opponents of such liberal court rulings have often developed counterclaims framed in exactly the same rights language as their opponents, and with two contending rights, resolution of the issue either judicially or legislatively becomes more difficult. Activists and members on both sides of the issue use congressional and media debate to denounce their opponents, and while the news media thrive on confrontation and controversy, the overall quality of congressional debate and deliberation diminishes (Uslaner 1993; Davidson 2001). According to Glendon (1991, 171): "Our stark, simple rights dialect puts a damper on the processes of public justification, communication, and deliberation upon which the continuing vitality of a democratic regime depends. It contributes to the erosion of the habits, practices, attitudes of respect for others that are the ultimate and surest guarantors of human rights."

Congressional debate and deliberation over gay rights during the second session of the 104th Congress (1995–97) provides a good example of the politics of rights in Congress today. Two major measures involving gay rights came before that Congress: the *Defense of Marriage Act* (DOMA) and the *Employment Non-Discrimination Act* (ENDA). DOMA, which allowed states and the federal government to refuse recognition to same-sex marriages that might be sanctioned in some states, was overwhelmingly passed, indicating an instance in contemporary American politics when rights claims have failed to prevail against communitarian concerns, in this case regarding the institution of marriage. Despite continuing widespread public and congressional political hostility toward gays and lesbians, the ENDA almost passed the Senate, largely because it appeared that the social consequences of granting employment protections on the basis of sexual orientation was not perceived as so threatening to the social fabric.

The remainder of this chapter will focus on the congressional politics of DOMA, and by association ENDA (the two bills were legislatively closely related), and attempt to draw some conclusions about how Congress deals specifically with issues involving gay and lesbian rights and with rights issues more generally. The conclusion is that while rights talk features prominently in congressional debate, social/communitarian considerations weigh more strongly in final legislative outcomes than is apparent in Glendon's analysis of judicial policy making.

THE GENESIS OF DOMA

In the classic model of "rights politics" a social movement dedicated to advancing a rights claim manages to get the issue on the congressional agenda by a combination of public pressure and court decisions, the enforcement of which

demands legislative and executive action. The case of the right of gays and lesbians to marry did not fit the traditional pattern. This issue came onto the
national political agenda because of a court decision in one state rather than pressure from national gay rights organizations. While the issue of gay marriage was
on the legal and political agendas of the major national gay and lesbian organizations, it had relatively low priority by comparison with repealing state anti-
sodomy laws, passing state and federal "hate-crimes" legislation, anti-workplace
discrimination legislation, and "domestic-partner" laws by which gay partners
would become eligible for the social benefits of employees (Lewis and Edelson
2000).

The issue of marriage had been extensively debated in the gay political community, however, with a school associated with commentators Andrew Sullivan
(1995) and Bruce Bawer (1993) recommending gay marriage as a demonstration
that gay relationships could be as loving and committed as heterosexual unions
and as a means of bringing gays and lesbians into the more socially conservative
mainstream of American society. In general, however, gay political strategists
held that the wider American public was more likely to endorse civil rights protections for gays rather than accept their right to marry, and opinion poll evidence corroborated their view (Wilcox and Wolpert 2000). While significant
numbers of Americans remained uncomfortable with homosexuality, a generally
growing majority indicated that they favored laws protecting gays and lesbians
from discrimination in the workplace. On issues such as marriage, however, that
touched upon deeply held traditional, communitarian beliefs, the public
remained heavily opposed during the 1990s. Thus, the pursuit of the right to
marry appeared to be a totally counterproductive strategy for gay and lesbian
organizations, and, while paying lip service to the principle, they generally
accorded it a relatively low priority, and the issue had never been debated in
Congress.

All these calculations were upset by the decision of the Hawaii Supreme Court
in the 1993 case of *Baehr v. Lewin* (CIV NO. 91-1394). Three gay and lesbian
couples sued the state of Hawaii after they were denied marriage licenses. The court
found that denial of such licenses on the basis of sex was subject to "strict scrutiny"
due to the Equal Rights Amendment in the Hawaiian constitution and sent the
case back to the lower court for the state to demonstrate that sex-based
classification for marriages was justified by a "compelling state
interest"—a "strict scrutiny" standard that governments can rarely meet in rights
cases (Lewis and Edelson 2000). The Hawaii decision attracted widespread
national media attention and launched the issue of gay marriage onto the national
political agenda. Opponents of gay rights sensed an issue that might benefit them
politically, while national gay rights organizations that had strategically accorded a
low priority to marriage, were now reluctantly compelled to advance the mar-

riage issue to the forefront of their national agenda. The main national gay legal organization—*Lambda Legal Defense and Education Fund* (LLDEF)—joined the Hawaii case as cocounsel.

Reaction to the Hawaii court's decision was swift. Even in traditionally liberal Hawaii (one state-by-state analysis determined that Hawaii had the most "pro-gay" public opinion of any state), public opinion was strongly opposed to same-sex marriage, and the state legislature immediately amended Hawaii law to state clearly that only opposite sex couples could get marriage licenses and proposed a constitutional amendment writing the legislature's right to do this into the state constitution (Lewis and Edelson 2000). But the issue reverberated far beyond the Pacific Island state. Opponents of gay marriage feared the "full faith and credit" clause in Article IV of the U.S. Constitution would compel all states to recognize any gay marriage performed after the likely legalization of gay marriage in Hawaii. Article IV, Section 1 of the federal Constitution states: "Full faith and credit shall be given in each State to the public acts, records and judicial proceedings of every other State. And the Congress may by general laws prescribe the manner in which such acts, records and proceedings shall be proved and the effect thereof."

Accordingly the general practice has been that all states recognize marriages performed in other states, and thus opponents of gay marriage argued that unless federal action were taken, the Hawaii court would effectively change the definition of marriage nationwide, because all fifty states would be compelled to recognize same-sex marriages of residents who went to Hawaii to marry, or of same-sex Hawaiian married couples who moved into another state. Thus the issue of same-sex marriage had moved from being a question of gay and lesbian rights to a major issue of federalism and states' rights. Supporters of the Hawaiian decision argued that the fears of opponents were groundless because of the widely recognized "strong public policy" exception whereby states can refuse to recognize public acts from other states if they violate that state's public policy (Lewis and Edelson 2000). For precisely this reason by early 1998 twenty-five states had rewritten their marriage laws to explicitly prohibit same-sex marriage, and similar legislation was pending in eleven more states.

While the *Baehr* case ground slowly through the Hawaiian court system (it was not heard again in lower courts until the fall of 1996), opponents of gay marriage mobilized their forces in opposition. The center of opposition to gay marriage hardly unsurprisingly came from the Christian right forces associated with the Republican Party. The religious right had long been the staunchest opponent of all gay rights measures in the United States, citing biblical prohibitions on homosexual acts and desire to protect the institution of the family as its rationale (Green 2000). At state and local levels the Christian right had had some considerable success in repealing or precluding gay rights laws and ordinances through referenda. However, at the national level vehemently anti-gay rhetoric, such as that used at the 1992 Republican convention by Patrick Buchanan and Pat Robertson, could backfire. Interestingly during the 1990s, anti-gay rights forces increasingly resorted to the rhetoric of "rights talk" by criticizing proposed antidiscrimination measures as demands for "special rights" for a "privileged elite" as opposed to "regular" civil rights.

Poll data demonstrated, however, that gay rights forces were more likely to prevail if they could frame issues in terms of discrimination, where there was more public sympathy for their position, but less likely to prevail if the demand of gay rights conflicted with a traditional social/political institution such as the military or, even more so, the family (Wilcox and Wolpert 2000). The fate of President Clinton's pledge to end discrimination against homosexuals in the U.S. military in early 1993 was evidence that even an issue framed in the favorable terms of antidiscrimination would not prevail if it ran against the mores of an entrenched and powerful social/political institution. The upshot of the whole "gays-in-the-military" debacle was the "Don't Ask Don't Tell Compromise" that left no one satisfied, and, it has been argued by some, actually intensified dismissals of gays and lesbians from the U.S. armed forces (D'Amico 2000). In fact, the success of institutional arguments in the "gays-in-the-military" debate illustrates that, institutional or communitarian arguments against rights claims are not always destined to fail in contemporary America.

In terms of same-sex marriage, the strong opposition demonstrated in polls nationally and in all states provided Christian right forces with an excellent political opening. Regardless of their stated fears about legitimating same-sex marriage nationally, the issue provided an excellent basis for mobilizing and fundraising and bringing Christian right concerns to the forefront of national attention. For the Republican Party more generally, the issue of same-sex marriage provided a basis to attack Democrats who were generally more supportive of gay rights, including marriage (although this issue was supported only on the more liberal wing of the party), as outside the "cultural" American mainstream. President Bill Clinton proved himself to be masterful in his 1992 campaign in diluting Republican attacks on Democratic cultural liberalism (which had proved fatal to Democratic presidential candidates in 1984 and 1988), by depicting himself as a "new kind of Democrat." His background as the Southern Baptist governor of a culturally conservative, "Bible Belt," Southern state reinforced this impression. In office, however, Clinton paid attention to his party's prevailing cultural liberalism, showed more concern for gay rights issues (at least rhetorically) than any previous president, and appointed openly gay and lesbian personnel to significant positions in his administration.

Clinton's apparent cultural liberalism was used against him in the 1994 midterm election campaign that returned the first Republican congressional majority since 1953. Although the Republicans' 1994 "Contract with America" did not highlight social issues, the new Republican majority was eager for issues on which they might embarrass the incumbent administration politically with a view to the 1996 election, and the issue of gay marriage seemed to fit the bill.

For these reasons the actions of the Hawaii court would become a central concern of Congress during the summer of 1996, and gay rights proponents, while suffering a major defeat, skillfully used the opportunity to almost achieve an unexpected victory.

THE DRAFTING OF DOMA

During the first session of the 104th Congress, the new Republican majority had concentrated on the largely economic issues contained in their 1994 election manifesto, the so-called Contract with America, instead of the highly divisive and polarizing social issues that gave rise to strident "rights talk" on each side, and had damaged the GOP in recent elections by identifying the national party too closely with the agenda of their Christian Right supporters. By the early summer of 1996, however, the Republicans were in the doldrums, having been bested by a resurgent Clinton administration in the budget debate and federal government shutdown at the end of 1995 (Rae 1998). Slender Republican majorities in both Houses looked precarious, and certain Republican presidential nominee, Senator Robert J. Dole (R-Kans.), was lagging in the polls. Since the advent of the Republican Congress, President Clinton and his closest electoral advisor, Dick Morris, had adopted a strategy of "triangulation" for the 1996 election campaign: doing enough to keep Democrats in line, while also taking opportunities to appeal to Republican-leaning constituencies on selected issues. As this strategy was proving to be successful for Clinton in recapturing the political center, Republicans in Congress decided to try and place the president on the spot by bringing forward federal legislation in defense of traditional opposite-sex marriage. Reckoning that they had more than enough votes to pass the bill over a potential Clinton veto, the GOP hoped to force Clinton to make a difficult choice between his enthusiastic backers in the gay and lesbian political community and the more traditionally minded centrist voters his triangulation strategy was intended to bring into the Democratic fold in November.

This is not to underestimate the genuine outrage felt by many conservative Republicans at the prospect of same-sex marriage (Killian 1998, 350–53). Lacking confidence that the "strong public policy" defense would protect states against the recognition of Hawaii marriages, and angered that a "liberal" judiciary appeared ready once again to foist its mores on American society, Republican conservatives were determined to do as much as they could to stifle the prospects of same-sex marriage. In addition Republican conservatives argued that federal legislation to protect marriage was necessary because the terms *marriage* and *spouse* were common in federal statutes without any clear definitions, and in the absence of the latter, gay marriages in Hawaii might pass legal muster although they ran counter to the intentions of those who had written the legislation (Lewis and Edelson 2000).

In May 1996 bills, entitled "The Defense of Marriage Act," stating that the federal government would only recognize marriages between persons of the opposite sex and permitting states not to recognize same-sex marriages legitimated in other states, were introduced in both chambers. The Senate legislation was sponsored by the newly elected Republican whip, Senator Don Nickles of Oklahoma, while the House version was sponsored by Representative Bob Barr (R-Ga.), thrice married, twice divorced, and sued by his second wife over unpaid medical bills for his children, but also a staunch social conservative and one of the members of the Republican freshman House class of 1994 most closely associated with the Christian right (Killian 2000).

The House Judiciary Committee's Subcommittee on the Constitution, chaired by Representative Charles T. Canady (R-Fla.), held a hearing on the legislation on May 15, 1996. Commentator and *New Republic* editor Andrew Sullivan made the case for society to accept gay marriage on conservative grounds: "Why would conservatives seek to oppose the same family values for gay people that they promote for everyone else?" (quoted in Idelson 1996a). Hawaii Democratic State Representative Terrance W. H. Tom spoke in favor of the bill, on the grounds that judges should not make such momentous decisions for society: "No single individual, no matter how wise or learned in the law, should be invested with the power to overturn fundamental social policies against the will of the people" (quoted in Idelson 1996a).

Subcommittee Chairman Canady clearly stated the socially conservative position in defense of the institution of marriage: "I hope that most Americans will think it quite odd that we are actually considering legislation to define marriage as an exclusively heterosexual and monogamous institution. Simply stated in the history of our country 'marriage' has never meant anything else" (quoted in Idelson 1996a).

Opponents of DOMA recognized that they found themselves in a weak position politically: a position that became even weaker when it became clear that the Justice department and the Clinton White House would not oppose the bill. Led by openly gay liberal Representative Barney Frank (D-Mass.), they based their arguments on the fact that the legislation was unnecessary, probably unconstitutional, and only intended to attack gays and drive a wedge in the Democratic Party (Idelson 1996a; Lewis and Edelson 2000; Campbell and Davidson 2000). Those who were prepared to base their case on a "right" to marry invoked antimiscegenation laws in the segregated South that were later held to be unconstitutional violations by the federal courts.

On May 30 the subcommittee voted 8 to 4 on a straight party line vote to send the bill to the full Judiciary Committee after a contentious mark-up session (Idelson 1996b). Democrats argued that the legislation was unnecessary because states could invoke the "strong public policy" rationale to refuse to recognize gay marriages, and even if they could not, Congress did not have the power under the constitution to give it to them. Representative Frank's amendment on those grounds was defeated by voice vote. Another Frank amendment removing the federal ban on recognition of gay marriages on the grounds that it was an unwarranted intrusion on states' rights regarding family law was also defeated 4 to 7. The views expressed by Judiciary Committee chair Henry J. Hyde (R-Ill.) represented the Republican majority: "The institution of marriage is trivialized by same-sex marriage. It legitimates something that is essentially illegitimate" (quoted in Idelson 1996b).

The full committee voted on the bill on June 12 after two days of debate, and it was defeated by 20 votes to 10. The only defectors from party ranks on the committee were Democrats John F. (Jack) Reed (R.I.) and Frederick C. (Rick) Boucher (Va.). Both the outcome and the debate reflected the degree to which the Judiciary Committee Democrats were to the left of House Democrats as a whole and the Clinton Justice Department, for it was already apparent that a majority of House Democrats would support the bill on the floor and that President Clinton would sign it (Idelson 1996c). Again Representative Canady stated the issue in terms of a traditional social institution—the family—without reference to rights: "What is at stake in this controversy? Nothing less than our collective moral understanding . . . of the essential nature of the family" (quoted in Idelson 1996c).

Opponents also by and large rejected arguments and rhetoric based on rights and attacked the legislation as an unwarranted federal intrusion into the business of the states, designed solely to damage the Democrats in an election year. Representative Frank mocked the title of the legislation: "This is not the defense of marriage but the defense of the Republican ticket" (quoted in Idelson 1996c). Frank again offered an amendment to remove the DOMA's federal definition of marriage as a male-female union and of a spouse as a person of the opposite sex, but was defeated 13 to 19, with Republican Representative Michael P. Flanagan (who represented a Chicago district with a significant gay population) breaking ranks. During the debate then-Representative Sonny Bono (R-Calif.) probably spoke for many Americans in his response to Frank's amendment: "I'm not homophobic, I simply can't handle it yet, Barney" (quoted in Idelson 1996c). Another Frank amendment that would have required the federal government to recognize gay marriages if approved by the legislature, a referendum, or a citizen initiative in a state (thus addressing the argument that a court might force gay marriage on an unwilling citizenry), was also defeated 8 to 14.

On July 12 DOMA was debated on the House floor and passed by the veto-proof margin of 342 to 67 (Idelson 1996d). The rhetoric on either side of the issue was incendiary, particularly on the part of Republican freshman conservatives in the "class of 1994":

> Representative Bob Barr (R-Ga.)—As Rome burned, Nero fiddled. The very foundations of our society are being burned. The flames of hedonism, the flames of narcissism, the flames of self-centered morality are licking at the very foundations of our society, the family unit. (quoted in Killian 1998, 351)

> Representative Andrea Seastrand (R-Calif.)—Traditional marriage is a house built on a rock. As shifting sands of public opinion and prevailing winds of compromise damage other institutions, marriage endures and so must its historically legal definition. This bill will fortify marriage against the storm of revisionism. (quoted in Killian 1998, 351)

> Representative David Funderburk (R-N.C.)—Homosexuality has been discouraged in all cultures because it is inherently wrong and harmful to individuals, families, and societies. The only reason it has been able to gain such prominence in America today is the near blackout on information about homosexual behavior itself. We are being treated to a steady drumbeat of propaganda echoing the stolen rhetoric of the black civil rights movement and misrepresenting science. (quoted in Killian 1998, 351)

The case for the opposition was made most passionately by two of the three openly gay members of the chamber, Representatives Frank and Steven C. Gunderson (R-Wis.), with arguments based more on tolerance for acts that do no harm to others rather than strident rights talk or arguments based on communitarian or moral concerns:

> Representative Barney Frank (D-Mass.)—People talk about their marriage being threatened. I find it implausible that two men deciding to commit themselves to each other threatens the marriage of people a couple of blocks away. (quoted in Killian 1998, 352)

> Representative Steve Gunderson (R-Wis.)—Why are we so mean? Why are we so motivated by prejudice, intolerance, and unfortunately in some cases, bigotry? Why must we attack one element of our society for some cheap political gain? Why must we pursue the politics of division, of fear, of hate? Frankly, I want to ask my colleagues, why should my partner of 13 years not be entitled to the same health insurance and survivor benefits that individuals around here, my colleagues with second and third wives, are able to give them? (quoted in Killian 1998, 352)

Voting patterns on DOMA followed predictable lines. Of the sixty-seven members who voted against, Gunderson was the sole Republican. Two hundred twenty-four Republicans and 118 Democrats (64 percent) voted in favor. The Democrats who voted against (36 percent) were from Northeastern and Pacific Coast states where the political culture was more sympathetic to gays and lesbians, or represented urban districts with large gay populations, or belonged to other minority groups that had traditionally suffered from discrimination, principally Jews and African Americans.

After a July hearing before the Judiciary Committee, the Senate measure was scheduled for floor debate in early September (Idelson 1996d). The outcome in that chamber would be similar to that in the House, with DOMA passing by an 85 to 14 margin, but Senate rules also allowed gay rights advocates to bring to the floor another critical piece of legislation: *The Employment Non-Discrimination Act* or ENDA, in conjunction with DOMA.

THE SENATE DEBATES DOMA AND ENDA

ENDA, prohibiting workplace discrimination on the basis of sexual orientation, had been hovering around Congress for some twenty years, since Representative Bella Savitzky Abzug (D-N.Y.) first introduced a version of it in 1975 (Campbell and Davidson 2000). The legislation had never been brought to the floor of either house, although it did get a hearing in 1993 when the then-chair, Senator Edward M. (Ted) Kennedy (D-Mass.), gave the issue a hearing before the Senate Labor and Human Resources Committee. The fact that it came to the floor of the Senate in September 1996 was due to legislative legerdemain by Senator Kennedy, who used the Senate's lax rules on germaneness to offer ENDA as an amendment to DOMA when the latter was brought to a vote on the Senate floor.

While the Democratic leadership had never brought ENDA to the floor of Congress during their years of control (despite a gay rights clause in the party's national platform since 1980), gay rights advocates and allies like Kennedy saw an opportunity to turn the same-sex marriage issue to advantage. As mentioned earlier, opinion polls had shown growing majorities in public opinion believing that homosexuals should not be fired from their jobs on account of their sexual preference, with the exception of particularly sensitive institutions such as the military and religious-based organizations. Many members of the public and members of Congress who would never countenance same-sex marriage were apparently inclined to support antidiscrimination measures.

In the Senate liberal Democrats and moderate Republicans who felt constituent pressures to vote for DOMA could dilute the impact of that vote by simultaneously supporting ENDA. It also allowed Democrats and the Clinton administration to conciliate the gay political community who might be offended by DOMA, but whose enthusiastic support and resources were necessary for the November presidential and congressional elections. The version of ENDA that the Senate debated together with DOMA on September 10, 1996, was also diluted to appeal to moderates, with exemptions from its provisions for the military, businesses with fewer than fifteen employees, and nonprofit religious organizations. "Quotas" and preferential policies for gays and lesbians were also barred in an attempt to deal with the "special rights" attacks of the bill's opponents (Weisman 1996).

DOMA passed the Senate by an 85 to 14 margin, with all fifty-three Republicans and thirty-two (68 percent) of the forty-seven Democrats supporting the bill. Almost all of the opponents of the bill were again from Pacific Coast and Northeastern liberal bastions where gays are a significant political force. With the outcome in no doubt, the Senate debate on DOMA was somewhat perfunctory, and familiar arguments were rehashed on both sides. Senator Kennedy led the opposition attacking DOMA as unnecessary, anti-gay, unconstitutional, and cynical: "We all know what is going on here. I regard this bill as a mean-spirited form of Republican legislative gay-bashing cynically calculated to try to inflame the public eight weeks before the November 5 election" (quoted in Carney 1996).

Senate Majority Leader Trent Lott (R-Miss.) defended DOMA as necessary defense against a judicially imposed liberal social agenda that did not reflect the popular will: "This is not prejudiced legislation. . . . It is a preemptive measure to make sure that a handful of judges in a single state cannot impose a radical social agenda upon the entire nation" (quoted in Carney 1996).

Defenders of DOMA also argued that without it federal and state governments might find themselves liable to a whole new category of beneficiaries—same-sex spouses.

With the outcome more open to doubt, the debate on ENDA was much more spirited. The measure failed to pass the Senate by a single vote—50 to 49. Democrats voted 41 to 5 in favor, and Republicans 45 to 8 against. The voting patterns reflected the much greater potential public support for ENDA. Twenty-seven Democrats who voted for DOMA voted for ENDA. The five holdouts—Senators Howell T. Heflin (Ala.), Samuel A. Nunn (Ga.), Wendell H. Ford (Ky.), Robert C. Byrd (W.Va.), and J. James Exon (Neb.)—were all from conservative states where gay rights were generally not popular. The eight Republican supporters of ENDA—Senators William S. Cohen (Maine), Olympia J. Snowe (Maine), Alfonse M. D'Amato (N.Y.), Mark O. Hatfield (Ore.), Arlen Specter (Pa.), John H. Chafee (R.I.), (then Republican) James M. Jeffords (Vt.), Alan K. Simpson (Wyo.)—were, with the exception of Simpson, from that already mentioned grouping of Northeastern and Pacific Coast states with significant gay rights lobbies. One Democrat, Senator David H. Pryor of Arkansas, who said he would have voted for ENDA, was at the bedside of his sick son in Arkansas. Had Pryor voted for ENDA, Vice President Al Gore would have broken the tie in favor of the measure.

The arguments of proponents of ENDA focused on the discrimination issue. According to Senator Charles S. (Chuck) Robb (D-Va.): "Those of us who support the Employment Non-Discrimination Act have a simple plea—let's end discrimination in the workplace. Each American worker—whether they build houses, pave roads, serve meals in country diners, or manage corporations—deserves to be judged by their dedication to their job and the quality of the workplace" (quoted in Weisman 1996).

Some opponents of ENDA, such as Senator Nancy L. Kassebaum (R-Kans.), focused on narrow legal objections: "I agree that discrimination does exist. However, our courts are already clogged with cases, which many times only lead to more divisiveness and disruption in the workplace. Relying on our legal system to resolve our differences can be not only counter productive but fraught with unintended consequences as well" (quoted in Campbell and Davidson 2000).

Others, like Senator Jesse Helms (R-N.C.), concentrated on the same traditional moral arguments against homosexual conduct that had been used in the debate on DOMA: "At the heart of this debate is the moral and spiritual survival of this nation" (quoted in Carney 1996).

The outcome of the congressional debates on DOMA and ENDA thus ended with all participants being able to claim a significant victory. Conservatives were able to raise the hurdles against the legal recognition of gay marriage at both the state and federal levels of government. By endorsing both DOMA (eventually signed on a plane in the middle of the night when the media were not paying attention) and ENDA President Clinton was able to simultaneously appeal to the traditional moral values of most voters, while pleasing his avid supporters in the gay political community: triangulation at its most agile.

For gay rights advocates the defeat of same-sex marriage, an issue on which they stood on very weak ground with the general public, may well be a long-term asset. National gay rights organizations could also take heart from the near passage of ENDA, which marked an apparent transformation of public and congressional attitudes to gay rights. As Elizabeth Birch, the executive director of the Human Rights Campaign, the major national gay rights political group, put it: "We have witnessed gay civil rights in the 1990s completely embraced by the civil rights community in general. We have firmly established that it is no longer a question of whether Congress will pass the employment nondiscrimination act for gay Americans. It's a question of when" (quoted in Weisman 1996).

CONCLUSION

While the "civil rights community" might have embraced gay civil rights, to date
there has been no further congressional action on ENDA, although Republican
margins in both houses of Congress have narrowed since 1996. In retrospect it
appears that the link with DOMA and the 1996 election campaign provided an
especially propitious opportunity for ENDA in the Senate. Congressional
Democrats and some moderate northeastern Republicans by and large supported
antidiscrimination measures for gays, but neither party's leadership seemed anx-
ious to bring the issue to the floor of either chamber again during the 105th
(1997–99) and 106th (1999–2001) Congresses—even in the Senate where it
would not have been that difficult for the Democratic minority to do so. The
major gay issue of these Congresses was the "holds" placed by conservative
Republican Senators—including then Senator John D. Ashcroft (R-Mo.)—on
the nomination of openly gay Chicago meatpacking heir and Democratic con-
tributor James Hormel to the post of Ambassador to Luxembourg, on the
grounds that Hormel would advance a "gay agenda" as U.S. emissary to the tiny
European state. Certainly as long as the Republicans control Congress, it appears
unlikely that ENDA will pass, since there seems to be little net electoral benefit
and much potential danger for Republicans on the gay rights issue.

Democratic control of both houses would probably see a better prospect for
ENDA, which was again included in the party platform for the 2000 election,
and presidential candidate Al Gore expressed strong and consistent support on
the stump and in televised presidential debates. Representative Frank expressed
optimism that a Democratic House would see the congressional passage of
ENDA: "As soon as the Democrats take over the House, we are going to pass it.
The current Republican leadership won't allow anything pro-gay to come up (on
the House floor). The votes for ENDA are there and in the Senate too, but in
the House the majority leadership has total control of what comes up" (author's
interview, May 5, 2001, Washington, D.C.).

It appears unlikely that President George W. Bush will sign such legislation,
however. His political career in Texas evidenced no particular sympathy for gay
rights claims, and Bush, while cultivating the image of a "compassionate conservative" on issues of social justice, has also taken pains to accommodate the vehemently anti-gay rights religious right segment of the Republican Party, as evidenced by his campaign stop at South Carolina's *Bob Jones University* and his
appointment of religious right stalwart and former Missouri Senator Ashcroft as
attorney general. Moreover, in response to a question on gay rights in the second
presidential debate, Bush deployed the concept of "special rights" frequently
invoked by opponents of gay antidiscrimination measures. On the other hand,
Bush did meet during the campaign with gay Republican groups, and in the vice

presidential debate, Republican candidate Richard (Dick) Cheney, who has a lesbian daughter, gave a surprisingly sympathetic if equivocal response. Perhaps if gay rights advocates can summon a significant degree of congressional and public support for ENDA, they might even persuade an apparently politically savvy Bush administration to endorse some version of the bill.

What does the mid-1990s' debate on gay rights tell us about how Congress approaches this issue and about the allegedly malign influence of "rights talk" over the American body politic? In general, gay rights are the kind of extremely sensitive moral/social issue that most members of Congress (aside from the committed activists on either side of the issue, who are representative neither of congressional nor public opinion)—and for that matter most of the American public—appear to be extremely uncomfortable discussing. As with advocates of many other rights-related issues in American politics, however, these advocates and vehement opponents of gay rights have public visibility out of all proportion to their numbers, because their organizations can raise money, deploy activists, and have a constituency of committed supporters who are likely both to vote and to vote on this particular issue alone. Moreover, the conflictual and sensationalistic manner in which the news media—now the primary arena of political debate for most Americans—approach this issue gives disproportionate attention to the extremes, as opposed to those who have a confused or nuanced approach to the issue.

Knowing that public opinion is in the middle, supporters and opponents of gay rights attempt to frame the issue in a manner that best favors their position. Religious right Republicans realized when same sex marriage came on to the political agenda after the 1993 Hawaii court decision that the issue was highly advantageous to them since public opinion was by no means ready to countenance such marriages being sanctioned nationwide by a state court decision.[1] In 1996 the Republican congressional leadership also spotted an opportunity to embarrass their Democratic opponents with an unpopular issue and thus let DOMA go forward. Unwilling to be perceived by the public as supporting court-imposed same-sex marriage, two-thirds of congressional Democrats and the Clinton administration went along. Proponents of gay rights, however, spotted an opportunity through the Senate's lax rules of debate to bring to the floor the issue of ending job discrimination against gays, to which the public is much more sympathetic, and the measure almost passed a Republican-controlled Senate. This political sleight of hand also diluted the impact of DOMA as a setback to the gay rights movement. The bottom line then is that the congressional response to gay rights is contingent on how the issue is framed and the willingness of congressional leaders to bring issues to the floor, which they will only do if they can see some benefit for their party (Sinclair 1995; Aldrich and Rohde 2000). In a sense gay rights and rights issues of all kinds have become part of the general struggle for partisan advantage in the contemporary Congress.

The contemporary approach to gay rights issues in the United States bears out some of Glendon's arguments about the use and effects of "rights talk" in current American politics, but undermines others. Certainly when gay rights issues are dealt with in the legal arena and issues perforce are made in terms of rights claims, then the rhetoric used by participants and in judgments is likely to be in terms of individual rights, because that is how contemporary American jurisprudence approaches such issues. Social and community "rights" appear to be only weakly recognized by the courts today. According to Glendon (1991, 110), with reference to the court decisions on burning and desecration of the American flag:

> The flag-burning dispute, to recur to a familiar example, elicited passionate defenses of freedom of expression on the one hand, and equally fervent protests against desecration of the national symbol on the other. The arguments for the former position were easy to make, fitting into familiar First Amendment grooves. They carried the day. The rebuttals tended to have a sputtering quality; they sounded more in emotion than in reason. The problem for the flag defenders, in part, was that the flag-burning controversy pitted individual rights against community standards. . . . The maintenance of a vital democratic society, a society with a creative tension between individual freedom and the general welfare, requires that a continuing debate take place about just such matters. If political discourse all but closes out the voices on one side of the debate, liberalism itself is at risk. Yet that is precisely what our simple rights dialect regularly does.

But judicial decisions are not necessarily the final word: statutes can be changed, new statutes can be introduced overriding existing ones interpreted by a court, and even state and federal constitutions may be altered if public opinion feels strongly enough. In fact, losing parties in such court decisions seek to sensationalize their impact and try to shift the debate to another political arena where their chances of political success are greater. When the public is not ready to endorse the rights claims successful in court, then the opponents of these claims are likely to resort to legislatures (or citizen initiatives) that by necessity hew more closely to public opinion on the issue. As far as Congress is concerned, the game becomes more one of congressional leaders framing the issue legislatively for the benefit of public opinion rather than trying to persuade a court of the constitutionality of a rights claim. In that debate the kinds of communitarian values mentioned by Glendon tend to weigh much more heavily because the public remains highly responsive to those values.

The case of gay marriage furnishes an excellent example of this. Congress and many states acted to suppress it by changing state constitutions or introducing statues, because the public was not ready to tolerate such a fundamental change in the ages-old social institution of marriage. The successful congressional opposition to same-sex marriage was not based on a rights counterclaim, but on appeal to "communitarian values," and the example shows that these are not invariably trumped by rights claims even if the claim has some judicial backing behind it. Moreover, opponents of DOMA made their arguments less in terms of rights than that the legislation was an unnecessary attack on states rights and a disadvantaged group—gays and lesbians—driven by political calculations. And contrary to some commentary at the time, the adverse reaction to the Hawaii decision and the widespread congressional and public support for DOMA appear to have put the issue of same-sex marriage to rest for the foreseeable future. In short, judicially mandated rights claims do not always have the upper hand in political debate and certainly do not always triumph politically. Outside the judicial arena then, "rights talk" may be less of a menace to the health of the polity than Glendon believes it to be.

On the wider issue of gay rights, the near success of ENDA in the Senate in 1996 illustrates that the current political situation is by no means hopeless for gay rights advocates as long as they can frame the issue in terms of discrimination and their cause appears to bear no strong threat to an entrenched social institution. In short, despite all the sound and fury of rights talk in the media, which exercises a distressing influence over our political debate, ultimate political outcomes are—by necessity in a system of free government—determined by what the overall society can bear politically. The framers of the U.S. Constitution saw the separation of powers between the branches of government as being the most likely governing framework to enable the participants to work out a broadly acceptable solution to political problems while protecting minorities and ensuring gradual social change when warranted. While this has not been the case with all issues in recent American politics, it appears to have been broadly corroborated by recent congressional action on gay and lesbian rights.

NOTES

The author would like to thank Bill Walker for his comments and suggestions.

1. In Hawaii the court proceedings were rendered moot by passage of a constitutional amendment in 1998, by more than two-thirds of Hawaii voters, amending the state's constitution to outlaw same-sex marriage.

PART THREE

Institutional Rights and Change

CHAPTER FIVE

The Emerging Rights of States: Revitalized Federalism

JOHN F. STACK, JR., AND COLTON C. CAMPBELL

Conflict between the enumerated powers of Congress and the reserved powers of the states began early and continued long. The Constitution gives to the legislative branch primacy over broad areas, including taxation and the regulation of interstate and foreign commerce, plus all powers "necessary and proper" for putting its specified authority into effect. But such qualified authority is occasionally clouded by the first ten amendments, which limit the role of the central government. Ratified in 1791 as part of the Bill of Rights, the Tenth Amendment declares that all powers not delegated by the Constitution to the federal government nor denied to the states are reserved to the states respectively or the people. Adding cushion is the Eleventh Amendment that grants states freedom from being unwillingly hauled into federal court by citizens having nonconstitutional complaints.

In this chapter we examine how the new judicial activism of the Supreme Court underscores the fluidity of states' rights (i.e., the prerogative power of a state to exercise its inherent authority as opposed to rights of the federal government), or "state rights," the prevalent usage proceeding the Civil War, in the congressional arena. For much of our nation's history states' rights were either the claimants of the party out of power (Current 1995) or almost exclusively equated with resistance to increasing civil rights protection, opposition to social legislation on a national level, and conservative economic benefits (Drake and Nelson 1999). Contemporary federal–state relations, however, are emerging in different ways. Central to the revitalized rights of states is the Supreme Court's new activism, which is defining new, unexpected rights for states (Stack and

Campbell 2001). In a series of landmark decisions, reinvigorating the Tenth Amendment and substantially defining the Eleventh Amendment, a bare majority of justices are redefining traditional federal–state relations, moving toward a dual federalist approach long abandoned since the late 1930s. The Supreme Court is also redefining long-established rights created under the Fourteenth Amendment's equal protection clause. This trend reflects historical periods when beliefs developed that states would better solve pressing matters as well as protect more effectively the rights of individuals.

STATES' RIGHTS AND THE MEANING OF THE TENTH AMENDMENT

The Constitution empowers the general, or national, government, while limiting its power to encroach on individual liberties. The founders hoped a system of federalism would achieve a "happy combination" of the relevant concerns of statesmen dedicated to providing new securities for "public good and private rights" in a manner that would "preserve the spirit and form of popular government" (Madison, in Hamilton, Madison, and Jay, *Federalist* No. 10). Madison and others held that governmental powers had to be distributed between state and national governments and that this division would serve as a balancing function of powers, a safeguard for individual liberties, and a promotion of the common good. The Tenth Amendment stresses the power relationship that exists between state and national governments. Often referred to as *reserved powers*, the Tenth Amendment provides that powers not given to the national government and at the same time not denied to the states belong to the states (Drake and Nelson 1999). In short, state governments have their own spheres of jurisdiction within which to perform and provide answers to critical issues.

Until well into the twentieth century, the Tenth Amendment was wielded, with varying degrees of success, to curtail federal power, particularly congressional power over the economy in areas claimed to be reserved for state regulation (Biskupic and Witt 1997). Initial erosion of the amendment began in 1895 when Congress passed an act forbidding the shipment of lottery tickets in interstate commerce. The purpose of the legislative act was only nominally a regulation of commerce: its real purpose was to restrict gambling, a matter that had always been the exclusive domain of states. In 1904 the Supreme Court, in *McCray v. United States*, upheld legislation imposing a prohibitive excise tax on oleomargarine. This action amounted to an exercise of a police power to protect the health of the citizenry, under the guise of a constitutional exercise of the power to levy taxes for "general welfare," as provided in Article I, Section 8 (McDonald 1992).

The increasing assertiveness of Congress in addressing complex issues of labor–management relations and in attempting to protect workers from the excesses of industrial life caused the Supreme Court to revitalize the Tenth Amendment. The Court used the Tenth Amendment in conjunction with the Fourteenth Amendment's due process clause as a way of limiting the activism of states and Congress. While underscoring the Court's solicitude for state sovereignty, the Tenth Amendment was used as a way of reinforcing laissez-faire economics at the expense of both Congress and state legislatures. In *Lochner v. New York* (1905) the New York legislature passed a law limiting the hours and other working conditions for bakers. Arguing that management and labor conducted business on a level playing field under conditions of free market capitalism, the Court interpreted the Fourteenth Amendment's due process clause as protecting the substantive right of "Liberty of Contract." Hence, the ability of management to contract for labor, and labor's freedom to accept an employment contract, received the protection of the U.S. Constitution. In dissent, Justice Oliver Wendell Holmes denounced the majority's preference for laissez-faire economics.

The Court's application of substantive due process, however, provided states and the federal government with some degree of latitude in safeguarding traditional concerns in the area of police powers, such as the health, safety, morals, and welfare of citizens. In *Jacobson v. Massachusetts* (1905) the Court upheld a state law requiring smallpox vaccinations, and in *Muller v. Oregon* (1908) justices unanimously upheld a state law limiting women to working in industries no more than ten hours a day (O'Brien 2000a, 943–44).

The doctrine that the Tenth Amendment limits the exercise of expressly delegated federal power was fully accepted by the Court in *Hammer v. Dagenhart* (1918). Here the Court invalidated the first child labor act of Congress as an invasion of the reserved rights of the states in the guise of regulating interstate commerce (Harris 1953). In the opinion of the Court, Justice William Rufus Day in effect amended the Tenth Amendment by declaring that "the powers not expressly delegated to the National Government" are reserved to the states or to the people (*Hammer v. Dagenhart*, 247 U.S. 251, 275). Dual federalism as a device to protect vested interests against national legislation reached its full fruition in three cases, which voided respectively the first Bituminous Coal Act and the first Agricultural Adjustment Act on the ground among others that they involved the reserved rights of the states (Harris 1953).

In *Carter v. Carter Coal Co.* (1936) the Court held that federal regulation of the soft coal industry was invalid because Congress invaded the reserved rights of the states, despite official protests of the attorneys general of coal-producing states that the rights of their states were not being invaded and that the legislation was needed. In *United States v. Butler* (1936), the Tenth Amendment attained its full development as a limit upon the power of Congress to tax (Harris

1953). Here the Court declared unconstitutional the processing taxes of the first Agricultural Adjustment Act, which were earmarked for the payment of benefits to farmers to curtail production. Associate Justice Owen J. Roberts, for the majority, concluded that Congress had no power to regulate agricultural production and that the tax was a mere incident of such regulation designed to pressure farmers into compliance to the subversion of the power reserved to the states (Harris 1953).

With President Franklin D. Roosevelt's threat to pack the Supreme Court in 1937 (increasing the number of seats from nine to fifteen) the High Bench's conservative majority collapsed. This, in turn, signaled a dramatic reassessment of the role of Congress in *West Coast Hotel v. Parrish* (1937), which endorsed state wage and hour restrictions. In the ensuing fifty-five years (1937 to 1992), the Supreme Court overturned only one statute that violated the Tenth Amendment, and that decision, itself, was later overturned.

Contemporary Interpretations of the Tenth Amendment

The Tenth Amendment has increasingly become a means of reviving state interests amid the harsh realities of the modern administrative state. The complexity of modern government, the requirements of extensive regulatory laws, an integrated economy, and the necessity of federal oversight seemingly made federal-dominated cooperative federalism, with its emphasis on centralized control, inevitable. However, the conservatism introduced into national politics during the Reagan presidency is reflected in a Supreme Court that increasingly hews to conservative principles (Stack and Campbell 2001). A bare majority of the current Court is pioneering new interpretations and tests that challenge long-established principles of federalism, which include circumscribing federal authority in areas of interstate commerce and the sovereign immunity of states. Table 5.1 illustrates a number of periods of judicial activism in which the Court struck down state laws. The period between 1910 to 1939 displays an activist Court defending free market capitalism. From 1960 to 1989 an activist Court continues the process of nationalizing law at the expense of states. But beginning in 1990, the Court's deference to state sovereignty dramatically increases.

Beginning with *National League of Cities v. Usery* (1976), the Court's new conservative justices have increasingly tried to restore the Tenth Amendment as a substantive limitation on Congress's commerce powers (Scheiber 1992). No single principal philosophical trajectory exists, but in the past two decades, a body of law and political philosophy have coalesced around the ideas attributed to, or associated with, the Tenth Amendment. *National League of Cities v. Usery* represents a bellwether of policy change in Commerce Clause jurisprudence (Foster and Leeson 1998). Moribund since the Court's rejection of dual federal-

TABLE 5.1 UNCONSTITUTIONAL STATE LAWS
AND LOCAL ORDINANCES, 1790–1999

Period	Number
1790–1799	0
1800–1809	1
1810–1819	7
1820–1829	8
1830–1839	3
1840–1849	9
1850–1859	7
1860–1869	23
1879–1879	36
1880–1889	46
1890–1899	36
1900–1909	40
1910–1919	118
1920–1929	139
1930–1939	93
1940–1949	57
1950–1959	61
1960–1969	149
1970–1979	193
1980–1989	162
1990–1999	61
Total	**1,249**

Source: Adapted from Lawrence Baum, *The Supreme Court,* 7th ed. (Washington, D.C.: CQ Press, 2000).

ism in the late 1930s, a 6 to 3 majority brought back to life an affirmative limitation on the ability of Congress to regulate economic relationships, expressing a new approach to federal–state relations. The Court voided a 1974 amendment to the Fair Labor Standards Act (FSLA), a statute to expand federal minimum wage provisions and maximum hours to state and local government employees. Then-Associate Justice William H. Rehnquist explained that those provisions made governments' basic and traditional functions, such as police protection, more expensive (O'Brien 2000a, 681). While acknowledging that the Tenth Amendment had been initially defined as a "truism," Rehnquist noted that Congress could not "exercise power in a fashion that impaired the States' integrity or their ability to function effectively in a federal system" (*National League of Cities v. Usery, 842* citing *Fry v. United States* [1975]). In stating a revitalized approach to dual federalism, Rehnquist reaffirmed the sovereignty that inheres in the nature of states:

> We have repeatedly recognized that there are attributes of sovereignty attaching to every state government which may not be impaired by Congress not because Congress may lack an affirmative grant of legislative authority to reach the matter, but because the Constitution prohibits it from exercising the authority in that manner. (*National League of Cities v. Usery* 1976, 845)

Rehnquist pointed to a state's ability to locate the seat of government or to determine how the seat of government may be changed as an example of the "separate and independent existence" of state sovereignty (*National League of Cities v. Usery* 1976, 845–46). Such functions, he interpreted, fell within the "plenary authority" of states (*National League of Cities v. Usery* 1976, 845–46). This decision elevated a state's sovereignty to the level of constitutional law, thus limiting the intrusive power of Congress under the Commerce Clause (O'Brien 2000a, 683).

In his concurrence, Associate Justice Harry A. Blackmun endorsed the Court's balancing approach as it addressed "the relationship between the Federal Government and our States" (*National League of Cities v. Usery* 1976, 856) The decision, he noted, did not "outlaw federal power" in an area like environmental protection, where federal interests necessarily predominate over those of the states (*National League of Cities v. Usery* 1976, 856).

National League of Cities v. Usery proved difficult to apply, however, because it opened up so many problems in its application (McDonald 1992). One such problem was the distinction between "traditional" and "essential" state activities, central to the Court's attempt to reinvigorate state sovereignty, which was never adequately defined (O'Brien 2000a, 683). This case did not provide a justification as to why the Court, rather than Congress, should defend state sovereignty (O'Brien 2000a, 683). The coalition supporting *Usery* disintegrated when Justice Blackmun reversed himself in *Garcia v. San Antonio Metropolitan Transportation Authority* (1985) and overruled *National League of Cities v. Usery*.

In her dissenting opinion, Justice Sandra Day O'Connor expressed concern about increasing congressional power to regulate interstate commerce, gradually erasing the diffusion of power between the federal government and the states (*Garcia v. San Antonio MTA* 1985, 584). States' inability to perform constitutionally mandated functions, she said, was rooted in the seemingly relentless power that industrialization, combined with transportation and communication systems as well as "unprecedented growth of federal regulatory activity," confers on interstate commerce. Citing federal mandates dictating the retirement age of state law enforcement personnel and an increasing maze of regulatory laws, O'Connor indicated the failure of the political process to protect states against federal encroachment. "With the abandonment of *National League of Cities*," she declared, "all that stands between the remaining essentials of state sovereignty and Congress is the latter's undeveloped capacity for self-restraint" (*Garcia v. San Antonio MTA* 1985, 588).

Reinvigorating the Tenth Amendment

Responding to studies showing that, in 1987, more than half a million students carried guns to school, members of Congress sought to turn the tide against firearm violence and drug activity. Part of the Gun-Free School Zones Act of 1990 prohibited individuals from possessing a firearm at a place that the individual knew, or had reasonable cause to believe, was a school zone: grounds of any public, private, or parochial school, or property within one thousand feet of such premises. Violators were subject to penalties up to five years in prison and a $5,000 fine.

During congressional hearings several witnesses addressed the impact of increasing firearms violence on the nation's educational system. None, however, specifically discussed the effects on interstate commerce. Neither the statute nor its legislative history contained express findings about the constitutional source of Congress's authority to enact the legislation (Foster and Leeson 1998). The bill nonetheless passed the 101st Congress (1989–91) with little opposition. However, President George Bush expressed reservation when signing the measure, noting that it intruded on the law enforcement responsibilities of the states (Jost 1995).

United States v. Lopez (1995) signaled the first time since the New Deal that the Court found Congress to have exceeded its constitutional discretion to regulate interstate commerce—in this case, the movement of guns across state lines that could end up in school playgrounds (Greenhouse 1999). Alfonso Lopez Jr. was a twelfth-grade student at Edison High School in San Antonio, Texas, who took a concealed .38 caliber handgun with five bullets to school. When confronted by school authorities, Lopez admitted to carrying a weapon, but noted that another student provided him the gun after school in a "gang war." Lopez also told officials that he was to receive $40 for delivering the gun. Lopez was nonetheless arrested and charged under Texas law with firearm possession on school grounds. The following day, the state charges were dismissed when federal agents charged the teenager with violating the 1990 Gun-Free School Zones Act. Lopez's lawyer decided to challenge the law on constitutional grounds.

Pivotal to the holding in *Lopez* was Chief Justice Rehnquist's reliance on a revitalized concept of dual federalism. The Constitution, he argued, creates a federal government of enumerated powers. Citing James Madison, Rehnquist stated: "the powers delegated by the proposed Constitution to the federal government are few and defined period. Those which are to remain in the State governments are numerous and indefinite" (*United States v. Lopez* 1995, 552). The chief justice then stressed the constitutionally mandated division of authority within the nature of federalism designed "to ensure protection of our fundamental liberties" (citing *Gregory v. Ashcroft* [1991]). Rehnquist raised dual federalism to the position afforded the separation and independence of these coordinate branches of the federal government, stating: "to prevent the accumulation of excessive power in any one branch, a healthy balance of power between the States and the Federal Government will reduce the risk of tyranny and abuse from either front" (*United States v. Lopez* 1995, 552, citing *Gregory v. Ashcroft* 1991, 458).

In a series of 5 to 4 decisions, the Supreme Court again invoked the Tenth Amendment to limit congressional power in *Printz v. United States* and *Mack v. United States* (1997). These cases stemmed from Congress's adoption of the Brady Handgun Violence Prevention Act of 1993, which amended the 1968 Gun Control Act by requiring the attorney general to establish a national instant criminal background check system by November 30, 1998. "It is incontestable that the Constitution established a system of 'dual sovereignty,'" Justice Antonin Scalia stated for the majority, in sharply condemning Congress's attempt to define the limits of state authority (*Printz v. United States* and *Mack v. United States* 1997, citing *Gregory v. Ashcroft* [1991]).

Scalia articulated a compelling vision of dual federalism, asserting that the Constitution "contemplates that a State's government will represent and remain accountable to its own citizens" (*Printz v. United States* 1997, 2377, citing *New York v. United States* 1992). This design, which he called a "great innovation," afforded American citizens a political system based on "two orders of government," possessing "its own direct relationship, its privity, its own set of mutual rights and obligations to the people who sustain it and are governed by it" (*Printz v. United States* 1997, 2377, citing *U.S. Term Limits, Inc. v. Thornton* [1995]), Associate Justice Kennedy concurring). Once again, a conservative justice invoked the words of Madison: "The local or municipal authorities form distinct and independent portions of the supremacy, no more subject, within their respective spheres, to the general authority than the general authority is subject to them, within its own spheres" (*Printz v. United States* 1997, 2377).

The ruling provoked strong reaction by some on Capitol Hill. Senator Herb Kohl (D-Wisc.) who sponsored the Gun-Free School Zones Act called the decision "legal nitpicking" (quoted in Jost 1995, 46). Kohl introduced a revised law to ban guns around schools that added some "findings" about the effects of guns in schools and required proof of some connection to interstate commerce for federal jurisdiction. The Clinton administration supported the new measure, but it faced opposition by many Republican members of Congress who favored a strengthened role for the states in the federal system.

BREATHING NEW LIFE INTO THE ELEVENTH AMENDMENT

A telling dimension of the revitalized concept of states' rights and a concomitant limitation on Congress's lawmaking authority over state sovereignty has been demonstrated in recent cases in which the Supreme Court has expanded the concept of the sovereign immunity of states by reviving the once-moribund Eleventh Amendment. Adopted in 1798, the Eleventh Amendment to the Constitution provides that federal courts do not have authority to hear cases brought against a state by an individual citizen of another state or of a foreign state. Although no one denied a state's right to bring a suit against an individual, Article III had not been interpreted in state ratifying conventions as permitting an individual to sue a state without its consent. The matter came to a head in 1793 when the Supreme Court in *Chisholm v. Georgia*, its first constitutional case, rejected Georgia's contention that it could not be sued. The case arose when two South Carolinians sued Georgia in the Supreme Court, invoking the jurisdiction granted to the Court by Article III. As executors of the estate of a man to whom money was owed by persons whose property the state of Georgia confiscated during the Revolutionary War, the South Carolinians asked the state of Georgia to pay the debt. The state of Georgia refused to appear before the High Bench, denying its authority to hear cases in which a state was the defendant.

No sooner had the Court handed down its decision than several states made clear their resistance to the assertion of a strong federal government. Georgia, Massachusetts, and other states led calls for a constitutional amendment to negate the ruling. Nearing the end of its lame-duck session, however, the 2d Congress (1791–93) did not act, and before the 3d Congress (1793–95) convened in late 1793, war resumed between Britain and France, which served to heighten popular anti-English sentiment. The dominant Federalists responded with the Eleventh Amendment, and in 1794 the proposed amendment passed the Senate by a vote of 23 to 2, and the House by a vote of 81 to 9. The amendment proposed by Congress was directed specifically toward overturning *Chisholm* and preventing suits against states by citizens of other states or by citizens or subjects of foreign jurisdictions.

Contemporary Interpretations of the Eleventh Amendment

Although the Eleventh Amendment was ratified more than two hundred years ago, the Supreme Court has decided more Eleventh Amendment cases in the past

TABLE 5.2 UNCONSTITUTIONAL LAWS DURING THE
1998–1999 TERM OF THE SUPREME COURT

Case	Law Challenged
Alden v. Maine	Fair Labor Standards Act (suit against states)
College Savings Bank v. Florida Prepaid Postsecondary Education Expense Board	Trademark Remedy Clarification Act
Florida Prepaid Education Expense Board v. College Savings Bank	Patent Remedy Act
Greater New Orleans Broadcasting Association, Inc. v. United States	Limits on broadcast advertising of casinos
Saenz v. Roe	Welfare reform law (authorizing different benefit levels for new state residents)

Source: Adapted from Kenneth Jost, 1998–1999 Supreme Court Yearbook (Washington, D.C.: CQ Press, 2000).

twenty-five years than it did in the entire preceding period (Fletcher 2000). In 1996, states' rights advocates found a legal victory in a less-than-obvious setting: Indian gambling. In 1999, three decisions on the final day of the Court's term cemented an extension of the doctrine of sovereign immunity to previously unimaginable limits. These fin de siècle decisions prompted the joke by many Court watchers that the Y2K bug hit the Supreme Court six months early, and the Court thought the year was 1900 (Sherry 2000). And in 2000 the Court reviewed a case that raised the issue of whether states can be subjected to private suits for violating the federal Age Discrimination in Employment Act. Table 5.2 illustrates the Court's willingness to strike down federal laws that compromise the rights of states.

Indian Gaming

By the 1990s gambling on Indian reservations grew from community-center bingo games to a multibillion-dollar business, with two hundred tribes operating more than one hundred casinos in twenty-four states (Jost 1996). For the Native American tribes, gambling had become an important source of revenue; for many states, it contradicted state laws.

The Supreme Court ruled in *Seminole Tribe of Florida v. Florida* (1996) that the Indian Gaming Regulatory Act, passed by Congress in the 1980s, allowing Indian tribes to sue states in federal court, violated the Eleventh Amendment. One provision of the law gave tribes the right to sue a state in federal court if it refused to negotiate over gambling issues. The Seminole Tribe invoked the law in 1990 to begin negotiations with Florida officials, but the talks faltered when the state refused to permit casinos. The Seminoles then sued Florida in federal court, claiming the "Sunshine State" had failed to negotiate "in good faith" as required by law. State officials denied the allegation of bad faith, but they also insisted the law violated the Eleventh Amendment's limitation on suits against states in federal court (Jost 1996, 43).

The state of Florida argued that the law infringed on the state's sovereignty. In a 5 to 4 ruling, the Court agreed, overturning the obscure congressional gaming act requiring states to negotiate with Indian tribes in good faith. In delivering the opinion of the Court, Chief Justice Rehnquist noted that notwithstanding Congress's clear intent to "abrogate the State's sovereign immunity," the Indian Commerce Clause did not grant Congress such power (*Seminole Tribe of Florida v. Florida* 1996). Therefore, Congress could not grant jurisdiction over a state that did not consent to being sued. Prior to *Seminole Tribe*, the Court had determined that Congress had the power to abrogate state sovereign immunity pursuant to Article I powers such as the Indian Commerce Clause or the Interstate Commerce Clause (*Seminole Tribe of Florida v. Florida*, 1996, citing *Pennsylvania v. Union Gas Co.*, 491 U.S. 1 [1989], 19–20). But the Court overruled this precedent, finding that Congress lacked the power to abrogate under Article I. Associate Justice Anthony M. Kennedy, who also sided with the state of Florida's argument, declared: "The states are separate, autonomous sovereignties within their spheres. . . . Congress doesn't order states to do anything" (*Seminole Tribe of Florida v. Florida* 1996).

State Sovereign Immunity

By a divided 5 to 4 decision, the Court, in *Alden v. Maine* (1999), sharply limited the power of Congress to authorize private citizen suits to enforce federal laws against state governments in state courts. A group of probation officers, seeking compensation for overtime, brought suit against the state of Maine for alleged violations of the Fair Labor Standards Act. The suit was originally filed in federal court, but was dismissed following the Supreme Court's *Seminole Tribe* decision. When the officers refiled the suit in Maine courts, the state took action to dismiss the case on grounds of state sovereign immunity. A lower court and the Maine Supreme Court both ruled in favor of the state.

In a closely divided, exhaustively argued decision, the Court broke new ground in defining additional limits on congressional intrusion into the sovereign affairs of states. The High Bench ruled that Congress has only limited power to override a state's sovereign immunity from suits in its own court (Jost 2000). Writing for the Court, Justice Kennedy maintained that "the powers delegated to

Congress under Article I of the United States Constitution do not include the power to subject nonconsenting States to private suits for damages in state courts" (*Alden v. Maine* 1999, 653). In dismissing the claim of Maine's probation officers, the Court reasoned that since Maine "had not consented to suits for overtime pay and liquidated damages" under the Fair Labor Standards Act, Congress lacked the power under Article I "to subject nonconsenting states to private suits for damages in state courts" (*Alden v. Maine* 1999, 2246).

Central to the Supreme Court's holding was the assertion that the Constitution defends state sovereignty in two ways. First, the "Nation's primary sovereignty" flows to states accompanied by the "dignity and essential attributes inhering" in that state. States "form distinct and independent portions of the supremacy, no more subject, within their respective spheres, to the general authority than the general authority is subject to them within its own sphere," declared Justice Kennedy while quoting *Federalist* No. 39 (*Alden v. Maine* 1999, 2247). Second, regarding the nature of dual federalism, the Court stated that with concern to the "competence of the National Government," the national constitutional framework:

> secures the founding generation's rejection of "the concept of a central government that would act upon and through States" in favor of "a system in which the State and Federal Governments would exercise concurrent authority over the people—who were, in Hamilton's words, 'the only proper objects of government'" (*Alden v. Maine* 1999, 2247, citing *Printz v. United States* 1997, 919–20). The residuary and inviolable sovereignty of the state, therefore, remains and is "not redelegated to the role of mere provinces or political corporations, but retain(s) the dignity, though not the full authority, of sovereignty." (*Alden v. Maine* 1999, 2247)

Justice Kennedy's majority opinion also invoked individual constitutional rights. In response to an argument in Justice David H. Souter's dissent, Kennedy argued that although state sovereign immunity is derived in part from common law, it is nonetheless a constitutional principle and as such unalterable by Congress (Sherry 2000). Like Justice Scalia, Kennedy turned to individual rights as an example:

> The text and the structure of the Constitution protect various rights and principles. Many of these, such as the right to trial by jury and the prohibition on unreasonable searches and seizures, derive from the common law. The common-law lineage of these rights does not mean they are defeasible by statute or remain mere common-law rights, however. They are, rather, constitutional rights, and form the fundamental law of the land. (*Alden v. Maine* 1999, 2256)

Throughout *Alden*, Justice Kennedy extended human emotions to states, worrying about the potential affront to the "dignity" of states were individuals permitted to sue them (Sherry 2000). Kennedy submitted that the Constitution "reserves to [the states] . . . the dignity and essential attributes" of primary sovereigns, and that they "retain the dignity, though not the full authority, of sovereignty" (*Alden v. Maine* 1999, 2247). He noted that immunity is "central to sovereign dignity" and that immunity from suit is essential to preserving the dignity of states (*Alden v. Maine* 1999, 2264). Congress, too, must consider the states' feelings: it must "respect" states and "accord" them the esteem due to them (*Alden v. Maine* 1999, 2264). Thus, by allowing Congress to subject states to private suits is "neither becoming or convenient," for it "denigrates" their sovereignty (*Alden v. Maine* 1999, 2263).

Continuing its efforts to rein in the federal government's power over state governments, a fractious Supreme Court ruled in February 2001 that state employees who say they suffered discrimination on the job because of their disabilities may not sue their employees for damages in federal court (Lane 2001). In a 5 to 4 ruling written by Chief Justice William H. Rehnquist, the Court held that Congress has no constitutional authority to subject lawsuits under the 1990 Americans with Disabilities Act. The case, *Board of Trustees of the University of Alabama v. Garrett* (2001), arose out of the job discrimination claims of a nurse at a state university hospital who was assigned a lower-paying job after returning from breast cancer treatment and a security guard with asthma who claimed that he was treated adversely on the job after demanding accommodations for his condition.

The Court struck down the portion of the Americans with Disabilities Act that provided a damages remedy against the states. The Court applied the logic of *Kimel v. Florida Board of Reagents* (2000), reasoning that since disability is not on the Court's own limited list of suspect classifications, Congress cannot add to the list and use the equal protection clause to remedy disability discrimination. The opinion by Rehnquist, which was joined by Associate Justices O'Connor, Kennedy, Scalia, and Clarence Thomas, said the evidence assembled by Congress of past state mistreatment of the disabled was insufficient to warrant federal intervention in the state employment context. "The legislative record . . . simply fails to show that Congress did in fact identify a pattern of irrational state discrimination in employment against the disabled," Rehnquist wrote (quoted in Lane 2001). State employment decisions regarding the disabled, which may be tinged by "negative attitudes or fear," do not alone compromise unconstitutional discrimination, the Court held, as long as they also contain a rational element related to a legitimate governmental purpose (Lane 2001).

Patent and Trademark Infringement

Beginning as one case in the same courtroom in New Jersey, *College Savings Bank v. Florida Prepaid Postsecondary Education Expense Board* and *Florida Prepaid Postsecondary Education Expense Board v. College Savings Banks* (1999) also reinvigorated states' rights under the Eleventh Amendment. Two largely unrelated trends converged to form the backdrop for these cases. First, states were engaging in expanding commercial ventures, becoming important players in intellectual property fields, such as acquiring valuable patents, copyrights, and trademarks through applications of scientific research. Second, the Supreme Court, with a conservative majority, was adopting stricter rules for Congress to follow before it could subject states to federal court suits for their business-like activities (Jost 2000).

Voting 5 to 4, the Court held in *Parden v. Terminal Railway of the Alabama State Docks Department* (1964) that states engaging in commercial activities relinquished their immunity from private federal court suits under the Eleventh Amendment. Congress, the Court declared, could have passed legislation specifically authorizing private suits against the state's railroad. Two decades later, with little fanfare, the Supreme Court tightened the rules for Congress, stating that Congress could "abrogate" or override states' immunity from suit only by "unambiguously" providing for private enforcement actions (*Atascadero State Hospital v. Scanlon* 1985). Over the next few years, following the Court's lead, lower federal courts were ruling in some cases that states could not be sued in federal court for copyright, patent, or trademark violations (Jost 2000, 41).

The 102d Congress (1991–93) responded by passing legislation to make trademark and patent laws applicable against states in light of court cases holding individual states immune under the Eleventh Amendment. Legal penalties were imposed on state governments for infringing on patent and trademark protections. "In an era in which we are working to craft international agreements to protect intellectual property rights, it is important that we set an example in our own country," declared Representative William J. Hughes (D-N.J.) at the introduction of the measure (*Congressional Record*, October 3, 1992, H11131). "We cannot permit States to evade liability to which private entities are subject."

Congressional action on the two laws—the Patent and Plant Variety Protection Remedy Clarification Act and the Trademark Remedy Clarification Act—coincided, and both measures were passed by voice vote with little controversy and no organized opposition from state governments (*Congressional Quarterly Almanac* 1992). The first measure stripped state governments of their claim of sovereign immunity from legal penalties for infringing on a patent. It specifically amended the 1970 Plant Variety Protection Act, which protected breeders of new varieties of plants, to allow an inventor who believed his or her patent had been violated by a state government or a state-sponsored university to sue the offending institution for damages (*Congress and the Nation* 1992, 792). The second measure held state governments similarly liable for trademark infringements. Congressional sponsors justified these statutes under powers delegated to them under Section 5 of the Fourteenth Amendment, which allows

Congress to pass legislation to enforce the provisions of the other clauses of the Fourteenth Amendment.

In *Florida Prepaid Postsecondary Education Expense Board v. College Savings Banks* (1999), the Court struck down on state sovereign immunity grounds aspects of the Patent Remedy Act that made patent laws applicable against states and state entities. The ruling nullified a patent infringement suit brought by the College Savings Bank in federal court against a Florida state agency, the Florida Prepaid Postsecondary Education Expense Board. College Savings Bank claimed that Florida Prepaid infringed its patented financing methodology when the agency began selling similar certificates of deposit to Florida residents. Florida moved to dismiss the suit on grounds of sovereign immunity under the Eleventh Amendment.

Voting 5 to 4, the Supreme Court held that the patent law could not be justified under Congress's power to enact remedial legislation protecting constitutional rights under the Fourteenth Amendment. Chief Justice Rehnquist reasoned that Congress demonstrated little evidence of patent infringements by states and had given no consideration to the availability of legal remedies against states in their own state courts (Jost 2000). Moreover, in applying *Seminole Tribe of Florida v. Florida,* Rehnquist declared "that Congress may not abrogate state sovereign immunity pursuant to its Article 1 powers (the patent clause, Article I, Section 8, clause 8 and the interstate commerce clause, Article I, Section 8, clause 3)" (*Florida Prepaid Postsecondary Education Expense Board v. College Savings Banks* 1999). "Congress retains the authority to abrogate state sovereign immunity pursuant to the Fourteenth Amendment." Rehnquist explained that the progressive expansion of the Fourteenth Amendment had "fundamentally altered the balance of state and federal power struck by the Constitution" (citing *Seminole Tribe of Florida v. Florida* 517 U.S. at 59). Relying on the reasoning in *City of Boerne v. Flores* (1997) the Court recognized that "legislation which deters or remedies constitutional violations can fall within the sweep of Congress's enforcement power even if in the process it prohibits conduct which is not itself unconstitutional and intrudes into 'legislative spheres of autonomy previously reserved to the states.'" As broad as the congressional enforcement power is it is not unlimited, wrote Rehnquist. "Congress does not enforce a constitutional right by changing what the right is. It has been given the power 'to enforce,' not the power to determine what constitutes a constitutional violation."

The Court, in *College Savings Bank v. Florida Prepaid Postsecondary Education Expense Board,* invalidated congressional efforts to subject states to federal court suits for trademark violations and false advertising. The High Bench barred a false advertising suit brought by the New Jersey–based College Savings Bank in federal court against a Florida state agency, the Florida Prepaid Postsecondary Education Expense Board, ruling that Congress had improperly attempted to abrogate the states' sovereign immunity (O'Connor 2000; Senkbeil 2000). The bank marketed certificates of deposit intended to shelter future costs of college tuition. The bank purported that Florida Prepaid made false claims about a competing product that the state agency sold to Florida residents. To bring the suit, the bank invoked the Trademark Remedy Clarification Act, which made trademark laws applicable against the states and state entities. The state of Florida challenged the constitutionality of the law under the Eleventh Amendment. The bank also argued that under the Court's 1964 decision, *Parden v. Terminal R. Co. of Alabama Docks Dept.*, Florida had waived its sovereign immunity by engaging in commercial activity (Jost 2000).

By a bare majority, the Court ruled that the trademark law was unconstitutional in providing for federal court suits against states and that Florida could not be subjected to federal court suit merely because it had engaged in commercial activity. Justice Antonin Scalia outlined his theory of federalism that sharply conflicted with the dissenters, particularly Justice Stephen G. Breyer. He denounced a concept of federalism that is rooted in the ability of Congress to determine the nature of shared governmental responsibility:

> The proposition that "the protection of liberty" is most directly achieved by "promoting the sharing among citizens of governmental decision-making authority" might well have dropped from the lips of Robespierre, but surely not from those of Madison, Jefferson, or Hamilton, whose north star was that governmental power, even—indeed, especially—governmental power wielded by the people, had to be dispersed and countered. And to say that the degree of dispersal to the States, and hence the degree of check by the States, is to be governed by Congress's need for "legislative flexibility" is to deny federalism utterly. (*College Savings Bank v. Florida Prepaid Postsecondary Education* 1999, 39–40)

In considering the question of whether the state's commercial activities should be construed as a waiver of its sovereign immunity, Scalia analogized the waiver to "other constitutionally protected privileges" (*College Savings Bank v. Florida Prepaid Postsecondary Education* 1999, 2229), including the Sixth Amendment right to counsel, the right to trial by jury protected by the Sixth Amendment in criminal cases and the Seventh Amendment in civil cases, and procedural due process (Sherry 2000).

Age Discrimination

States' rights were also at issue in *Kimel v. Florida Board of Regents* (2000). The Age Discrimination in Employment Act (ADEA) enacted by Congress in 1967 subjected states to suits by individuals by outlawing employer discrimination against any individual with respect to his or her compensation. The ambit of ADEA's coverage was expanded over the years by amendment, ultimately embracing the treatment of state employers and employees. A number of current and former professors and librarians at Florida State University and Florida International University sued the Florida Board of Regents (BOR). The suit was filed when the BOR refused to require the two state universities to allocate funds to provide previously agreed upon market adjustments to the salaries of eligible university employees. The unwillingness of the universities to provide funds, it was contended, offended the ADA and the Florida Civil Rights Act of 1992 (*Kimel v. Florida Board of Regents* 2000, 534). Lawyers for the BOR responded that the law exceeded Congress's power because there was no evidence of widespread age discrimination by the states and no need for preventive legislation since most states had laws on the books prohibiting discrimination on the basis of age anyway.

The Court's analysis proceeded on two fronts. In the first instance, the Court applied a "simple but stringent test." "Congress," Justice O'Connor argued, "may abrogate the State's constitutionally secured immunity from suit and federal court only by making its intentions unmistakably clear in the language of the statute" (*Kimel v. Florida Board of Regents* 2000, 640, citing *Dellmuth v. Muth* [1989]). Drawing on the Court's earlier decision in *Seminole Tribe of Florida v. Florida* (1996), the Court declared that Congress under Article I does not possess the power to abrogate a state's sovereign immunity. "Even when the Constitution vests in Congress complete lawmaking authority over a particular area," declared Justice O'Connor, "the Eleventh Amendment prevents congressional authorization of suits by private parties against unconsenting States" (*Seminole Tribe of Florida v. Florida* 1996, 72). In a clear attempt to compel congressional acquiescence in *Seminole Tribe of Florida v. Florida*, the majority stated that Congress could not "extract constructive waivers of sovereign immunity" via Article I powers. Thus, the Court sought to close what it considered to be a loophole implicit in Article I's commerce power (*Kimel v. Florida Board of Regents* 2000, 643).

The Court's logic also extended to consideration of Section 5 of the Fourteenth Amendment, which allows Congress to pass legislation to enforce the provisions of the other clauses of the Fourteenth Amendment. Here the Court relied on its earlier decision in *City of Boerne v. Flores* (1997), interpreting Section 5 as an affirmative grant of power to Congress. "It is for Congress in the first instance to 'determine whether and what legislation is needed to secure the guarantees of the Fourteenth Amendment,' and its conclusions are entitled to much deference," stated Justice O'Connor (*City of Boerne v. Flores* 1997, 536).

Invoking the negative implications doctrine, the Court reasoned that the enforcement provision of Section 5 of the Fourteenth Amendment also "serves to limit that power" (*City of Boerne v. Flores* 1997, 644). Justice O'Connor went on to proclaim: "The ultimate interpretation and determination of the Fourteenth

Amendment's substantive meaning remains the province of the judicial branch."
Drawing on the "congruence and proportionality tests" of *City of Boerne* (*Kimel v.
Florida Board of Regents* 2000, 645–47), the Court declared that state-based age
discrimination did not violate the Fourteenth Amendment if "the age classification
in question is rationally related to a legitimate state interest. The rationality commanded by the Equal Protection Clause does not require states to match age dis-
tinctions and legitimate interests they serve with razorlike precision" (*Kimel v.
Florida Board of Regents* 2000, 543).

CONCLUSION

Just as increasing polarization in Congress (Patterson and Caldeira 1987; Hurley
and Wilson 1989; Smith 1993; Patterson 1995; Ornstein et al. 1997; Rae and
Campbell 2001) has incurred gridlock (Binder 1996) and stimulated the use of
message politics (Sellers 2000; Evans and Oleszek 2001), thereby limiting both
the flexibility and creativity of that venerable institution, the insistence by five
members of the Supreme Court of new interpretations of the Tenth and Eleventh
Amendments have introduced new tension between Congress and the Court in
the area of states' rights. The Supreme Court's majority—led by Chief Justice
Rehnquist and Associate Justices O'Connor and Scalia—has pioneered new
approaches to federalism. The Tenth and Eleventh Amendments' surfacing
prominence underscores the Court's belief that the nature of state sovereignty is
deserving of respect, reducing fifty years of expanding federal regulation in nearly
all areas of American life.

Congress's reliance on the Interstate Commerce Clause to compel state compliance in a number of unregulated areas, such as minimum wages and working
conditions for state and local governmental employees and gun control has gal-
vanized a majority of the Supreme Court sympathetic to the rights of states.
Beginning with the Court's 1976 decision in *National League of Cities v. Usery*,
the ability of states as sovereign entities in partnership with the federal government were revitalized and expanded. Chief Justice Rehnquist's concern for the
prerogatives and respect due a coequal sovereign laid the foundation for new theories for states' rights. Despite the inability of lower federal courts to apply the
Usery tests, and despite the overturning of *Usrey* nine years later in *Garcia v. San
Antonio Metropolitan Transportation Authority*, the commitment of Justices
Rehnquist, O'Connor, Scalia, and Kennedy held firm.

In the area of state sovereignty, as defined by the Eleventh Amendment, the
Rehnquist majority has carved out increasing zones of deference for states, holding that states, as sovereign entities on par with the federal government, enjoy
immunity from individual suits. In such areas as Indian gaming, patent and

trademark infringement, and issues of age discrimination for state workers, the Court has increasingly immunized states from suit in federal courts. Congress may abrogate this immunity, the Court has said, only when its intent to do so is clear, the evidence of state discrimination is substantial, and the remedy created by Congress is congruent and proportional to the harm done by the state. These cases highlight a decentralized approach to federalism that provides states with far greater latitude in shaping major issues of public policy.

The Court's interpretation of Section 5 of the Fourteenth Amendment places issues of states' rights within a broader institutional context. In the *Boerne* case the Supreme Court held that Congress may not create new fundamental rights but, rather, may enact remedial or preventative legislation "that enforce the amendment's guarantee of civil rights" (Long 2001, 89). Here, Justice Kennedy asserted the High Bench's exclusive, or sole, prerogative to interpret the Constitution. The Court's institutional role therefore as a coequal branch of the federal government, and its philosophical commitment to the defense of states' rights, ushers in a new chapter in American constitutional law, the full parameters of which are not yet fully apparent. But such activism that characterizes *Marbury v. Madison* (1803) has asserted itself in the face of congressional attempts to circumvent judicial review. This may explain in part why Justices Ruth Bader Ginsburg and John Paul Stevens joined their colleagues Rehnquist, Kennedy, and Thomas in the *Boerne* decision.

CHAPTER SIX

Representing Congress: Protecting Institutional and Individual Members' Rights in Court

REBECCA MAE SALOKAR

R esearch that examines congressional interest and activity in the area of rights is typically framed in the context of the institution's lawmaking function. In its legislative capacity, Congress engages in defining rights not otherwise spelled out in the Constitution or expounded upon by the courts, and the output is generally in some form of protective legislation. Through these legislative initiatives, Congress develops strategies for protecting and enforcing the rights of individuals or groups—strategies that necessitate executive enforcement and action. However, relying solely on this lawmaking lens for an examination of congressional interests in the development of rights is limiting. Beyond such a view is Congress's interest in protecting and defending its own institutional rights and the rights of its members.

In this chapter I explore how Congress, as an institution, defends the rights accorded it and its members by the United States Constitution through litigation. Given the scholarly fascination with those political intersections where conflict is most likely to take place in our system of separated and shared powers, namely, those points where the branches must interact, surprisingly little research has been devoted to understanding how and why Congress goes to court (Salokar 1993; Tiefer 1998). Published work on lawyers in the national legislature has generally focused on the workload of attorneys assigned to committees and the ethical decisions involved in advising legislators on policy decisions (Clark 1998; Glennon 1998; Miller 1995; Yoo 1998). Case studies have incidentally touched on congressional legal activity in court (Craig 1988), and constitutional law texts unevenly include Supreme Court opinions that address

Congress's power to legislate, investigate, and delegate (Ducat 1995; Nowak and Rotunda 2000). But the mechanics of how those constitutional cases get before our nation's courts, who represents or advocates on behalf of Congress's legal interests, and how those arguments are made has not been subject to rigorous examination. This chapter begins to build a base of knowledge on the legal interests of Congress by discussing the history of the offices of legal counsel in the House and Senate, exploring the roles of those lawyers tasked as advocates for the institution of Congress, and by identifying when and how Congress finds its way to court.

CONGRESSIONAL COUNSELS

There is no dearth of lawyers in Congress. Legally trained professionals abound within the hallways and offices of the nation's capitol, serving not only as staff support to committees and elected members, but in the highest of offices as elected senators and representatives (Miller 1995). Historically, when the legal interests of the legislative institution were raised in the nation's courts, Congress would depend on either the attorneys at the Department of Justice, outside counsel, or on one of its own members for legal representation.

Reliance by Congress on the attorney general and the Department of Justice for legal representation began somewhat awkwardly in 1818, with the case of *Anderson* v. *Dunn* (1821). Having initiated contempt and breach of privileges proceedings, Speaker Henry Clay (R-Ky.) ordered the House of Representatives' Sergeant at Arms Thomas Dunn to bring John Anderson to the House for investigation. Subsequently, Anderson filed suit against Dunn for bodily trespass, assault and battery, and false imprisonment, and the House of Representatives authorized the speaker to provide for Dunn's legal defense. For the fee of $500, Speaker Clay hired the U.S. attorney general, who, as a private citizen, represented Dunn and the legal interests of the House all the way to the Supreme Court (U.S. Senate 1977).

The attorney general has long been authorized to serve as the legal voice of the "United States," and since 1875, that executive officer was expressly required to "defend an 'officer' of either House of Congress for acts performed in the 'discharge of his official duty'" (2 *U.S.C.* §118). But allowing the executive branch to represent its coequal partner is like inviting the fox to guard the henhouse. Questions of robust representation by the executive branch and conflicts of interest between the branches finally came to a head in 1926 in the case of *Myers* v. *United States*.

In *Myers*, Solicitor General James Beck argued on behalf of the executive branch that the Tenure of Office Act of 1867 was an unconstitutional restraint on executive power because the statute predicated the president's removal of certain postal officials upon "the advice and consent of the Senate" (107). The intestate appellant, a nongovernmental litigant, had sought reinstatement of lost wages in the Court of Claims for the allegedly illegal dismissal of a first-class postmaster; the Senate had not given its advice or consent to Myers's dismissal in accordance with the Tenure of Office Act. When the Supreme Court recognized the legislative interests involved in the case, it invited the United States Senate to participate as an amicus curiae with a written brief and an oral argument. Senator George Wharton Pepper received the assignment, and the uniqueness of his participation drew notice of the petitioner:

> In the 136 years that have passed since the Constitution was adopted, there has come before this court for the first time . . . a case in which the Government, through the Department of Justice, questions the constitutionality of its own act. We find the Solicitor General appearing as a representative of the Executive Department of the Government. And we have Senator Pepper, as amicus curiae, who . . . represents another branch, the Legislative branch, of the Government. (Will King, Counsel for the Petitioner *Myers* 1926)

Even Chief Justice William Howard Taft made special note of Senator Pepper's participation in the concluding statements of the majority opinion, despite ultimately ruling against the legislative branch.[1]

The *Myers* case, however, did not result in a change in litigation practices for Congress, although suggestions of the need for a legislative attorney general were noted. Generally, Congress trusted the work of the Department of Justice in representing its interests as was apparent not more than three years after *Myers* when the attorney general of the United States aptly presented what would become one of the most important cases for reinforcing the investigative reach of Congress through its contempt powers *(McGrain v. Daugherty* 1927). In a somewhat ironic twist, the issue at the heart of the congressional investigation involved the actions of the former attorney general and the practices of the Department of Justice. Congress continued to rely on the litigation skills of the executive branch, and when necessary either hired private counsel or engaged one of their own members to represent the institution's legal interests in the nation's courts. While proposals occasionally surfaced to institute a formal policy or procedure for employing legal counsel, bicameral participation or perceived threats to leadership power prevented action (Salokar 1993). Legal representation of Congress remained ad hoc until the late 1970s.

A rash of cases found their way to the nation's courts in the late 1960s and early 1970s that directly impacted congressional power and highlighted the need for institutionalizing some form of in-house legal expertise (*United States v. Johnson* 1966; *Powell v. McCormack* 1969; *Gravel v. United States* 1972; *United*

States v. Brewster 1972; *Senate Select Committee v. Nixon* 1974; *Kennedy v. Sampson* 1974). Hearings held by a Senate subcommittee of the Committee on the Judiciary in late 1975 and early 1976 acknowledged and documented the failures of contracted private counsel, less than adequate representation by its own members, and blatant conflicts of interest by the Department of Justice (U.S. Senate 1976). A proposal for a joint office of congressional legal counsel was subsequently imbedded in the proposed Public Officials Integrity Act of 1977.

There were other events in the late 1960s and early 1970s that also supported the development of an in-house legal advisor for Congress. From questionable antitrust prosecutions by the Department of Justice, the firing of Special Prosecutor Archibald Cox by then-Acting Attorney General (and Solicitor General) Robert Bork to the embarrassing resignation of a president, Congress had good cause to question both the ability and motives of the Department of Justice when it came to representing congressional interests. Additionally, the Nixon administration had more visibly used its solicitor general as a tool for crafting legal policy on social issues like the environment and civil rights, frustrating, in some instances, the very policy directions that Congress had set in legislation (Salokar 1992). The development of an independent legal voice for Congress became a critical need in the context of separation of powers and a system of checks and balances.

The proposal for a joint office of congressional legal counsel was ultimately rejected by the House of Representatives. The Senate, however, moved ahead and established its own Office of Senate Legal Counsel as part of the Ethics in Government Act (1978). Because its powers and responsibilities were originally defined in the context of a joint office, the Office of the Senate Legal Counsel was crafted to be nonpartisan with clear responsibilities and specific duties. From its inception, the Senate legal counsel has been dependent upon the Joint Leadership Group of the Senate for authorization to act and in some cases, it must secure Senate approval in order to litigate. On the House side, however, the development of an in-house litigator in the late 1970s was less formal and tied directly to the speaker, Thomas P. (Tip) O'Neill (D-Mass.).

Both the House and the Senate had employed some form of legal expertise prior to the 1970s for the purposes of contract review and personnel management. In the House, the general counsel to the clerk of the House of Representatives had served those functions and the office was simply invigorated by Speaker O'Neill's hiring of a former staff member, Stanley M. Brand, in the mid-1970s. According to Brand, Speaker O'Neill urged him to develop a more active role for the General Counsel's Office and thus, he began taking cases for individual lawmakers who needed legal representation. "I thought Members ought to be defended; they ought to be represented and they ought to be represented by people who understood the institutional and political background of Congress" (Salokar 1993). This personalized development of the office took several years as Speaker O'Neill and Brand identified tasks that logically fit with the function of an "attorney general" for the House of Representatives.

The lack of formal institutionalization and procedures, however, gave rise to some partisan divisiveness over the work of the House general counsel through its first decade of existence. It was not until 1993 that the 102d Congress (1991–93) officially recognized the Office of the General Counsel in the Rules of the House of Representatives (H. Res. 5). While the rule included a directive that the office be nonpartisan, it tied the general counsel directly to the speaker who is responsible for hiring the staff and setting their pay, and "who shall consult with a Bipartisan Legal Advisory Group" (H. Res. 5). The *Congressional Record* reflects that a Republican substitute was offered that would have made the office more directly accountable to and dependent on the bipartisan legal advisory group and mandated full House action on certain litigation (1993, H19). The amendment was not adopted.

The development of formal litigation expertise within the House of Representatives and the Senate gives Congress the ability to argue on its own behalf before any court in the United States. What we do not know, however, is when and to what degree the congressional legal counsels have allowed Congress to become a more active participant in the nation's courts. To approach these questions, I explore the types of legal issues that have historically drawn Congress into court and thus, the issues where these lawyers are most likely to represent their institutional client.[2]

CONGRESS GOES TO COURT

Congress, like most participants in litigation, finds itself in need of legal representation in court through fairly routine processes. One path to the courtroom is seen when the institution, one of its members, officers, employees, or committees is named as a defendant or respondent in a lawsuit. Congress may also be drawn into litigation when members, personnel, or committees receive subpoenas to appear as witnesses or to produce documents in an ongoing suit between nonlegislative parties. A third method of engaging in litigation comes about when the House or Senate (or both) intervenes in an existing case where institutional interests may be in jeopardy, and Congress can meet the standing thresholds before the court. Finally, Congress may file an amicus curiae brief in a matter where it simply wants its voice heard. What is generally not seen, however, is Congress—the institution—venturing out on its own as a plaintiff by filing suits against other parties, public or private.[3]

Because of their separate developments, the Senate legal counsel and House general counsel are governed by different internal rules regarding their decisions to litigate either as a party or as an amicus. Under 2 *U.S.C.* 288h, the Senate legal counsel is directed to defend challenges that would affect the Senate's constitutional interests. In order to do so, they may enter litigation as an intervenor, thus achieving the rank of a named party to the case, or simply speak as an amicus by filing a brief. The *Ethics Act* that established the office also provided the Senate legal counsel with an automatic right to participate in pending litigation provided that they meet the standing requirements, that their participation is not untimely, and that their involvement would not unnecessarily delay the litigation as determined by the court.

The Senate legal counsel's decision to participate in litigation is subject to approval by either the Joint Leadership Group (JLG) of the Senate or by Senate resolution, depending on the nature of the participation. A bipartisan group, the JLG is made up of the president pro tempore, the majority and minority leaders, the chair and ranking minority member of the Committee on the Judiciary, and the chair and ranking minority member of the Senate committee that has control of the contingent fund of the Senate (generally, the Committee on Rules and Administration).[4] A two-thirds vote by the JLG or a resolution by the Senate is necessary for the Senate legal counsel to defend the institution or one of its committees, officers, members, or employees in court. Additionally, the legal counsel may intervene or file an amicus brief only with the approval of the Senate by resolution. The Senate may also direct the legal counsel to either pursue a civil action to enforce a subpoena issued by the Senate or one of its committees or request immunity from a judicial forum for a witness testifying before the Senate or one of its committees. In short, the Senate legal counsel does not enjoy much independence in litigating on behalf of the Senate. At the same time, however, the lawyer for the Senate does know that when she goes into court, she has the support of the institution she represents.

The House general counsel faces no such constraints in their litigation activity. Directly responsible to the speaker, the Rules of the House require that the speaker consult the Bipartisan Legal Advisory Group with respect to the general counsel's functions (H.R. Rules 2000). The Bipartisan Legal Advisory Group is made up of members who hold the majority and minority leadership posts. But the rule seems not to bind the general counsel to seek the group's approval. Thus, the general counsel may enter litigation on behalf and at the direction of the speaker, the Bipartisan Legal Advisory Group, or by resolution of the House of Representatives. In practice, however, the House general counsel is expected to engage in legal activities necessary to protect the institution's interests with little direct supervision by the leadership, operating more like in-house counsel at a large private corporation (Interview 2001).

For most of its twenty-year history, the House general counsel lacked the automatic statutorily based authority to appear before any court in the nation. Previously, the general counsel would have to seek the approval of the two parties in a case in order to submit an amicus curiae brief and obtain leave of the court to appear if not admitted to the bar in the event that the case was in state jurisdiction. In September 1999, Congress included a provision in its annual legislative appropriations bill that statutorily granted the general counsel and her staff the right to appear in any court (except the Supreme Court), regardless of admission to practice requirements (2 *U.S.C.* §130f). Like the Senate, the House must also meet the standing requirements in order to intervene as a party.

Tradition accounts for much in governmental practices, and evidence of the long-term relationship between the Department of Justice and the U.S. Congress is still seen today. As noted earlier, the attorney general is charged with representing "the United States" in all legal actions in any court of the nation. Since 1875, the legal arm of the executive branch has been obligated by law to represent congressional leadership in litigation over their official duties (2 *U.S.C.* §118). The Department of Justice also manages lawsuits filed under the Federal Tort Claims Act that involve congressional personnel or occur in an area under the legislative branch's jurisdiction (like the Library of Congress). By tradition rather than statute, the Department of Justice has also responded to requests from individual legislators and committees for legal representation on congressional (but not personal) matters. Thus, even today, congressional interests are occasionally defended by the executive branch before the nation's courts.

The task of defending the constitutionality of statutes nearly always falls to the Department of Justice even when the most basic issues in dispute tug at the core of congressional power. In *United States v. Lopez* (1995)[5] and *United States v. Morrison* (2000), for example, we find the solicitor general of the United States vigorously defending the constitutionality of the Gun-Free School Zones Act of 1990 and the Violence Against Women Act of 1994. These constitutional challenges struck at the heart of Congress's power to regulate through the Commerce Clause and in both cases, the solicitor general's defense of congressional interests was ultimately unsuccessful. While these types of cases might impact the most substantive matters affecting government, the expertise and experience of the Department of Justice generally fulfills the representational needs of Congress, and the in-house attorneys play no role in litigation. But this is not always the case.

In 1989, the executive branch failed to argue against a challenge to the constitutionality of several provisions of the False Claims Act in *United States ex rel. Stillwell v. Hughes Helicopter, Inc.* It sent no legal representation to the bar. Instead, the United States Senate filed an amicus curiae brief in support of the act and thus argued the interests of the United States and in particular, the interests of the executive branch.[6] The court took note:

> This challenge is something of an anomaly, because the executive branch—whose authority is purportedly undermined by this law—has not appeared in this action to contest the statutory scheme. As amicus curiae the United States Senate points out, and as this Court's review of the case law confirms, no reported decision has ever invalidated a statute because of undue intrusion on executive branch authority when the executive has expressly declined to oppose the law. Thus, the defendants ask this Court to entertain a separation of powers challenge . . . without the participation of the affected branch. (*United States ex rel. Stillwell v. Hughes Helicopter, Inc.* 1989, 1086–87)

Since the inception of the Senate legal counsel, the attorney general has been statutorily obligated to notify Congress if the Department of Justice decides not to defend the constitutionality of a congressional action (2 *U.S.C.* §288k). This notification was extended to specifically include the House general counsel in 1999, with the codification of the office (2 *U.S.C.* §130f). Upon the attorney general's notification, the congressional attorneys may then determine whether or not they want to defend the statute or resolution. Should they assume the case, the attorney general is required to transfer all documentation to the legislative body and is relieved of any representational responsibilities in the matter, although the Department of Justice may appear later as an amicus curiae. Cases where the Department of Justice fails to defend the constitutionality of a statute are infrequent, but when they arise they are generally rooted in separation of powers issues or policy decisions based on the administration's preferences.

In yet other cases, Congress may find that it is best served by complementing the work of the Department of Justice. Unsure of the Bush administration's commitment to defending the Flag Protection Act of 1989, both the House general counsel and the Senate legal counsel filed amicus curiae briefs supporting the legislation in *United States v. Eichman* (1990). And more recently in a line item veto case, the solicitor general's arguments on the merits were supplemented by a joint brief from both the House Bipartisan Leadership Group and the Senate as amici curiae (*Raines v. Byrd* 1997).

Full agreement and cooperation is another pattern of litigation between the branches. This was seen, for example, in the litigation stemming from the impeachment of District Judge Alcee L. Hastings, where Hastings argued against the constitutionality of the impeachment proceedings (*Hastings v. United States* 1992).[7] The Department of Justice with the Senate legal counsel submitted a single brief in the case that was the product of close cooperation between the two branches. Other examples of interbranch cooperation are seen in *Boehner v. Anderson* (1994) and *Schaffer v. Clinton* (2001), cases where individual members of Congress sued their legislative institution and the executive branch, alleging that the cost-of-living provisions of the Ethics Reform Act violated the Twenty-seventh Amendment to the Constitution. In both instances, the congressional legal counsels and their Department of Justice counterparts prevailed.

The Department of Justice and congressional counsels may also concur on some aspects of a pending legal matter while disagreeing with each other on other issues in the case. Litigation over the Balanced Budget and Emergency Deficit Act of 1985 gave rise to just such a scenario where the Department of Justice and Congress agreed on the constitutionality of the act, but disagreed over the role of the comptroller general (*Bowsher v. Synar* 1986). The comptroller (Bowsher) was represented by the solicitor general, while the House and Senate were each named parties in the two companion cases and presented their own distinct arguments.

Perhaps the most interesting cases are where the Department of Justice, representing the executive branch, and Congress are on opposite sides of a case. This is the classic separation of powers model at work—two branches of government battling each other before the third. Cases such as these are not commonly accepted by the nation's courts since they tend to invoke "political questions" that courts generally try to avoid. However, depending on the court and judges or justices, some of these cases do find their way to the docket.

The classic example of interbranch conflict in court was seen in *Immigration and Naturalization Service v. Chadha* (1983), the legislative veto case. While the case was on appeal at the Ninth Circuit, both the House of Representatives and the Senate were invited by the court to submit their views as amici (*Chadha v. Immigration and Naturalization Service* 1980). The appellate court had found itself in the somewhat odd position of having only one party represented since the Department of Justice on behalf of the Immigration and Naturalization Service (INS) had sided with Chadha, arguing that the veto was unconstitutional.

As lawyers for the amici, the House general counsel and Senate legal counsel vigorously posited that the issue was nonjusticiable for several reasons. First, they argued that the case raised a political question rooted in separation of powers issues that courts should not decide. Second, the congressional counsels submitted that Chadha did not have standing since he "has suffered no injury in fact, that he is asserting a nonjusticiable generalized government grievance, and that he is impermissibly asserting the rights of others" (*Chadha* 1980, 15). But finally, the lawyers for the legislature noted that the litigation failed to meet the "case or controversy" standard as to adverseness since no fully recognized party stood before the court in opposition to Chadha's arguments; the congressional counsels were merely representing amici and thus, could not appeal to the Supreme Court if the appellate court ruled the statute unconstitutional. The Ninth

Circuit rejected Congress's arguments at every turn and, on the merits, ruled the legislative veto unconstitutional.

Despite prevailing at the lower court, the Department of Justice appealed to the U.S. Supreme Court seeking to broaden the applicability of the ruling beyond the Ninth Circuit. The congressional legal counsels independently secured approval from their respective bodies to intervene in the case (S. Res. 40 1981; H.R. Res. 49 1981) and became fully recognized parties before the Court. However, the Supreme Court rejected their arguments both as to the justiciability of the case (specifically on the issues of political questions and adverseness) and on the standing threshold of *Chadha*. The Court ultimately ruled against Congress on the merits as well, and the legislative veto was declared unconstitutional. But the representational issues surrounding *Chadha* are the exception rather than the norm.

Since developing an in-house legal expertise and learning how to use that resource to its advantage, Congress has increasingly found itself in court defending its interests without the presence of the solicitor general or the U.S. Attorney's Office. The Senate and the House as institutions, and the members in their official capacities are regularly named parties in cases docketed before the nation's courts. For the most part, the in-house legal counsels ably handle this litigation without reliance on the executive branch.

Filing suit in federal court is not a terribly complicated or expensive process. As a result, court dockets are sometimes used as forums for public statements in the form of lawsuits that range from the very serious and worthy of public attention to the frivolous, petty rantings of a misguided soul that are not worth the time that it will take the legal staff to prepare and file an answer. Yet the even hand of justice must take each case seriously although most litigation in the latter category will likely not proceed far along the judicial path toward remedy and resolution.

Consider the 1994 case of *Adams v. Richardson,* where a constituent sued in the District Court of the District of Columbia to block then-Representative William B. Richardson (D-N.M.) from taking office. Employing the shotgun approach to litigation (allege everything and hope that something is founded), the *pro se* plaintiff charged that the apportionment of New Mexico's congressional districts were "created under conditions of fraud"; that Representative Richardson's failure to participate in debates and "to visit his district or confront his constituents as frequently as Mr. Adams believes was necessary to inform the electorate" suppressed citizens' voting rights; that local newspapers allegedly received tax breaks and thus engaged in a "constructive bribe" since all but one endorsed Representative Richardson; and that public officials of New Mexico were engaged in an armed insurrection against the United States, to which Richardson was aiding and abetting by his failure to notify Congress about the "insurrection" (*Adams v. Richardson* 1994, 44–45). As impertinent as the allegations in this case were, the House general counsel was obliged to respond to the complaint and filed a motion to dismiss arguing for Richardson's immunity under the speech or debate clause. Judge Paul L. Friedman agreed, finding that the plaintiff's claims, "are conclusory, without merit, insubstantial, frivolous and far-fetched" (45).

Congressional interests might also arise when individual members, committees, employees, or officers are subpoenaed for deposition or receive a subpoena duces tecum or deposition duces tecum[8] with respect to documents or materials related to their official work. This may occur in cases where the United States or a member is a named party or where legislators receive demands to appear in litigation between private parties. Often a simple phone call to the litigant who is demanding discovery by one of the attorneys on the congressional counsel's staff is sufficient to exact a voluntary withdrawal of the subpoena (Interview 2001). On other occasions, however, these subpoenas may necessitate a motion to quash and court argument by staff attorneys. For example, when the U.S. government sued to recover the costs incurred in the identification and transportation of bodies and the collection of evidence associated with the Jonestown tragedy, subpoenas filed by the respondent sparked the need for congressional legal representation (*United States v. Peoples Temple of the Disciples of Christ* 1981). As part of the discovery process necessary to prepare its legal defenses, Peoples Temple wanted to question two members of Congress who had been involved in a congressional investigation of the Jonestown tragedy. House General Counsel Brand, representing the two representatives, successfully persuaded the D.C. District Court that the speech or debate clause protected members of Congress from questioning in all venues even in the face of a litigant's right to acquire evidence on his own behalf.

The types of issues that prompt Congress to depend on its own legal representation stem, in large part, from the constitutional clauses that provide specific authority and exclusive responsibility to Congress and are powers not shared by the other branches. In the following section, I discuss these substantive areas that provide Congress with rights and powers that typically prompt congressional litigation and representation by in-house counsel.

WHENCE CONGRESSIONAL RIGHTS?

Of the six substantive articles in the Constitution, Article I is by far the most extensive; it is also the most explicit of the three articles outlining each of the branches of national government. The Framers of the Constitution were rigorous in providing specificity to the legislative power, especially in the context of lawmaking as seen in Article 1, Sections 7, 8, and 9. But what was also important to the drafters was to protect the legislative branch by imbedding certain rights for its members that are unique to their position as legislators. Moreover, the Founders provided for distinctive procedural aspects of the legislative institutions as to the impeachment process, selection of internal officers (Sections 2 and 3), selection and eligibility of members of Congress (Sections 2, 3, and 4), and institutional operations (Section 5). These latter components of the constitutional outline of legislative authority have become important because they insulate Congress from the other branches. Additionally, the courts have recognized the legislature's power to investigate as implied in the legislative power defined under Article 1, Section 1 and operationalized through the rule-making clause of Section 5.

The lawmaking powers of Congress found in Sections 7, 8, and 9 are most regularly defended in our nation's courts by the Department of Justice. These cases are those in which the constitutionality of congressional outputs in the form of public laws are directly questioned. Consider the Supreme Court's decision in *Board of Trustees of the University of Alabama v. Garrett* (2001), where the Court curtailed the reach of the interstate commerce clause and found that Congress had violated the Eleventh Amendment of the Constitution by making applicable to state governments the Americans with Disabilities Act. While such a decision strikes at the heart of Congress's lawmaking abilities under Section 8 of Article 1, it is the responsibility of the executive branch to defend the constitutionality of all laws in our nation's courts. Once Congress legislates, its interests are generally over.

Only on rare occasions do the congressional legal counsels find themselves at the bar arguing for the constitutionality of a statute of general applicability. As mentioned earlier, these are likely to be instances where Congress must fill the shoes of the "United States" because the Department of Justice has chosen not to, or where Congress suspects that the executive branch will not provide a hearty defense of the law despite its appearance. Even less frequently will the congressional counsels find themselves pitted against the Department of Justice and executive branch over the constitutionality of a statute as they did in *Bowsher v. Synar* (1986) or *Chadha*, as discussed earlier.

Where the real work of the congressional legal counsels is found is when they litigate the rights of the members of Congress provided for under Article 1, Section 6. Clause 1 provides that:

> The Senators and Representatives shall receive a Compensation for their Services, to be ascertained by Law, and paid out of the Treasury of the United States. They shall in all Cases, except Treason, Felony and Breach of the Peace, be privileged from Arrest during their Attendance at the Session of their respective Houses, and in going to and returning from the same; and for any Speech or Debate in

either House, they shall not be questioned in any other place. (*U.S. Constitution, Article* 1, Sec. 6, cl. 1)

While the privileges accorded to members of Congress under the arrest and speech or debate clauses are fairly settled areas of law, the latter is still regularly litigated in our nation's courts.

The privilege from arrest was first addressed early in our nation's history (*Coxe v. McClenachan* 1798), and cases have been brought on this issue intermittently as courts attempted to determine the scope of the privilege and its exceptions. Generally, the arrest privilege has been narrowly interpreted as protecting a legislator from liability directly resulting from his or her actions and words in the legislative arena, but it does not extend to criminal arrest or those cases arising from private, nonlegislative matters. The "treason, felony or breach of peace" exception to the privilege has been broadly defined to include all criminal offenses (*Williamson v. United States* 1908) and exempts members from arrest in civil cases only during session (*Gravel v. United States* 1972). But civil arrests are an antiquated practice in American law, meaning there is little need for the privilege.

The ultimate constitutional protection afforded only to the legislative branch is rooted in the speech or debate clause. The contours of this privilege are continually litigated in our nation's courts and as such, remain a key area of legal work for congressional legal counsels. Time and again, the courts have recognized the broad sweep of this clause and its importance in protecting legislative activities from intrusion by the other branches (*United States v. Johnson* 1966; *United States ex rel. Hollander v. Clay* 1976). The speech or debate clause reaches beyond simply speeches given on the floor of Congress to voting, participation in committee hearings, and the preparation of committee reports (*Dickey v. CBS, Inc.* 1975). And that protection has been extended to aides and legislative staff to the extent that their work is integral to the legislative process (*Browning v. Clerk, U.S. House of Representatives* 1986) and confined to acts that would be immune had the member performed them (*Gravel v. United States* 1972).

Courts have also recognized that members engage in both legislative and political work; the former is protected (*United States v. Johnson* 1966), the latter is not (*United States v. Brewster* 1972; *Hutchinson v. Proxmire* 1979). It is for this reason that courts must examine each case individually and determine whether or not the speech, debate, or action is protected activity under the legislative sphere (*McClellan v. McSurely* 1976). If there is a rational legislative purpose to the member's words or actions, it will likely be protected by the constitutional privilege.

Much of the litigation over the speech or debate clause has taken place since the 1970s. As a result, the congressional legal counsels have had a direct hand in shaping the judicial decisions in this legal arena and the lawyers in these offices pride themselves on being experts on speech or debate law. Stanley Brand, the first House general counsel and now a private practitioner, still litigates cases involving speech or debate issues and the privileges afforded the legislators under the Constitution. He has been hired by individual members of Congress in cases where the congressional legal counsels could not provide representation because the litigation involved former members' personal legal matters (*Federal Election Commission v. Wright* 1991; *United States v. Oakar* 1996).

A less-recognized clause found at the beginning of Article 1, Section 6 is the ascertainment clause, which relates to the compensation of congressional members. Historically, Congress set its own pay scale and thus, there was no litigation as the legislative body was protected from lawsuits by its internal rulemaking function under the Constitution. In 1967, however, Congress passed and the president signed into law the Federal Salary Act, which delegated to the executive branch the power to set salaries for Congress, federal judges, and some senior executives. In separate actions, Senator Larry Pressler (R-S.D.) and 140 federal judges subsequently filed suit, both claiming that the act was an unconstitutional delegation of power to the executive (*Pressler v. Simon* 1976; *Atkins v. United States* 1977). The courts disagreed, noting that "Congress continues to be responsible to the public for the level of pay its members receive" (*Pressler* 1976, 306).

Shortly after the legislative veto was declared unconstitutional in *Chadha* (1983), Congress modified the Federal Salary Act to remove the legislative veto in that legislation. As a result, the executive branch was given even more power over pay scales for members of Congress. This sparked a lawsuit by Senator Gordon Humphrey and five members of the House who asserted an argument similar to *Pressler* (1976) and *Atkins* (1977). But the United States Court of Appeal again ruled that "Congress retains the power . . . to supplant that process with specific legislation at any time. The Article I branch thus continues to bear political responsibility for whatever appropriations actions it takes" (*Humphrey v. Baker* 1988, 14). In short, the courts recognize that ultimately Congress retains authority over its own compensation.

Judicial notice of the ascertainment clause in recent years has been incidental to litigation over the Twenty-seventh Amendment. Adopted in 1992, the amendment provides that "No law, varying the compensation for services of the Senators and Representatives, shall take effect until an election of Representatives shall have intervened." Two cases filed by individual legislators against Congress and other governmental parties questioned the application of the Twenty-seventh Amendment to cost-of-living pay increases and necessitated a discussion of the ascertainment clause by the courts (*Schaffer v. Clinton* 2001; *Boehner v. Anderson* 1994).

Article 1, Section 5 outlines several institutional concerns for Congress that have been addressed through litigation. Clause 1 states that "Each House shall

be the Judge of the Elections, Returns and Qualifications of its own Members."
The courts have generally read this provision broadly, affording Congress full
and exclusive rights to determine the validity of elections and the qualifications
of its members (*Barry v. U.S. ex. rel. Cunningham* 1929). Most litigation in this
constitutional venue took place in the first half of the 1900s and by 1970, could
be cast as well-settled law. But the most recent cases over Clause 1 of Section 5
occurred in 1985, as a result of a single election that spawned litigation in state
court, two federal district courts, two federal courts of appeal, and ultimately, the
Supreme Court.

The State of Indiana's race on November 6, 1984, for the Eighth Congressional
District resulted in a statistical dead heat between Republican Richard D.
McIntyre and Democrat Francis X. McCloskey. Election night returns showed
McCloskey ahead with seventy-two votes, but after the state applied its recount
procedures, it declared McIntyre the winner by a margin of thirty-four votes and
certified the election. The House of Representatives, however, instituted its own
recount and determined that McCloskey had won the election by four votes and
seated McCloskey. McIntyre had first filed suit against McCloskey in state court
over the state's recount procedures, but the case was removed to federal court once
Congress began its investigation. McIntyre subsequently lost any hope of attaining
office when the federal appellate court recognized that the action by the House of
Representatives under Article 1, Section 5, Clause 1, preempted any judicial ruling
to the contrary:

> The House is not only "Judge" but also final arbiter. Its decisions about which
> ballots count, and who won, are not reviewable in any court. . . . Nothing we say
> or do, nothing the state court says or does, could affect the outcome of this elec-
> tion. Because the dispute is not justiciable, it is inappropriate for a federal court
> even to intimate how Congress ought to have decided. (*McIntyre v. Fallahay*
> 1985, 1081)

While the House general counsel was not involved in the original suit, he was
brought into the two other cases in U.S. District Court. One was filed by an
aggrieved absentee voter who sued the speaker of the House, members of the
House task force that reviewed the election returns, the majority leader and
whip, and the clerk of the House, claiming a denial of due process and equal protection and a deprivation of rights, privileges, and immunities because his absentee ballot was not counted in the House of Representatives' recount (*Barkley v.
O'Neill* 1985). McIntyre also filed suit against Speaker O'Neill, two Democratic
Party leaders, and the 247 Democratic members of the House who voted to seat
McCloskey (*McIntyre v. O'Neill* 1985). In both cases, the House general counsel
provided representation and successfully persuaded the courts to recognize the
constitutional power granted to the House under Article 1, Section 5, Clause 1,

to sit as "judge of the elections, returns and qualifications of its Members." As a result of Congress's actions in seating McCloskey, the courts ruled the matter as beyond review.

Congress, in establishing procedures by which to carry out its power as "judge of the elections," established the Federal Contested Elections Act (FCEA). In a case of first impression with respect to the discovery procedures imbedded in that act, the general counsel of the House of Representatives submitted an amicus brief that defended the constitutionality of the subpoena provisions of the act and provided the court with the history of the FCEA (*Dornan v. Sanchez* 1997). Judge Gary L. Taylor's decision reflects the careful deference afforded the legislative body when it invokes its constitutional powers in determining elections.

Also imbedded in Section 5 of Article 1 is a proviso that grants the legislative bodies the power to craft their own procedural rules and to establish disciplinary measures for the membership. This has prompted some of the more interesting litigation in recent years as disaffected minority members of the House have attempted, albeit unsuccessfully, to use the courts as a remedy for their lack of power in the chamber. While courts recognize that they have the power to determine whether the rules fashioned by Congress violate the Constitution or fundamental rights (*Vander Jagt v. O'Neill* 1982, 1170; *Michel v. Anderson* 1993; *Skaggs v. Carle* 1997), the judiciary has been less inclined to intervene in internal disputes that are rooted in party politics. But these kinds of cases prove to be interesting work for the House general counsel. The Senate legal counsel, on the other hand, has not seen cases of this ilk simply because they have not been filed by the Senate's members who have fewer rules to contest generally. The rule-making clause was also invoked by members of Congress who were prosecuted criminally in connection with the House Post Office and banking scandals in the 1990s with little success as a defensive strategy (*United States v. Rostenkowski* 1995; *United States v. Oakar* 1996).

The right of Congress to establish its own rules combined with the grant of legislative power found in Section 1 of Article 1 has served as the basis for a range of investigative activities undertaken by the legislative branch. The power of Congress to subpoena witnesses, to compel their testimony, and to punish those who fail to respond by findings of contempt of Congress have been recognized by the federal judiciary as elements essential to the investigative aspects of the legislative function. As a corollary to these powers, Congress also secured by statute the power to request a federal court grant immunity to those who testify before it (18 *U.S.C.* §6005). Typically, staff attorneys for the committees involved in investigations assume responsibility for initiating subpoenas and contempt or immunity orders and work closely with their respective legal counsels to ensure the institution's interests are protected (*In re Grand Jury Investigation of Ven-Fuel* 1977). The work for the general counsel's staff might involve a court appearance to secure an immunity order, reviewing subpoenas, and answering legal questions, for example. But when unusual circumstances arise or institutional interests are invoked such as in the ABSCAM investigation or during the Iran-Contra Affair of the 1980s, congressional legal counsels may find themselves engaged in ongoing litigation.

Congress also enjoys further powers over elections under Section 4, Clause 1 of Article 1, where it may preempt state legislative action with respect to the time, place, and manner of congressional elections. While this clause has been vigorously litigated, most of the litigation has been of a private nature as in the case of contested elections and election irregularities. Alternatively, cases that implicate Congress's power over elections directly have been managed by the Department of Justice. For example, in *U.S. Term Limits v. Thornton* (1995), the solicitor general participated as amicus, and in the case challenging the National Voter Registration Act of 1993, the Civil Rights Division of the Department of Justice represented the national government, and especially, Congress's interests (*Association of Community Organizations for Reform Now v. Miller* 1997). While congressional interests may well be challenged in cases involving elections, this has not been a major area of work for the congressional legal counsels.

Where Congress truly has a unique role to play, however, is in the area of impeachment. Sections 2 and 3 speak to the power of the House to impeach and the responsibilities of the Senate for impeachment trials and punishment upon conviction. While impeachment activities have not been regular events for either body, the impeachments of federal judges Alcee L. Hastings and Walter L. Nixon Jr. prompted litigation in the late 1980s and early 1990s that demanded involvement by the congressional legal counsels. In the Nixon case, the Senate legal counsel worked hand in hand with the solicitor general in crafting the briefs and arguments before the U.S. Supreme Court (*Nixon v. United States* 1993). When Judge Hastings initially filed his suit, he named directly the U.S. Senate, the Impeachment Trial Committee, the secretary of the Senate, and others (*Hastings v. U.S. Senate* 1989). Even the House's power to impeach was at issue when the House Judiciary Committee sought the grand jury records of the Hastings criminal investigation in Miami, Florida. There, however, the general counsel for the House committee played the lead role in obtaining those records (*In re Grand Jury Proceedings of Grand Jury No. 81-1* 1987).

Like other aspects of the Constitution and its amendments, the contours of Article 1 with respect to the powers of the legislative branch are regularly examined by the judiciary. In order to guarantee that Congress's interests are fully and fairly represented, this cursory review of litigation over constitutional power suggests that the legislative branch ought not fully depend on the executive for all of its representational needs in court. Having its own independent legal expertise is logical in the context of the separation of powers.

THE CONGRESSIONAL LEGAL AGENDA, 1996–2000

Litigation over major constitutional questions is but one aspect of the work of the general counsel for the House of Representatives and the Senate legal counsel. Often, counsel will be drawn into routine matters simply to protect the interests of their institution. To more fully understand the nature of the litigation work of these legal advisors, I identified all federal cases in which they participated over the past five years.[9] The resulting portrait of their activity reflects a mix of the routine with the pathbreaking, as the congressional legal counsels found their way to court on a variety of matters.

The House general counsel and Senate legal counsel were noted as attorneys of record or as amicus curiae in twenty different federal cases decided by published opinion between January 1996 and December 2000.[10] Litigation took place at both the Circuit Court of Appeals (nine cases) and at the District Court (trial) level (eleven cases). The House was involved in sixteen cases; the Senate in eight. This difference in litigation rates is not surprising, considering that the House has more "clients" with 435 members to the Senate's one hundred. Additionally, the House general counsel has more freedom in litigation than the Senate legal counsel, who must obtain an endorsement by the full Senate in order to intervene or act as an amicus curiae.

In four cases of the twenty, congressional counsel for both the House and the Senate were participants. It would be easy to assume that these would be the more important cases during the time period studied since they demanded the attention of both houses of Congress. While mostly true, one of the cases is easily classified as a nuisance suit by a *pro se* claimant who burdened not only the district and appellate courts' resources, but also the congressional counsels with his frivolous jailhouse claims (*Magee v. Hatch* 1998). His case was finally dispatched by the District Court for the District of Columbia when he failed to respond to a court-ordered request to substantiate his informa pauperis application.

The other three cases that merited the attention of both legal counsels during this time period were of some significance to Congress and its constitutional powers. In *Byrd v. Raines* (1997), four senators and two representatives challenged the constitutionality of the line item veto. At issue in *Schaffer v. Clinton* (2001) was a challenge by a member of Congress who claimed that the cost-of-living raises granted to members violated the Twenty-seventh Amendment. The suit named both the House clerk and secretary of the Senate as defendants to the action. Finally, in *Adams v. Clinton* (2000), citizens of the District of Columbia decried their lack of representation in the House of Representatives and U.S. Senate as an unconstitutional deprivation of their right to vote.

The Senate legal counsel's other four cases ranged from internal personnel employment matters *(Singer v. Office of the Senate Sergeant at Arms* 1999; *Office of the Sergeant at Arms v. Office of Senate Fair Employment Practices* 1996) to rules on cloture and another line item veto case filed by the City of New York. In *Page v. Shelby* (1998), a *pro se* citizen sued all 100 members of the Senate as well as the parliamentarian, the secretary of the Senate, and the Senate's sergeant at arms, challenging the Senate's rules on cloture as unconstitutional. While not characterized as a frivolous suit, the court took pains to carefully dismiss the case for Page's lack of standing. The *City of New York v. Clinton* (1998) case, on the other hand, proved to be a valid constitutional battle over the line item veto, which eventually wound its way to the Supreme Court. The Senate legal counsel participated at the district court hearings and filed an amicus brief in the Supreme Court case.

The House general counsel found itself engaged in a number of frivolous suits during the five years under review. In *Slangal v. Cassel* (1997), the general counsel simply filed a motion to dismiss, which was granted by the court. Slangal, a *pro se* claimant, had filed six such suits and provoked the federal district court judge in Nebraska to rule, "The complaint is patently frivolous and malicious. . . . Plaintiff names 44 judges, lawyers, law enforcement officers, elected officials, and others as defendants without stating what any of these people did to warrant being sued" (1216). Similarly, in *Banks v. United States* (1997), a *pro se* plaintiff alleged that "Congressman Thomas M. Barrett failed to fulfill unspecified responsibilities to his constituents." This case also required a motion to dismiss, which was readily granted by the court.

Protecting individual members' rights, both as legislators and public officials, as well as the institution's right to investigate were at the heart of several cases involving the House general counsel. In *X-men Security, Inc. v. Pataki* (1997a), a member of Congress had been named as a defendant in a civil rights lawsuit. Recognizing that the speech or debate clause provided absolute immunity for some of Representative Peter T. King's (R-N.Y.) actions, the federal trial judge dismissed a number of complaints levied against the congressman, but permitted others to remain in play. The general counsel's office assisted King with a motion to reconsider, which was subsequently denied (*X-men Security, Inc. v. Pataki* 1997b), and then worked with the U.S. attorney on crafting a successful appeal. On review, the Court of Appeals reversed the district court's denial of qualified immunity to Representative King on the remaining claims (*X-men Security, Inc. v. Pataki* 1999). In *Nix v. Hoke* (1999) and *Albanese v. Federal Election Commission* (1996), individual members were also defended by the general counsel.

Three cases on the House side invoked institutional rights that extend to staff members and committees. In *Pentagen Technologies v. Committee on Appropriations*

(1998), the general counsel successfully invoked the speech or debate clause and prevented a private party from obtaining documents that a House committee possessed as a product of its investigations but had not yet released publicly. In the second case, both a former staff member of a congressional committee and the institution itself were named in a Federal Tort Claims Act *(Popovic v. United States* 1998). While the speech or debate clause was claimed as a mantle for the former staffer, the court ruled on the more narrow qualified immunity afforded to federal employees. And in a third case, the general counsel successfully persuaded the Court to recognize that the speech or debate clause required dismissal of the claims against the Executive Committee of Correspondents, an administrative body that issues credentials to the press galleries of the Congress (*Schreibman v. Holmes* 1999).

The House general counsel submitted an amicus brief in two cases, *United States v. McDade* (1995) and *Beverly Enterprises v. Trump* (1999). The first case involved the criminal prosecution of Representative Joseph M. McDade (R-Pa.) for allegedly accepting bribes and illegal gratuities from defense contractors and lobbyists. Ultimately acquitted of all charges in 1996, McDade unsuccessfully tried to use the speech or debate clause in early motions to dismiss the indictment. The general counsel's interest as amicus was to provide the court with its expertise and understanding of the reach of the speech or debate clause focusing, in part, on the intent of Congress in the crafting the Racketeer Influenced and Corrupt Organization Act (RICO).

The amicus brief filed by the general counsel in *Beverly Enterprises* (1999) was also designed to inform the court of the scope of legislative activities protected under both the speech or debate clause and tort law. Sparked by statements made by Rosemary Trump at a town hall meeting held by members of Congress in Pennsylvania, Beverly Enterprises sued Trump for defamation. The general counsel's office argued that the town hall meeting involved "communications preliminary to a [legislative] proceeding" and statements made by Trump should therefore be privileged under the law of torts (*Restatement [Second] of Torts* § 590A 1976). Further, since the speech or debate clause protected both the congressional members and their aides who were present at the town hall meeting, the general counsel advised the court that certain portions of discovery anticipated by the plaintiffs would be prohibited. The appellate court ruled on behalf of Trump by dismissing the complaint, but on grounds other than those raised by the general counsel.

Like the Senate, the House general counsel occasionally engages in litigation involving employees and labor issues, but this is less likely because of the establishment of an office specifically for legal representation on employee matters. During the five-year period under study, only one case of this nature was litigated in court by the general counsel. The Office of the Chief Administrative Officer of the House of Representatives was named as a defendant when an employee appealed a negative finding by the Board of Compliance, alleging that he did not receive accurate notice of termination under the Congressional Accountability Act (*Schmelzer v. Office of Compliance* 1998). The findings of the board were upheld by the Court of Appeals.

Perhaps the most interesting case to be handled by the House general counsel during this time period involved a suit filed by twenty-seven members of the House against Robin H. Carle, the clerk of the House. The plaintiffs challenged two rules of the House that impacted federal income tax legislation by requiring a minimum three-fifths vote. Defending the clerk, the House general counsel successfully persuaded the district court to avoid the tangles of such a political question. As that court noted,

> Whether expressed in terms of a failure of standing, or "equitable" or "remedial" discretion, the fundamental consideration underlying those decisions is one of prudent self-restraint: federal courts should generally refrain, as a matter of policy, from intruding in the name of the Constitution upon the internal affairs of Congress at the behest of lawmakers who have failed to prevail in the political process. (*Skaggs v. Carle* 1995, 2)

However, the United States Court of Appeal for the District of Columbia Circuit sent a message that it might consider such a case and afford the members a full hearing on the merits if only they had something more than a hypothetical case (*Skaggs v. Carle* 1997). At the urging of the general counsel the court ultimately dismissed the matter for lack of standing.

The legal counsels for the House of Representatives and the Senate seem to be highly successful in defending both their individual clients as well as their institutional ones at all stages of litigation. With the exception of the line item veto cases, the congressional legal counsels prevailed by getting cases dismissed where appropriate by invoking the speech or debate clause or by persuading the court on the merits. While their litigation agenda is not as vigorous during this time period as one might have expected, further data collection and analysis is necessary to provide a more robust depiction of the work of the congressional legal counsels over the past twenty-five years.

CONCLUSION

The litigation activities of the congressional legal counsels revolve around entrenched principles of constitutional design and tread near the fuzzy outlines of power afforded to each of the branches under our system of divided government. Practitioners of law, these lawyers defend and protect the rights and powers of both individual legislators and the institutional actor in the judicial arena. As we have seen, these legal battles can occasionally pair the legislative and executive branches in a constitutional headlock that must be refereed by the third branch of government.

To more fully understand the importance of these lawyers to the legislative branch, future research must move beyond litigation activities and explore their work as advisors to both individual members of each legislative body and to institutional entities like committees and the leadership. Understanding the work of these lawyers in the context of government attorneys can provide some comparative understandings on case selection for amicus participation and strategies for institutional representation. Through interviews with current and past officeholders, we should be able to discern how the lawyers for the legislature identify the institutional interests and best represent their clients.

To truly play a role as a coordinate branch of government, afforded the rights and responsibilities outlined in the U.S. Constitution, Congress must have an independent advocate in the nation's courts. The Office of the General Counsel in the House of Representatives and the Office of the Senate Legal Counsel provide the legal representation that the legislative branch demands. As students of the political process, we have yet to fully capture the importance and influence of these offices in the array of constitutional government.

NOTES

The author wishes to thank Geraldine R. Gennet, General Counsel of the House of Representatives, and her staff for their insight and comments on this chapter.

1. "Before closing this opinion we wish to express the obligation of the court to Mr. Pepper for his able brief and argument as a friend of the court. Undertaken at our request, our obligation is none the less, if we find ourselves obliged to take a view adverse to his" (*Myers* 1926, 176).

2. Both the Senate legal counsel and the general counsel for the House have a range of responsibilities within their respective institutions, only one of which is litigation. This chapter focuses only on their work in the nation's courts as representatives of the legislative branch.

3. But see *United States Department of Commerce v. United States House of Representatives* (1999), involving the use of statistical sampling by the Department of Commerce in completing the census. In this instance, Congress statutorily authorized the House of Representatives to originate legal action under the 1998 Appropriations Act (1997).

4. The Committee on Rules and Administration is also charged under Senate Standing Rules, Rule 25.1, to "identify any court proceeding or action which, in the opinion of the Committee, is of vital interest to the Congress as a constitutionally established institution of the Federal Government and call such proceeding or action to the attention of the Senate."

5. An amicus curiae brief urging reversal was filed on behalf of sixteen members of the United States Senate. It did not have the institutional endorsement of the Office of the Senate Legal Counsel.

6. The Federal Civil False Claims Act includes a *qui tam* provision whereby a private citizen may bring suit to enforce public rights in the name of the United States. The English origin of *qui tam* is generally understood to be one "who brings the action for the king as well as for himself." Thus, one would not normally expect the executive branch to participate in *qui tam* litigation. What is significant in this case is that the challenge to the constitutionality of the federal law should have provoked some response by the Department of Justice, the agency charged with defending the constitutionality of the nation's laws, if only in the form of an amicus curiae brief.

7. The saga of Alcee L. Hastings is among the more bizarre in the annals of American politics. District Court Judge Hastings was tried for bribery and solicitation of bribes, but was later acquitted by a trial jury. He was nonetheless impeached by the House of Representatives, convicted in the Senate in 1989, and removed from office. In 1993, he took his seat in the House of Representatives as a duly elected Democratic member of Congress representing south Florida's 23d district.

8. *Duces tecum* generally means "bring with you" as in documents, evidence, or some item to be inspected by the court (subpoena) or at deposition.

9. Data for this section were drawn from an electronic search of the Lexis-Nexis Academic Universe database, limited by date (1/1/1996–12/31/00) and by attorney (using names of attorneys working in both offices during this time period, the words *Senate* and *House,* and the variations of terms used to describe the leadership groups of the House over time). The resulting case list was screened for misidentified cases, which were discarded.

10. The data count cases not opinions. On several matters, there were multiple rulings and decisions at both trial and appellate levels.

PART FOUR

Comparative Rights

CHAPTER SEVEN

Rights in America through a Comparative Lens

MARY L. VOLCANSEK

Americans tend toward a reverential view of their Constitution and its appended Bill of Rights, even though many are ignorant of their contents. Scholars, judges, and pundits argue over the original intent behind the Bill of Rights and deplore or applaud its treatment in the hands of judges and legislators. This discussion occurs too often in a vacuum, as though the United States were not a part of a larger world or that only people living north of the Rio Grande contemplate human rights. In this chapter, I place the U.S. conception of rights into a larger comparative and historical context. The term *human rights* is, after all, now part of the vocabulary of politicians the world over, though the rights so designated and the lenses through which they are viewed are often quite different from the U.S. conception. Indeed, the United States' large neighbor to the north (Canada) only enacted its own national Charter of Rights in 1982 (Mandel 1989), and its perception of how human rights is defined is distinct from that of the United States.

Aristotle supposed that politics could best be understood by classifying and categorizing regime types and constitutions, and since his *Politics* was written "the notion of comparing political systems has lain at the heart of political science" (Mair 1996, 309). Differences among countries may be identified and, hopefully, explained through the comparative method. Application of this notion to a discussion of rights in the hands of U.S. judges and legislators is intended as an antidote to the view that the United States is a unique entity.

Constitutions abound throughout the world; some are ignored, while others truly constitute parchment barriers. The United Kingdom has endured for centuries with no written constitution, but in 2000 it absorbed a European regional charter of rights. Constitutions differ, as Ulrich Preuss (1993, 75) notes, "according to the tradition, physical, economic and social conditions, world view, culture and historical experience of the people who create them." What constitutions have in common is their goal of limiting the power of government, and this is typically achieved through some combination of division of power and guarantees of individual rights. The rights to be protected and the precise divisions of governmental power tend to vary by the experiences of the generations in which they were written. They change, in other words, over time.

Since chronology offers a major demarcating point in how rights are perceived, I suggest that Samuel Huntington's (1991) "three waves" of democratization offer useful time frames for examining the various generations of rights. Though some notions of rights, notably the Magna Carta, predate modern times, the twin concepts of democracy and of individual rights at the nation-state level are largely products of the modern era. Developments in how rights are conceived run roughly parallel to Huntington's waves of democratization. There are three categories of rights that also have evolved over time: civil and political rights, social, cultural and economic rights, and the third generation or collective rights (Davidson 1993). Because of the coincidence of when they became commonly recognized, Huntington's taxonomy can serve as a template for a description. Huntington argues that the first wave of democratization can be observed in the early nineteenth century, a second following World War II, and a third beginning in 1974 (Huntington 1991). Whereas he proposes that a reverse wave follows each forward wave in the process of democratization, a similar phenomenon is not necessarily relevant to a discussion of rights. The first wave of rights focused on civil and political rights, and they were first acknowledged as deserving protection from the nation-state circa 1800, contemporaneous with the initial wave of democratization. The post–World War II period witnessed the ascendancy of social and economic rights, and the third generation began with a bridge in the 1970s, but became a wave a decade later as democratization occurred in Africa and redemocratization in Latin America; in the 1990s it continued as parts of the former Soviet Union, Eastern Europe, and pockets in Asia moved toward democracy.

POLITICAL AND CIVIL RIGHTS

When the American colonies declared their independence from Britain in 1776, the thoughts of some of the colonists turned to questions of individual rights. Three weeks before the Declaration of Independence was promulgated, Virginia adopted a Declaration of Rights, the first in North America to restrain all branches of government (Levy 1986). The philosophical underpinnings of that document, as well as of Jefferson's Declaration of Independence, were essentially liberal in character and directed at protection of life, liberty, and property. Interestingly, however, when the delegates met in Philadelphia eleven years later to reconsider the Articles of Confederation, the Constitution they crafted did not include a similar enumeration of rights. Near the end of the deliberations in 1787, George Mason argued that the document would be improved by a bill of rights as a preface, but other delegates countered that the state constitutions included the requisite guarantees for individual rights. The efficacy of the state documents must have appeared sufficient, since the motion to include a bill of rights failed unanimously (Van Doren 1948).

Debates in the states on ratification of the Constitution and, specifically, the opposition of the Anti-Federalists, served as catalysts for what would become known as the Bill of Rights. State after state in their ratifying conventions proposed a series of amendments to the proposed constitution, with two main goals: to protect individual liberties and to limit the powers of the national government. The list of amendments coming from Massachusetts, New Hampshire, Virginia, and North Carolina were all remarkably similar, though New Hampshire was the first to include common law protections for the accused in criminal procedures (Lienesch 1989). The essence of the repeated objections is perhaps best captured by George Mason, whose primary objection to the Constitution was the absence of enumerated rights. "[Since] the Laws of the general Government being paramount to the Laws and Constitutions of the several states," he observed, "the Declaration of Rights in the separate States are no security" (Mason [1787] 1989, 116). Consequently, to achieve ratification, the Federalists were forced to propose such amendments. Twelve amendments were presented in 1789, and ten of them were ratified by 1791 and became known collectively as the Bill of Rights (Hall et al. 1991). Of note, another of those amendments was ratified in 1992, 203 years after its companions, and became the Twenty-seventh Amendment (O'Brien 2000b).

The driving ideas behind the protections appended to the U.S. Constitution in 1791 were already in evidence in some state constitutions, in particular the Virginia Declaration of Rights. The foundation underlying them all was John Locke's liberalism. Locke had articulated a secular derivation for the natural rights of mankind, and they constituted one element of the social contract among people when moving from the state of nature into a political society. These rights were asserted as universal and existed without reference to a constitution or jurisprudential precedent (Henkin 1990). Some of those rights found their way into the U.S. Bill of Rights. Amendments One through Four are essentially civil rights, including those of religion, press, speech, and assembly, along with freedoms from government intrusions through searches and seizures or quartering of soldiers; the now troublesome Second Amendment provides for militias and their arms. Amendment Five is a blend of common law criminal protections and one essential liberal value, protection of property; it provides that life, liberty, and property can only be taken through due process of law. Amendments Six, Seven, and Eight reaffirm a number of common law guarantees involving both criminal and civil law, and the omnibus Amendment Nine refers to other rights retained by the people, even if not specified. Amendment Ten constitutes an affirmation of a role for the states and not a declaration of another individual right.

The Constitution and Bill of Rights were written at the end of the eighteenth century and, are, therefore, inconsistent with Huntington's time frame of the mid-nineteenth century. In actuality, although the rights of the generation of the American Founders were widely embraced in their era, neither the judiciary nor the legislature breathed life into them until the twentieth century. Even so, they stood as a backdrop and articulated aspirations if not realities. When discussing human rights, a similar disjuncture between ideal and actualities too often emerges as a theme. How those rights were eventually expanded or contracted is the subject of the other contributions to this collection, and I will refrain from repeating what is more thoroughly addressed elsewhere.

On the other side of the Atlantic, another revolution occurred and another set of rights and aspirations were born. Whereas the United States was strongly influenced by Lockean conceptions of political community, the French Revolution and its attendant Declaration of the Rights of Man and Citizen bore the mark of Jean Jacques Rousseau. Where Locke emphasized liberty, Rousseau championed equality (Preuss 1993). The American version essentially codified the recognized rights of Englishmen at the time, albeit in an expanded and clarified fashion. It drew on the Lockean tradition and built "a ring fence around individuals which no government can touch" (Finer 1997, 1506).

The essential intent of the French declaration was to establish a nation grounded on the general will of all citizens. The Declaration was proclaimed by the French National Assembly in 1789 and added as a preface to the French Constitution of 1791. The seventeen articles of the French document differed from those of the United States in a number of important respects. First, the rule of law, mentioned explicitly in nine articles, places rights squarely in a legal framework, but were curiously also treated as statements of intent rather than claims that one could invoke in court. Second, the French declaration established a nation, the property of its citizens, and the capability of disposing of itself according to the general will. It provides for the "inviolability of private property," while also declaring complete juridical equality of all its citizens. Equality was notably absent from the U.S. document until 1868 and then was ensured by

Amendment Fourteen only from breaches by the various states. In sum, the French document contains contradictions, one of which was deadly: all authority flows from the general will, but each individual holds natural and inviolable rights; "the two are *not compatible*" (Finer 1997, 1541).

Perhaps the inconsistencies of the declaration, as well as the tenuous nature of the new regime, condemned France to instability. The First Republic was short-lived and followed by the Reign of Terror, the directory, and then a consulate, which was supplanted by the First Empire under Napoleon I in 1804. In all, France has had eleven political systems since 1789; five of them, republics (Safran 1995). Napoleon's ascension in 1804 ended any constitutional or legal authority for the Declaration of Rights of Man and Citizen, though it was later incorporated via preambles into the Fourth (1946) and the Fifth Republics (1958). Portions of the Declaration of Rights were later constitutionalized by the Constitutional Council in 1986 (Stone 1992). Despite its fallow existence in France for two centuries, the Declaration of Rights of Man and Citizen had a long reach and has influenced every subsequent modern constitution that was created for the purpose of establishing new institutions (Finer 1997).

COLD WAR ERA OF SOCIAL AND ECONOMIC RIGHTS

At the conclusion of World War II, a so-called Age of Rights was ushered onto the stage, and "human rights acquired the full value of an ideology" (Cassese 1990, 159). One of the most striking characteristics of this new consciousness was that human rights were "internationalized," whereby "the idea of constitutional rights in a few countries [were transformed] to a universal conception and a staple of international politics and law" (Henkin et al. 1999, 276). Contemporaneously, a number of new national constitutions were written in Europe that included not only an enumeration of rights, but also a mechanism designed to put teeth into them—judicial review. The European reverence for popular sovereignty expressed through parliament had long stood as an impediment to judicial review as something that would allow another institution of government the power to overrule acts of the people's representatives in parliament. If courts can do this, it "means that they can supervise the legislature" (Blondel 1995, 348); popular or parliamentary sovereignty is trumped by independent judges.

Indeed, *sovereignty* was the concept most affected by the international dimension in post–World War II notions of rights. The very idea of an international declaration of rights implied a limitation on how a state, within its territorial sovereignty, could treat its own citizens. Previously, "concerns for individual welfare was framed and confined with the state system" (Henkin et al. 1999, 278). The international arena was populated by nations, and individuals had no part in it; the only bodies involved were sovereign and independent states (Cassese 1990). There had been a number of treaties or other international agreements prior to World War II that had addressed certain individual rights, but only when the United Nations Charter came into force in 1945 was there an impetus and an incentive to pursue universal recognition of basic human rights. The motivation behind the United Nations (UN) and the protection of human rights is obvious: Nazi atrocities and genocide. The victorious Allies in World War II concluded that a just and stable international order was predicated on an international vehicle for protection of human rights when national governments had none (Davidson 1993).

The UN charter contained references to human rights in several passages, but the Universal Declaration of Human Rights, promulgated in May 1948, constituted a first effort to enumerate those rights essential to the "inherent dignity and the equal and inalienable rights of all members of the human family." The thirty articles encompass some of the rights found in the U.S. Bill of Rights and the French Declaration of Rights of Man and Citizen, but many others reflected both the experiences of the nineteenth and twentieth centuries and changes in expectations. For example, slavery and torture were prohibited, and family, marriage, work, equal pay, social protection, and trade union membership were protected. Similarly, freedom of travel and a right to asylum are listed, along with rights to vote and to a free education. Discrimination based on "race, color, sex, language, religion, political or other opinion, national or social origin, property, birth or other status" was condemned in Article Two. The idealism of the Declaration was obvious and, a half-century later, it is apparent that its articulated goals have hardly been achieved around the world. Indeed, the Universal Declaration's statement of equality of sexes and of races predated serious attempts in the United States to foster equal protection regardless of race or gender.

The changing perceptions of inherent rights were further reflected in a second document passed by the United Nations later in 1948: the Convention on the Prevention and Punishment of the Crime of Genocide. In it genocide was defined and condemned, and measures for punishing the crime were specified. The annihilation of whole peoples had likely been contemplated or attempted on some scale prior to World War II, but consciousness of it escalated after Nazi atrocities were exposed. New rights were recognized, along with new categories of criminal behavior. As more and more international or regional agreements are concluded to protect human rights, that pattern emerges repetitively: when some heinous act by a state government occurs, something previously unfathomable, then a new right is envisioned that requires protection.

Protection of human rights at the national and international levels is intimately connected, and United Nations conventions specifically directed protection of rights and punishment for their violation to national courts wherever possible. Antecedents for those rights embodied in the Universal Declaration of Human Rights lay in national legal systems, and domestic constitutional regimes are the cornerstones of its enforcement. "International mechanisms operate to reinforce domestic protections of human rights," according to Scott Davidson (1993, 1), "and to provide redress when the domestic system fails or is found wanting." Not surprisingly, a new catalogue of rights can be found in the national constitutions that are of the same Cold War vintage as the United Nations declaration.

The second wave of human rights protection tended to be limited to the West and to places influenced by the West, such as Japan and the Philippines. Perhaps the most notable examples of a second generation of rights can be found in the vanquished Axis powers after World War II, Germany, Italy, and Japan. Italy had, in fact, broken its ties to Nazi Germany in 1943 and had allied itself to Britain, France, and the United States, but because of the ongoing German occupation, Italy reached the end of the war with its political regime in disrepute. All three nations wrote new constitutions, with lengthy catalogues of rights, in the years immediately following the war. The authors of these documents were motivated by past mistakes and a desire to guard against their repetition. This has, consequently, been described as "negative revolutions," intended to counter previous experiences (Johnson 1993, 27).

A defining feature of the post–World War II national constitutions, like the international documents, is a lengthy catalogue of rights. These enumerations are not afterthoughts and appendages, but rather introduce the whole. Rights are, in other words, primary, and their protection from government infringement constitutes the foremost aspiration of the constitution. The Basic Law of the Federal Republic of Germany begins with nineteen such articles; the Italian Republic's constitution has some fifty articles, divided into categories of fundamental principles, civil rights, ethical and social relations, economic relations, and political rights. In both documents, marriage, work, education, unionization, gender relations, and other policies are included as rights. This listing would have seemed quite strange to those writing in the eighteenth and nineteenth centuries. Unlike civil, political, and criminal rights that set limits on government, the new topics appear to envision or even demand specific government actions. Preuss calls these "teleological constitutions" in an effort to capture their policy-oriented components; such goal setting is, he argues, contrary to the notion of liberal constitutions. The intent of the policy items is not to limit government, but to propel it (Preuss 1993, 78). Put differently, liberal rights of the earlier generation were conceived as freedoms, whereas the "new rights" required a positive government action (Blondel 1995). New rights embodied aspirations more than limitations. That perception led, in the Italian case, to an argument that all of the rights were mere proclamations, without juridical force to transform them into meaningful limitations on or responsibilities for the national government (Mény and Knapp 1998). The Italian Constitutional Court, in its very first decision countered that by invalidating a series of laws that infringed Article 21's guarantee of freedom of expression (Volcansek 2000). The vagueness and ambiguity of the Italian constitution, like the conflicting requirements contained in the preamble of 1958 French constitution, conspired to prevent direct enforcement in courts of all of the enshrined rights.

Implicit in my discussion of rights in Western Europe is that the will or authority of the Constitutional Court—in the French case, the Constitutional Council—gave meaning and force to constitutional rights. The absence of a body with binding authority defanged the United Nations Universal Declaration. Yet, courts had different impacts on the efficacy of rights elsewhere. For example, the post–World War II Japanese Constitution included in Article 20, for example, a guarantee that "freedom of religion is guaranteed to all," and that "no person shall be compelled to take part in any religious acts, celebration, rite or practice." Yet, with the agreement of the Supreme Court, war heroes were enshrined in a Shinto service over the objections of relatives whose religious beliefs opposed the Shinto practice (O'Brien 1996). Conversely, the State of Israel has built a constitution incrementally, passing a Freedom and Dignity Basic Law only in 1993. There, the civil courts and the Supreme Court attempted to define and protect certain rights in the absence of a government and fundamental law from which to derive them (Edelman 1994).

A third feature of the Age of Rights that began after World War II was the recognition of rights and creation of bodies to protect them on a regional level. The European Council was the first, with its European Convention for the Protection of Human Rights and Fundamental Freedoms, which went into effect in 1953. That list of rights was binding only on nations that accepted compulsory jurisdiction, and all did not. Further, implementation depended on a dual institutional structure of a commission and a court, with the former emphasizing diplomatic strategies for resolution of complaints and serving as the gatekeeper to the more formal procedure of adjudication (Jackson 1997). Only well into the era of the new generation of rights were such shortcomings overcome. In 1998, the commission was abolished, placing all authority for resolution of alleged breaches into the formal process of adjudication before the European Court of Human Rights, and by 1999, all members of the European Council were parties to the convention. The court continues to lack, however, any police power to enforce its decisions (Henkin et al. 1999).

Limitations similar to those initially imposed on the European Court of Human Rights were placed on its sister organization in the Americas. The Organization of American States (OAS) adopted the American Convention on

Human Rights in 1969, but the convention did not enter into force until 1978. It also relied on nations' accepting its authority, and notably the United States has never done so. Its commission also served as a dispute resolution arm that filtered the cases that could reach the Inter-American Court for formal adjudication. Few cases were heard by the court as a result, and even now the court is far behind its European counterpart in effectiveness, though it has rendered some important decisions (Henkin et al. 1999).

Huntington marks the beginning of the third wave of democratization with the end of dictatorships in Portugal and Spain. In terms of rights, however, the Spanish and Portuguese transitions are best seen as bridges to the third generation of rights that were asserted beginning in the 1980s when the democratization wave grew to tidal proportions across the globe. Spain began its journey toward democracy with the death of General Francisco Franco in 1975, and its new democratic constitution went into effect three years later. The by-then-usual catalogue of political and civil rights were noted, and a number of the expected social and economic ones were included. The stretch toward more novel, policy-oriented rights were found in guarantees of adequate housing, protections for the handicapped, pensions for the elderly, and protection of the environment (Newton 1997). At the same time, Portugal dismantled its dictatorship. A new constitution was in place in 1976 but underwent several revisions during the first six years. Consolidation of democracy in Portugal was slower than it had been in Spain, but the rights included in the constitution were reflective of the post–World War II era. Notably, the highest court, the Constitutional Tribunal, dealt minimally with issues of individual rights during its first ten years, 1983–92 (de Araújo 1997).

THIRD GENERATION

As democracy became more the norm in Latin America, Eastern Europe, portions of Africa, and in parts of the old Soviet Union, new constitutions were written and new listings of rights were incorporated into them. This movement has been so vast and, in many ways, so disparate, that it is difficult if not impossible to generalize about it. Earlier eras had been largely Western phenomena; beyond the Western Hemisphere, democratization had generally occurred in countries strongly influenced by the West through colonial status or, as in Japan, occupation. With more than 170 nation-states in the world that met UN standards by the late 1990s, uniformity in how human rights are conceived is notably absent among the newest democracies. The older configurations of rights are often adopted, but regarded as less central. Some balance between "state power and individual and collective rights" is surely a part of constitutionalism for the newer democracies, but the "American and Western European universalistic constitutional models were not persuasive in many parts of the world, including some parts of Europe" (Katz 1993, 15). Certain individual rights from earlier eras are included, but alongside them are often found a "third generation" of rights. These are so-called solidarity or collective rights that may take several forms. Particularly in developing nations, solidarity rights are attempts to stake a claim for fairer treatment of the nation in the larger world order (Davidson 1993). In this sense, they are also assertions of rights to self-determination of a people, rights to economic development, rights to peace, or rights to a healthy environment. But, collective rights can have another connotation: they may be subversive of individual rights and demand that the rights of society override those of individuals. For example, national security or public order may preempt individual or minority rights (Henken et al. 1999). The inversion of logic from earlier generations of rights is obvious: individual rights for protection from a potentially overpowering state was the goal of the first generation, whereas the third generation allows for the collective to assume priority over the individual.

Another characteristic of many of the newer democracies is their invocation of the language of human rights even while harboring suspicion about it. The concept of human rights, whether the language comes naturally or is imposed from outside, has been viewed as a thinly disguised attempt by the Western powers to mask discussions of power with the discourse of rights; rights are but "an imperialist Trojan Horse" (Mamdani 1993, 175). External imposition of human rights, whether by rhetoric, persuasion, or force, is a means of controlling or directing national development. It can be employed to justify the status quo of national dependency or of class or race ascendancy.

What further complicates discussions of rights in the third wave of democratization is the basic fragility of democracy in so many states. The success of democratic experiments seems to be intimately connected to the strength of a nation's economy, but rarely are human rights included in discussions of transitions to democracy. Economic factors, distribution of wealth, the role of the military, amnesty for crimes of previous regimes, and other nonrights-based topics dominate. Rights emerge as a goal—perhaps—of democratization, but not the means to arrive at or to consolidate a democratic state. To get a better grip on the varied expressions of rights among the new democracies, it is useful to tackle the subject by region, where at least some historical, cultural, or economic variables may be constant.

Conditions in Eastern Europe would be expected to resemble more closely those in the established democracies of Western Europe, but even there, a single picture does not emerge. Rights were part of the negotiated new constitution in Hungary, but the whole of the constitution was amended six times during its first year of existence. A constitution with such easy flexibility does not augur well for entrenching rights that might become episodically unpopular in the hands of the ruling majority. Moreover, any protection for human rights in a constitutional regime usually requires some other mode of limiting government power, such as federalism or separation of powers. Yet all of those features were in question early in the democratic regimes of Hungary, the Czech Republic, Poland, and Bulgaria (Sajó and Losonci 1993). The range of potential implications for human rights is likely linked also to the new nation's sense of its past. Hungary can, for example, point to its constitutional past, whereas Slovakia has no such tradition since it only had a brief brush with autonomy during World War II. The Poles can and do point to constitutionalism in their distant past, before 1791. The Czech Republic inherited a history it refers to as "legal nihilism" (Katz 1993, 19).

The situation is quite different in the new democracies of Latin America. One survey of rights in Latin American democracies found that most reflected a pronounced ideological flavor, but the "determinant factor is not [the existence of a catalogue of rights], but the quality and content of these freedoms and rights" (Frühling 1993, 87). They range from authoritarian declarations to liberal ones, and virtually all include exceptions. Those periods of "exceptions" can be particularly damaging. The exceptions are typically related to two qualities of Latin American democracies: the role of the military (Rouquié 1991) or the pervasiveness of political violence (Hakim and Lowenthal 1993). Closely linked to both is the lack of economic stability that would allow democracy and human rights to flourish without the threat of military intervention or the rise of civil strife (Hakim and Lowenthal 1993). Democracies in Latin America, though often giving lip service to human rights' protections, sit under the dangling sword of possible "violent disloyal opposition." Measures taken in defense of democracy, "even when legally enacted by democratic majorities in the legislature, can be and have been questioned from a strict civil libertarian point of view" (Linz 1978, 94).

On the vast and varied continent of Africa, yet another view of human rights can be discerned among the emerging democracies. In 1995, there were twenty-five democratic nations or ones at least committed to democratic change there, and they spanned half of the continent. Rights in the African context have been rendered secondary to the overarching theme of resurrecting some form of national self-determination. The goal of human rights and that of self-determination often collide. Even where they do not, patterns of discrimination may accompany self-determination, and existing discrimination on economic, religious, and cultural lines may effectively deny some minorities human rights. Self-determination can feed ethnic oppression, but even where it does not, marginalized groups remain oppressed or displaced (Joseph 1993). For democracy and rights to take root in Africa, a number of other obstacles must be removed:

economic crisis, national fragmentation, and tenuous state legitimacy (Hutchful 1993).

If the nature of rights protection in Africa can be captured at all, I believe the 1981 African Charter on Human and People's Rights is instructive. This multi-national treaty was signed in 1981 and became effective in 1986. While it enumerates the normal civil and political rights that one might expect, it also, as its title implies, seeks protection of solidarity rights or those of an entire people. In doing so, it necessarily sets minority and majority rights on a potential collision course. The treaty's enforcement hinges on strictly diplomatic actions aimed at achieving consensus without coercion (Davidson 1993). The two forms of rights need not be in conflict, but they too often are. As Henkin et al. (1999, 476) point out, collective rights are "really values asserted by the society as a whole to override individual or minority claims[;] . . . they are not human rights."

THE EVOLUTION OF HUMAN RIGHTS

Notions of human rights, whether derived from divine or secular origins, have been the source of contemplation at least since John Locke and Jean Jacques Rousseau. Their conceptions were linked to protections from unwarranted intrusions by government and were first proclaimed at a national level in 1791, almost simultaneously in the United States and in France. In the past fifty years, the concept has found voice, if not protection, in international forums that rely largely on domestic enforcement, but pretend to take effect when domestic remedies falter. How rights have been viewed has evolved substantially, both in content and in reach. Yet, in other ways, the content of human rights has remained quite constant. Questions about human rights, their content and their efficacy, remain much today as they did at the end of the eighteenth century.

As the rights enshrined in constitutions and treaties subsequent to the U.S. and French ones are surveyed, the most striking element is that they tend to be additive. The civil and political rights that were embraced by political leaders on both sides of the Atlantic two centuries ago tend to be repeated in the later documents. Constitutions in the second wave did not jettison any of the basic rights to participate in government, to assemble peaceably, to hold property, to be free from government intrusion into one's home, to due process of law, and others. Rather, they added a series of economic and social rights, perhaps acknowledging that one's ability to exercise the earlier rights was conditioned largely by economic and social circumstances. Of course, the second wave of rights was also influenced clearly by a vision of a larger state responsibility in providing for human development. Notably, the second wave also acknowledged that protections were necessary to protect from sexual, racial, and linguistic discrimination.

Even as the third wave of rights followed in the 1980s and 1990s, many of the rights articulated in the first two waves were repeated. Again, there was more addition than subtraction. Whereas many national and even international statements of human rights in the second wave had recognized both individual and collective rights, some of the newer versions chose to highlight collective rights. In doing so, of course, they moved the focus away from the individual, which is where the notion of rights had its genesis.

CONCLUSION

Human rights' protections gain efficacy only in certain types of governmental systems. Though authoritarian nations often recite a litany of rights, their claims are transparently hollow. Democratic regimes appear to be a necessary, though not necessarily sufficient, condition for the protection of human rights. Constitutionalism seems to be the second necessary feature. Notably, constitutionalism and democracy are not synonymous. Indeed, the two can find themselves at cross-purposes. "Democracy is more willing to chance injuries that can flow from majoritarian domination," Walter Murphy (1993, 20) explains, while "constitutionalism is more willing to risk harms that can flow from restricting government power." Human rights are by definition protected from the whim or will of the majority, and constitutionalism involves establishing limits on government by restricting its power, even the power to act with a democratic majority mandate. The connection "between democracy and promotion of human rights is not perfect" (Sorensen 1993, 87).

Meshing democracy with constitutionalism has the potential to ensure the first generation of liberal rights from infringement, provided that appropriate mechanisms are designed. However, the second generation of rights included more than limits on the scope of government; they committed government to accomplish a number of positive actions. These require implementation and must be established over time, if at all. The distance between the stated ideals and the current realities run the risk of rising expectations that cannot be fulfilled, at least not immediately (Blondel 1995). That discrepancy between aspirations and actualities is even greater when the third generation of rights is considered, for collective rights of peace, self-determination, and environmental health frequently will find their fruition predicated on actions beyond national boundaries.

Rights that constitute only restrictions of government power are hardly self-actuating. Limits on government can only be enforced in a few ways. Typically, the government checks itself, the majority recognizes self-limitation, or there is some external mechanism to control the power of government. Constitutionalism, with its protection of human rights, is usually linked to the legal process or the rule of law (Lev 1993), but Western judicial mechanisms are hardly the only means of controlling government. Indeed, the rule of law can be observed where those who wield power believe that the constitution is controlling, as is the case in Great Britain, and a constraining legal process is not imperative. Britain is, of course, the quintessential majoritarian government system, with a historically unitary system, a single lawmaking chamber, a flexible constitution, and weak judicial review. The majority holds the reins of government, with little or no restriction. This would lead in many cases to wholesale violation of rights, but not necessarily. Conversely, the checks that inhere in consensus models of government—federalism, second chambers, rigid constitutions, and strong judicial review—should be more inclined to ensure individual rights. Exceptions to that formula can also be found rather facilely, usually in times of "emergency."

What, therefore, does any of this say about the U.S. Bill of Rights, as it has been shaped and formed in the hands of legislators and judges over the past two hundred years? The U.S. experience, both at the time of independence and now, is centered on the individual. It "began and continues as the most anti-statist, legalistic and rights-oriented nation" (Lipset 1996, 20). Not surprisingly, the Bill of Rights that was ratified in 1791 pits the individual against the state and places the burden of asserting rights on the individual. European rights emerged differently, and as the Old World of aristocratic privilege and domination of economic and social norms was ushered out, a different face would be placed on the new regime. The French Declaration of Man and Citizen in 1791 placed the nation and the general will above the individual, even while listing a number of protections for the individual. When democracy finally took root on the Continent after World War II and began the second wave, the state was not the enemy, but the servant of popular sovereignty—the general will—and was given responsibility for creating a better life in real economic and social terms. Human rights in the second wave cast the state as a partner or a vehicle. The third wave of rights can be seen as an attempt by newer democracies to claim development rights in economic, social, and environmental terms from the developed world. Conversely, it can be viewed as a formula for chauvinistic nationalism and ethnic or religious strife. The past decade has testified to both possibilities.

The Bill of Rights that was ratified in 1791 was hardly a model of egalitarianism, as women, nonwhites, non-property owners, and adherents of some religions were denied citizenship and even the most basic access to political, social, and economic participation. Most of its tenets of civil and political rights have, however, found their way in more modern guises into most declarations of rights in the second and third generations. The Bill of Rights served primarily as a protection for economic interests until the twentieth century, but it has been interpreted by both Congress and the courts in ways that have allowed it to retain some currency. Human equality and human dignity are the two themes that characterize the second generation of rights, and these are still far from achieved in the United States. The third generation of rights centers on elements somewhat alien to American individualism. They may, however, highlight the paradoxes that are implicit in the U.S. system of rights. Lipset (1996) devotes two chapters of his book on American exceptionalism to the racial and ethnic divides in the United States. Rights are individual, but discrimination often follows group lines. Economic inequities tend to track racial, ethnic, gender, and sexual orientation; the role of the state in the taking of life is debated by opponents of abortion and, at the other end of the political spectrum, by those who challenge the death penalty. Is the individual or the larger collective society primary? Are there rights to a healthy environment, to peace, and to security? Can government policies to achieve social goals override individual rights? Much of the world has been instructed by the example of the United States, but can the United States also learn some lessons about rights from the rest of the world?

The United States Constitution

We the people of the United States, in order to form a more perfect union, establish justice, insure domestic tranquility, provide for the common defense, promote the general welfare, and secure the blessings of liberty to ourselves and our posterity, do ordain and establish this Constitution for the United States of America.

Article I

Section 1.

All legislative powers herein granted shall be vested in a Congress of the United States, which shall consist of a Senate and House of Representatives.

Section 2.

The House of Representatives shall be composed of members chosen every second year by the people of the several states, and the electors in each state shall have the qualifications requisite for electors of the most numerous branch of the state legislature.

No person shall be a Representative who shall not have attained to the age of twenty five years, and been seven years a citizen of the United States, and who shall not, when elected, be an inhabitant of that state in which he shall be chosen.

Representatives and direct taxes shall be apportioned among the several states which may be included within this union, according to their respective numbers, which shall be determined by adding to the whole number of free persons, including those bound to service for a term of years, and excluding Indians not taxed, three fifths of all other Persons. The actual Enumeration shall be made within three years after the first meeting of the Congress of the United States, and within every subsequent term of ten years, in such manner as they shall by law direct. The number of Representatives shall not exceed one for every thirty thousand, but each state shall have at least one Representative; and until such enumeration shall be made, the state of New Hampshire shall be entitled to chuse three, Massachusetts eight, Rhode Island and Providence Plantations one, Connecticut five, New York six, New Jersey four, Pennsylvania eight, Delaware one, Maryland six, Virginia ten, North Carolina five, South Carolina five, and Georgia three.

When vacancies happen in the Representation from any state, the executive authority thereof shall issue writs of election to fill such vacancies.

The House of Representatives shall choose their speaker and other officers; and shall have the sole power of impeachment.

Section 3.

The Senate of the United States shall be composed of two Senators from each state, chosen by the legislature thereof, for six years; and each Senator shall have one vote.

Immediately after they shall be assembled in consequence of the first election, they shall be divided as equally as may be into three classes. The seats of the Senators of the first class shall be vacated at the expiration of the second year, of the second class at the expiration of the fourth year, and the third class at the expiration of the sixth year, so that one third may be chosen every second year; and if vacancies happen by resignation, or otherwise, during the recess of the legislature of any state, the executive thereof may make temporary appointments until the next meeting of the legislature, which shall then fill such vacancies.

No person shall be a Senator who shall not have attained to the age of thirty years, and been nine years a citizen of the United States and who shall not, when elected, be an inhabitant of that state for which he shall be chosen.

The Vice President of the United States shall be President of the Senate, but shall have no vote, unless they be equally divided.

The Senate shall choose their other officers, and also a President pro tempore, in the absence of the Vice President, or when he shall exercise the office of President of the United States.

The Senate shall have the sole power to try all impeachments. When sitting for that purpose, they shall be on oath or affirmation. When the President of the United States is tried, the Chief Justice shall preside: And no person shall be convicted without the concurrence of two thirds of the members present.

Judgment in cases of impeachment shall not extend further than to removal from office, and disqualification to hold and enjoy any office of honor, trust or profit under the United States: but the party convicted shall nevertheless be liable and subject to indictment, trial, judgment and punishment, according to law.

Section 4.

The times, places and manner of holding elections for Senators and Representatives, shall be prescribed in each state by the legislature thereof; but the Congress may at any time by law make or alter such regulations, except as to the places of choosing Senators.

The Congress shall assemble at least once in every year, and such meeting shall be on the first Monday in December, unless they shall by law appoint a different day.

Section 5.

Each House shall be the judge of the elections, returns and qualifications of its own members, and a majority of each shall constitute a quorum to do business; but a smaller number may adjourn from day to day, and may be authorized to compel the attendance of absent members, in such manner, and under such penalties as each House may provide.

Each House may determine the rules of its proceedings, punish its members for disorderly behavior, and, with the concurrence of two thirds, expel a member.

Each House shall keep a journal of its proceedings, and from time to time publish the same, excepting such parts as may in their judgment require secrecy; and the yeas and nays of the members of either House on any question shall, at the desire of one fifth of those present, be entered on the journal.

Neither House, during the session of Congress, shall, without the consent of the other, adjourn for more than three days, nor to any other place than that in which the two Houses shall be sitting.

Section 6.

The Senators and Representatives shall receive a compensation for their services, to be ascertained by law, and paid out of the treasury of the United States. They shall in all cases, except treason, felony and breach of the peace, be privileged from arrest during their attendance at the session of their respective Houses, and in going to and returning from the same; and for any speech or debate in either House, they shall not be questioned in any other place.

No Senator or Representative shall, during the time for which he was elected, be appointed to any civil office under the authority of the United States, which shall have been created, or the emoluments whereof shall have been increased during such time: and no person holding any office under the United States, shall be a member of either House during his continuance in office.

Section 7.

All bills for raising revenue shall originate in the House of Representatives; but the Senate may propose or concur with amendments as on other Bills.

Every bill which shall have passed the House of Representatives and the Senate, shall, before it become a law, be presented to the President of the United States; if he approve he shall sign it, but if not he shall return it, with his objections to that House in which it shall have originated, who shall enter the objections at large on their journal, and proceed to reconsider it. If after such reconsideration two thirds of that House shall agree to pass the bill, it shall be sent, together with the objections, to the other House, by which it shall likewise be reconsidered, and if approved by two thirds of that House, it shall become a law. But in all such cases the votes of both Houses shall be determined by yeas and nays, and the names of the persons voting for and against the bill shall be entered on the journal of each House respectively. If any bill shall not be returned by the President within ten days (Sundays excepted) after it shall have been presented to him, the same shall be a law, in like manner as if he had signed it, unless the Congress by their adjournment prevent its return, in which case it shall not be a law.

Every order, resolution, or vote to which the concurrence of the Senate and House of Representatives may be necessary (except on a question of adjournment) shall be presented to the President of the United States; and before the same shall take effect, shall be approved by him, or being disapproved by him, shall be repassed by two thirds of the Senate and House of Representatives, according to the rules and limitations prescribed in the case of a bill.

Section 8.

The Congress shall have power to lay and collect taxes, duties, imposts and excises, to pay the debts and provide for the common defense and general welfare of the United States; but all duties, imposts and excises shall be uniform throughout the United States;

To borrow money on the credit of the United States;

To regulate commerce with foreign nations, and among the several states, and with the Indian tribes;

To establish a uniform rule of naturalization, and uniform laws on the subject of bankruptcies throughout the United States;

To coin money, regulate the value thereof, and of foreign coin, and fix the standard of weights and measures;

To provide for the punishment of counterfeiting the securities and current coin of the United States;

To establish post offices and post roads;

To promote the progress of science and useful arts, by securing for limited times to authors and inventors the exclusive right to their respective writings and discoveries;

To constitute tribunals inferior to the Supreme Court;

To define and punish piracies and felonies committed on the high seas, and offenses against the law of nations;

To declare war, grant letters of marque and reprisal, and make rules concerning captures on land and water;

To raise and support armies, but no appropriation of money to that use shall be for a longer term than two years;

To provide and maintain a navy;

To make rules for the government and regulation of the land and naval forces;

To provide for calling forth the militia to execute the laws of the union, suppress insurrections and repel invasions;

To provide for organizing, arming, and disciplining, the militia, and for governing such part of them as may be employed in the service of the United States, reserving to the states respectively, the appointment of the officers, and the authority of training the militia according to the discipline prescribed by Congress;

To exercise exclusive legislation in all cases whatsoever, over such District (not exceeding ten miles square) as may, by cession of particular states, and the acceptance of Congress, become the seat of the government of the United States, and to exercise like authority over all places purchased by the consent of the legislature of the state in which the same shall be, for the erection of forts, magazines, arsenals, dockyards, and other needful buildings;—And

To make all laws which shall be necessary and proper for carrying into execution the foregoing powers, and all other powers vested by this Constitution in the government of the United States, or in any department or officer thereof.

Section 9.

The migration or importation of such persons as any of the states now existing shall think proper to admit, shall not be prohibited by the Congress prior to the year one thousand eight hundred and eight, but a tax or duty may be imposed on such importation, not exceeding ten dollars for each person.

The privilege of the writ of habeas corpus shall not be suspended, unless when in cases of rebellion or invasion the public safety may require it.

No bill of attainder or ex post facto Law shall be passed.

No capitation, or other direct, tax shall be laid, unless in proportion to the census or enumeration herein before directed to be taken.

No tax or duty shall be laid on articles exported from any state.

No preference shall be given by any regulation of commerce or revenue to the ports of one state over those of another: nor shall vessels bound to, or from, one state, be obliged to enter, clear or pay duties in another.

No money shall be drawn from the treasury, but in consequence of appropriations made by law; and a regular statement and account of receipts and expenditures of all public money shall be published from time to time.

No title of nobility shall be granted by the United States: and no person holding any office of profit or trust under them, shall, without the consent of the Congress, accept of any present, emolument, office, or title, of any kind whatever, from any king, prince, or foreign state.

Section 10.

No state shall enter into any treaty, alliance, or confederation; grant letters of marque and reprisal; coin money; emit bills of credit; make anything but gold and silver coin a tender in payment of debts; pass any bill of attainder, ex post facto law, or law impairing the obligation of contracts, or grant any title of nobility.

No state shall, without the consent of the Congress, lay any imposts or duties on imports or exports, except what may be absolutely necessary for executing its inspection laws: and the net produce of all duties and imposts, laid by any state on imports or exports, shall be for the use of the treasury of the United States; and all such laws shall be subject to the revision and control of the Congress.

No state shall, without the consent of Congress, lay any duty of tonnage, keep troops, or ships of war in time of peace, enter into any agreement or compact with another state, or with a foreign power, or engage in war, unless actually invaded, or in such imminent danger as will not admit of delay.

Article II

Section 1.

The executive power shall be vested in a President of the United States of America. He shall hold his office during the term of four years, and, together with the Vice President, chosen for the same term, be elected, as follows:

Each state shall appoint, in such manner as the Legislature thereof may direct, a number of electors, equal to the whole number of Senators and Representatives to which the State may be entitled in the Congress: but no Senator or Representative, or person holding an office of trust or profit under the United States, shall be appointed an elector.

The electors shall meet in their respective states, and vote by ballot for two persons, of whom one at least shall not be an inhabitant of the same state with themselves. And they shall make a list of all the persons voted for, and of the number of votes for each; which list they shall sign and certify, and transmit sealed to the seat of the government of the United States, directed to the President of the Senate. The President of the Senate shall, in the presence of the Senate and House of Representatives, open all the certificates, and the votes shall then be counted. The person having the greatest number of votes shall be the President, if such number be a majority of the whole number of electors appointed; and if there be more than one who have such majority, and have an equal number of votes, then the House of Representatives shall immediately choose by ballot one of them for President; and if no person have a majority, then from the five highest on the list the said House shall in like manner choose the President. But in choosing the President, the votes shall be taken by States, the representation from each state having one vote; A quorum for this purpose shall consist of a member or members from two thirds of the states, and a majority of all the states shall be necessary to a choice. In every case, after the choice of the President, the person having the greatest number of votes of the electors shall be the Vice President. But if there should remain two or more who have equal votes, the Senate shall choose from them by ballot the Vice President.

The Congress may determine the time of choosing the electors, and the day on which they shall give their votes; which day shall be the same throughout the United States.

No person except a natural born citizen, or a citizen of the United States, at the time of the adoption of this Constitution, shall be eligible to the office of President; neither shall any person be eligible to that office who shall not have attained to the age of thirty five years, and been fourteen years a resident within the United States.

In case of the removal of the President from office, or of his death, resignation, or inability to discharge the powers and duties of the said office, the same shall devolve on the Vice President, and the Congress may by law provide for the case of removal, death, resignation or inability, both of the President and Vice President, declaring what officer shall then act as President, and such officer shall act accordingly, until the disability be removed, or a President shall be elected.

The President shall, at stated times, receive for his services, a compensation, which shall neither be increased nor diminished during the period for which he shall have been elected, and he shall not receive within that period any other emolument from the United States, or any of them.

Before he enter on the execution of his office, he shall take the following oath or affirmation:—"I do solemnly swear (or affirm) that I will faithfully execute the office of President of the United States, and will to the best of my ability, preserve, protect and defend the Constitution of the United States."

Section 2.

The President shall be commander in chief of the Army and Navy of the United States, and of the militia of the several states, when called into the actual service of the United States; he may require the opinion, in writing, of the principal officer in each of the executive departments, upon any subject relating to the duties of their respective offices, and he shall have power to grant reprieves and pardons for offenses against the United States, except in cases of impeachment.

He shall have power, by and with the advice and consent of the Senate, to make treaties, provided two thirds of the Senators present concur; and he shall nominate, and by and with the advice and consent of the Senate, shall appoint ambassadors, other public ministers and consuls, judges of the Supreme Court, and all other officers of the United States, whose appointments are not herein otherwise provided for, and which shall be established by law: but the Congress may by law vest the appointment of such inferior officers, as they think proper, in the President alone, in the courts of law, or in the heads of departments.

The President shall have power to fill up all vacancies that may happen during the recess of the Senate, by granting commissions which shall expire at the end of their next session.

Section 3.

He shall from time to time give to the Congress information of the state of the union, and recommend to their consideration such measures as he shall judge necessary and expedient; he may, on extraordinary occasions, convene both

Houses, or either of them, and in case of disagreement between them, with respect to the time of adjournment, he may adjourn them to such time as he shall think proper; he shall receive ambassadors and other public ministers; he shall take care that the laws be faithfully executed, and shall commission all the officers of the United States.

Section 4.

The President, Vice President and all civil officers of the United States, shall be removed from office on impeachment for, and conviction of, treason, bribery, or other high crimes and misdemeanors.

Article III

Section 1.

The judicial power of the United States, shall be vested in one Supreme Court, and in such inferior courts as the Congress may from time to time ordain and establish. The judges, both of the supreme and inferior courts, shall hold their offices during good behaviour, and shall, at stated times, receive for their services, a compensation, which shall not be diminished during their continuance in office.

Section 2.

The judicial power shall extend to all cases, in law and equity, arising under this Constitution, the laws of the United States, and treaties made, or which shall be made, under their authority;—to all cases affecting ambassadors, other public ministers and consuls;—to all cases of admiralty and maritime jurisdiction;—to controversies to which the United States shall be a party;—to controversies between two or more states;—between a state and citizens of another state;—between citizens of different states;—between citizens of the same state claiming lands under grants of different states, and between a state, or the citizens thereof, and foreign states, citizens or subjects.

In all cases affecting ambassadors, other public ministers and consuls, and those in which a state shall be party, the Supreme Court shall have original jurisdiction. In all the other cases before mentioned, the Supreme Court shall have appellate jurisdiction, both as to law and fact, with such exceptions, and under such regulations as the Congress shall make.

The trial of all crimes, except in cases of impeachment, shall be by jury; and such trial shall be held in the state where the said crimes shall have been committed;

but when not committed within any state, the trial shall be at such place or places as the Congress may by law have directed.

Section 3.

Treason against the United States, shall consist only in levying war against them, or in adhering to their enemies, giving them aid and comfort. No person shall be convicted of treason unless on the testimony of two witnesses to the same overt act, or on confession in open court.

The Congress shall have power to declare the punishment of treason, but no attainder of treason shall work corruption of blood, or forfeiture except during the life of the person attainted.

Article IV

Section 1.

Full faith and credit shall be given in each state to the public acts, records, and judicial proceedings of every other state. And the Congress may by general laws prescribe the manner in which such acts, records, and proceedings shall be proved, and the effect thereof.

Section 2.

The citizens of each state shall be entitled to all privileges and immunities of citizens in the several states.

A person charged in any state with treason, felony, or other crime, who shall flee from justice, and be found in another state, shall on demand of the executive authority of the state from which he fled, be delivered up, to be removed to the state having jurisdiction of the crime.

No person held to service or labor in one state, under the laws thereof, escaping into another, shall, in consequence of any law or regulation therein, be discharged from such service or labor, but shall be delivered up on claim of the party to whom such service or labor may be due.

Section 3.

New states may be admitted by the Congress into this union; but no new states shall be formed or erected within the jurisdiction of any other state; nor any state be formed by the junction of two or more states, or parts of states, without the consent of the legislatures of the states concerned as well as of the Congress.

The Congress shall have power to dispose of and make all needful rules and regulations respecting the territory or other property belonging to the United States; and nothing in this Constitution shall be so construed as to prejudice any claims of the United States, or of any particular state.

Section 4.

The United States shall guarantee to every state in this union a republican form of government, and shall protect each of them against invasion; and on application of the legislature, or of the executive (when the legislature cannot be convened) against domestic violence.

Article V

The Congress, whenever two thirds of both houses shall deem it necessary, shall propose amendments to this Constitution, or, on the application of the legislatures of two thirds of the several states, shall call a convention for proposing amendments, which, in either case, shall be valid to all intents and purposes, as part of this Constitution, when ratified by the legislatures of three fourths of the several states, or by conventions in three fourths thereof, as the one or the other mode of ratification may be proposed by the Congress; provided that no amendment which may be made prior to the year one thousand eight hundred and eight shall in any manner affect the first and fourth clauses in the ninth section of the first article; and that no state, without its consent, shall be deprived of its equal suffrage in the Senate.

Article VI

All debts contracted and engagements entered into, before the adoption of this Constitution, shall be as valid against the United States under this Constitution, as under the Confederation.

This Constitution, and the laws of the United States which shall be made in pursuance thereof; and all treaties made, or which shall be made, under the authority of the United States, shall be the supreme law of the land; and the judges in every state shall be bound thereby, anything in the Constitution or laws of any State to the contrary notwithstanding.

The Senators and Representatives before mentioned, and the members of the several state legislatures, and all executive and judicial officers, both of the United States and of the several states, shall be bound by oath or affirmation, to support this Constitution; but no religious test shall ever be required as a qualification to any office or public trust under the United States.

Article VII

The ratification of the conventions of nine states, shall be sufficient for the establishment of this Constitution between the states so ratifying the same.

Amendment I (1791)

Congress shall make no law respecting an establishment of religion, or prohibiting the free exercise thereof; or abridging the freedom of speech, or of the press; or the right of the people peaceably to assemble, and to petition the government for a redress of grievances.

Amendment II (1791)

A well regulated militia, being necessary to the security of a free state, the right of the people to keep and bear arms, shall not be infringed.

Amendment III (1791)

No soldier shall, in time of peace be quartered in any house, without the consent of the owner, nor in time of war, but in a manner to be prescribed by law.

Amendment IV (1791)

The right of the people to be secure in their persons, houses, papers, and effects, against unreasonable searches and seizures, shall not be violated, and no warrants shall issue, but upon probable cause, supported by oath or affirmation, and particularly describing the place to be searched, and the persons or things to be seized.

Amendment V (1791)

No person shall be held to answer for a capital, or otherwise infamous crime, unless on a presentment or indictment of a grand jury, except in cases arising in the land or naval forces, or in the militia, when in actual service in time of war or public danger; nor shall any person be subject for the same offense to be twice put in jeopardy of life or limb; nor shall be compelled in any criminal case to be a witness against himself, nor be deprived of life, liberty, or property, without due process of law; nor shall private property be taken for public use, without just compensation.

Amendment VI (1791)

In all criminal prosecutions, the accused shall enjoy the right to a speedy and public trial, by an impartial jury of the state and district wherein the crime shall have been committed, which district shall have been previously ascertained by law, and to be informed of the nature and cause of the accusation; to be confronted with the witnesses against him; to have compulsory process for obtaining witnesses in his favor, and to have the assistance of counsel for his defense.

Amendment VII (1791)

In suits at common law, where the value in controversy shall exceed twenty dollars, the right of trial by jury shall be preserved, and no fact tried by a jury, shall be otherwise reexamined in any court of the United States, than according to the rules of the common law.

Amendment VIII (1791)

Excessive bail shall not be required, nor excessive fines imposed, nor cruel and unusual punishments inflicted.

Amendment IX (1791)

The enumeration in the Constitution, of certain rights, shall not be construed to deny or disparage others retained by the people.

Amendment X (1791)

The powers not delegated to the United States by the Constitution, nor prohibited by it to the states, are reserved to the states respectively, or to the people.

Amendment XI (1798)

The judicial power of the United States shall not be construed to extend to any suit in law or equity, commenced or prosecuted against one of the United States by citizens of another state, or by citizens or subjects of any foreign state.

Amendment XII (1804)

The electors shall meet in their respective states and vote by ballot for President and Vice-President, one of whom, at least, shall not be an inhabitant of the same state with themselves; they shall name in their ballots the person voted for as President, and in distinct ballots the person voted for as Vice-President, and they shall make distinct lists of all persons voted for as President, and of all persons voted for as Vice-President, and of the number of votes for each, which lists they shall sign and certify, and transmit sealed to the seat of the government of the United States, directed to the President of the Senate;—The President of the Senate shall, in the presence of the Senate and House of Representatives, open all the certificates and the votes shall then be counted;—the person having the greatest number of votes for President, shall be the President, if such number be a majority of the whole number of electors appointed; and if no person have such majority, then from the persons having the highest numbers not exceeding three on the list of those voted for as President, the House of Representatives shall choose immediately, by ballot, the President. But in choosing the President, the votes shall be taken by states, the representation from each state having one vote; a quorum for this purpose shall consist of a member or members from two-thirds of the states, and a majority of all the states shall be necessary to a choice. And if the House of Representatives shall not choose a President whenever the right of choice shall devolve upon them, before the fourth day of March next following, then the Vice-President shall act as President, as in the case of the death or other constitutional disability of the President. The person having the greatest number of votes as Vice-President, shall be the Vice-President, if such number be a majority of the whole number of electors appointed, and if no person have a majority, then from the two highest numbers on the list, the Senate shall choose the Vice-President; a quorum for the purpose shall consist of two-thirds of the whole number of Senators, and a majority of the whole number shall be necessary to a choice. But no person constitutionally ineligible to the office of President shall be eligible to that of Vice-President of the United States.

Amendment XIII (1865)

Section 1. Neither slavery nor involuntary servitude, except as a punishment for crime whereof the party shall have been duly convicted, shall exist within the United States, or any place subject to their jurisdiction.

Section 2. Congress shall have power to enforce this article by appropriate legislation.

Amendment XIV (1868)

Section 1. All persons born or naturalized in the United States, and subject to the jurisdiction thereof, are citizens of the United States and of the state wherein they reside. No state shall make or enforce any law which shall abridge the privileges or immunities of citizens of the United States; nor shall any state deprive any person of life, liberty, or property, without due process of law; nor deny to any person within its jurisdiction the equal protection of the laws.

Section 2. Representatives shall be apportioned among the several states according to their respective numbers, counting the whole number of persons in each state, excluding Indians not taxed. But when the right to vote at any election for the choice of electors for President and Vice President of the United States, Representatives in Congress, the executive and judicial officers of a state, or the members of the legislature thereof, is denied to any of the male inhabitants of such state, being twenty-one years of age, and citizens of the United States, or in any way abridged, except for participation in rebellion, or other crime, the basis of representation therein shall be reduced in the proportion which the number of such male citizens shall bear to the whole number of male citizens twenty-one years of age in such state.

Section 3. No person shall be a Senator or Representative in Congress, or elector of President and Vice President, or hold any office, civil or military, under the United States, or under any state, who, having previously taken an oath, as a member of Congress, or as an officer of the United States, or as a member of any state legislature, or as an executive or judicial officer of any state, to support the Constitution of the United States, shall have engaged in insurrection or rebellion against the same, or given aid or comfort to the enemies thereof. But Congress may by a vote of two-thirds of each House, remove such disability.

Section 4. The validity of the public debt of the United States, authorized by law, including debts incurred for payment of pensions and bounties for services in suppressing insurrection or rebellion, shall not be questioned. But neither the United States nor any state shall assume or pay any debt or obligation incurred in aid of insurrection or rebellion against the United States, or any claim for the loss or emancipation of any slave; but all such debts, obligations and claims shall be held illegal and void.

Section 5. The Congress shall have power to enforce, by appropriate legislation, the provisions of this article.

Amendment XV (1870)

Section 1. The right of citizens of the United States to vote shall not be denied or abridged by the United States or by any state on account of race, color, or previous condition of servitude.

Section 2. The Congress shall have power to enforce this article by appropriate legislation.

Amendment XVI (1913)

The Congress shall have power to lay and collect taxes on incomes, from whatever source derived, without apportionment among the several states, and without regard to any census of enumeration.

Amendment XVII (1913)

The Senate of the United States shall be composed of two Senators from each state, elected by the people thereof, for six years; and each Senator shall have one vote. The electors in each state shall have the qualifications requisite for electors of the most numerous branch of the state legislatures. When vacancies happen in the representation of any state in the Senate, the executive authority of such state shall issue writs of election to fill such vacancies: Provided, that the legislature of any state may empower the executive thereof to make temporary appointments until the people fill the vacancies by election as the legislature may direct.

This amendment shall not be so construed as to affect the election or term of any Senator chosen before it becomes valid as part of the Constitution.

Amendment XVIII (1919)

Section 1. After one year from the ratification of this article the manufacture, sale, or transportation of intoxicating liquors within, the importation thereof into, or the exportation thereof from the United States and all territory subject to the jurisdiction thereof for beverage purposes is hereby prohibited.

Section 2. The Congress and the several states shall have concurrent power to enforce this article by appropriate legislation.

Section 3. This article shall be inoperative unless it shall have been ratified as an amendment to the Constitution by the legislatures of the several states, as provided in the Constitution, within seven years from the date of the submission hereof to the states by the Congress.

Amendment XIX (1920)

The right of citizens of the United States to vote shall not be denied or abridged by the United States or by any state on account of sex. Congress shall have power to enforce this article by appropriate legislation.

Amendment XX (1933)

Section 1. The terms of the President and Vice President shall end at noon on the 20th day of January, and the terms of Senators and Representatives at noon on the 3d day of January, of the years in which such terms would have ended if this article had not been ratified; and the terms of their successors shall then begin.

Section 2. The Congress shall assemble at least once in every year, and such meeting shall begin at noon on the 3d day of January, unless they shall by law appoint a different day.

Section 3. If, at the time fixed for the beginning of the term of the President, the President elect shall have died, the Vice President elect shall become President. If a President shall not have been chosen before the time fixed for the beginning of his term, or if the President elect shall have failed to qualify, then the Vice President elect shall act as President until a President shall have qualified; and the Congress may by law provide for the case wherein neither a President elect nor a Vice President elect shall have qualified, declaring who shall then act as President, or the manner in which one who is to act shall be selected, and such person shall act accordingly until a President or Vice President shall have qualified.

Section 4. The Congress may by law provide for the case of the death of any of the persons from whom the House of Representatives may choose a President whenever the right of choice shall have devolved upon them, and for the case of the death of any of the persons from whom the Senate may choose a Vice President whenever the right of choice shall have devolved upon them.

Section 5. Sections 1 and 2 shall take effect on the 15th day of October following the ratification of this article.

Section 6. This article shall be inoperative unless it shall have been ratified as an amendment to the Constitution by the legislatures of three-fourths of the several states within seven years from the date of its submission.

Amendment XXI (1933)

Section 1. The eighteenth article of amendment to the Constitution of the United States is hereby repealed.

Section 2. The transportation or importation into any state, territory, or possession of the United States for delivery or use therein of intoxicating liquors, in violation of the laws thereof, is hereby prohibited.

Section 3. This article shall be inoperative unless it shall have been ratified as an amendment to the Constitution by conventions in the several states, as provided in the Constitution, within seven years from the date of the submission hereof to the states by the Congress.

Amendment XXII (1951)

Section 1. No person shall be elected to the office of the President more than twice, and no person who has held the office of President, or acted as President, for more than two years of a term to which some other person was elected President shall be elected to the office of the President more than once. But this article shall not apply to any person holding the office of President when this article was proposed by the Congress, and shall not prevent any person who may be holding the office of President, or acting as President, during the term within which this article becomes operative from holding the office of President or acting as President during the remainder of such term.

Section 2. This article shall be inoperative unless it shall have been ratified as an amendment to the constitution by the legislatures of three-fourths of the several states within seven years from the date of its submission to the states by the Congress.

Amendment XXIII (1961)

Section 1. The District constituting the seat of government of the United States shall appoint in such manner as the Congress may direct:

A number of electors of President and Vice President equal to the whole number of Senators and Representatives in Congress to which the District would be entitled if it were a state, but in no event more than the least populous state; they shall be in addition to those appointed by the states, but they shall be considered, for the purposes of the election of President and Vice President, to be electors appointed by a state; and they shall meet in the District and perform such duties as provided by the twelfth article of amendment.

Section 2. The Congress shall have power to enforce this article by appropriate legislation.

Amendment XXIV (1964)

Section 1. The right of citizens of the United States to vote in any primary or other election for President or Vice President, for electors for President or Vice President, or for Senator or Representative in Congress, shall not be denied or abridged by the United States or any state by reason of failure to pay any poll tax or other tax.

Section 2. The Congress shall have power to enforce this article by appropriate legislation.

Amendment XXV (1967)

Section 1. In case of the removal of the President from office or of his death or resignation, the Vice President shall become President.

Section 2. Whenever there is a vacancy in the office of the Vice President, the President shall nominate a Vice President who shall take office upon confirmation by a majority vote of both Houses of Congress.

Section 3. Whenever the President transmits to the President pro tempore of the Senate and the Speaker of the House of Representatives his written declaration that he is unable to discharge the powers and duties of his office, and until he transmits to them a written declaration to the contrary, such powers and duties shall be discharged by the Vice President as Acting President.

Section 4. Whenever the Vice President and a majority of either the principal officers of the executive departments or of such other body as Congress may by law provide, transmit to the President pro tempore of the Senate and the Speaker of the House of Representatives their written declaration that the President is unable to discharge the powers and duties of his office, the Vice President shall immediately assume the powers and duties of the office as Acting President.

Thereafter, when the President transmits to the President pro tempore of the Senate and the Speaker of the House of Representatives his written declaration that no inability exists, he shall resume the powers and duties of his office unless the Vice President and a majority of either the principal officers of the executive department or of such other body as Congress may by law provide, transmit within four days to the President pro tempore of the Senate and the Speaker of the House of Representatives their written declaration that the President is unable to discharge the powers and duties of his office. Thereupon Congress shall decide the issue, assembling within forty-eight hours for that purpose if not in session.

If the Congress, within twenty-one days after receipt of the latter written declaration, or, if Congress is not in session, within twenty-one days after Congress is required to assemble, determines by two-thirds vote of both Houses that the President is unable to discharge the powers and duties of his office, the Vice President shall continue to discharge the same as Acting President; otherwise, the President shall resume the powers and duties of his office.

Amendment XXVI (1971)

Section 1. The right of citizens of the United States, who are 18 years of age or older, to vote, shall not be denied or abridged by the United States or any state on account of age.

Section 2. The Congress shall have the power to enforce this article by appropriate legislation.

References

BOOKS AND ARTICLES

Ackerman, Bruce. 2000. *We the People: Transformations.* Cambridge, Mass.: Harvard University Press.

Aldrich, John H., and David W. Rohde. 2000. "The Consequences of Party Organization in the House: The Role of the Majority and Minority Parties in Conditional Party Government." In *Polarized Politics: Congress and the President in a Partisan Era,* ed. Jon R. Bond and Rich Fleisher. Washington, D.C.: CQ Press.

Association of American Colleges. 1978. Project on the Status and Education of Women, *Sexual Harassment: A Hidden Issue.* Washington, D.C.: Association of American Colleges.

Barnett, James D. 1908. "The Delegation of Legislative Power by Congress to the States." *American Political Science Review* 2(3): 347–77.

Baum, Lawrence. 2000. *The Supreme Court,* 7th ed. Washington, D.C.: CQ Press.

Bawer, Bruce. 1993. *A Place at the Table: The Gay Individual in American Society.* New York: Simon and Schuster.

Bennett, Colin J. 1992. *Regulating Privacy: Data Protection and Public Policy in Europe and the United States.* Ithaca, N.Y.: Cornell University Press.

Binder, Sarah A. 1997. *Minority Rights, Majority Rule: Partisanship and the Development of Congress.* New York: Cambridge University Press.

———. 1996. "The Disappearing Political Center." *The Brookings Review* 15 (Fall): 36–39.

Binder, Sarah, and Steven S. Smith. 1997. *Politics or Principle: Filibustering in the United States Senate.* Washington, D.C.: Brookings Institution.

Bird, Caroline. 1970. *Born Female.* New York: Pocket Books.

Biskupic, Joan, and Elder Witt. 1997. *Guide to the Supreme Court,* 3d ed. 2 vols. Washington, D.C.: Congressional Quarterly.

Blondel, Jean. 1995. *Comparative Government.* London: Prentice-Hall.

Bloustein, Edward J. 1964. "Privacy as an Aspect of Human Dignity." *New York University Law Review* 39: 962–1007.

Brenton, Myron. 1964. *The Privacy Invaders.* New York: Coward-McCann.

Bullock, Charles S., III, and Charles M. Lamb. 1984. *Implementation of Civil Rights Policy.* Monterey. Calif.: Brooks/Cole.

Bushkin, John. 2000. "Our Data, Ourselves." *Wall Street Journal.* 17 April 2000, R34.

167

Campbell, Colton C., and Roger H. Davidson. 2000. "Gay and Lesbian Issues in the Congressional Arena." In *The Politics of Gay Rights*, ed. Craig A. Rimmerman, Kenneth D. Wald, and Clyde Wilcox. Chicago: University of Chicago Press.

———. 1998. "Coalition Building in Congress: The Consequences of Partisan Change." In *The Interest Group Connection: Electioneering, Lobbying, and Policymaking in Washington*, ed. Paul S. Herrnson, Ronald G. Shaiko, and Clyde Wilcox. Chatham, N.J.: Chatham House.

Carney, Dan. 1996. "GOP Bill Restricting Gay Unions Clears . . . Nut Does Not Yield Political Dividends." *Congressional Quarterly Weekly Report*, 14 September 1996, 2598–99.

Carr, Raymond. 1980. *Modern Spain: 1875–1980*. New York: Oxford University Press.

Cassata, Donna. 1995. "Swift Progress of 'Contract' Inspires Awe and Concern." *Congressional Quarterly Weekly Report*, 1 April 1995, 909–19.

Cassese, Antonio. 1990. *Human Rights in a Changing World*. Philadelphia: Temple University Press.

Center for Democracy and Technology. 1999. *Behind the Numbers: Privacy Practices on the Web*. July. http://www.cdt.org/privacy/990727privacy.pdf.

Chrisman, Robert, and Robert L. Allen, eds. 1992. *For the Black Scholar, Court of Appeal: The Black Community Speaks Out on the Racial and Sexual Politics of Thomas vs. Hill*. New York: Ballantine.

Clark, Kathleen. 1998. "The Ethics of Representing Elected Representatives." *Law and Contemporary Problems* 61: 31–45.

Clinton, William J., and Albert Gore Jr. 1997. *A Framework for Global Electronic Commerce*. http://www.iitf.nist.gov/eleccomm/ecomm.htm

Congress and the Nation. 1992. Vol. VIII, 1989–1992. Washington, D.C.: Congressional Quarterly.

Congressional Record. 2000. 106th Cong., 2d sess., vol. 146, July 26, S7671.

———. 2000. 106th Cong., 2d sess., vol. 146, July 26, S7672.

———. 2000. 106th Cong., 2d sess., vol. 146, July 26, S7669.

———. 1998. 105th Cong., 2d sess., vol. 144, July 17, S8483.

———. 1998. 105th Cong., 2d sess., vol. 144, October 1, E1861.

———. 1997. 105th Cong., 1st sess., vol. 144, January 7, E8.

———. 1992. 102nd Cong., 2nd sess., vol. 138, October 3, H11131.

———. 1992. 102nd Cong., 2nd sess., vol. 138, January 27, S443.

Congressional Quarterly. 1999. "Conservative True Believers: Bob Barr." In *CQ 50: 50 Ways to Do the Job of Congress*. Washington, D.C.: Congressional Quarterly.

Congressional Quarterly Almanac. 1992. 102nd Congress, 2nd sess., vol. XLVIII. Washington, D.C.: Congressional Quarterly.

Craig, Barbara. 1988. *Chadha*. Berkeley: University Press of California.

Cranor, Lorrie Faith, Joseph Reagle, and Mark S. Ackerman. 1999. *Beyond Concern: Understanding Net Users' Attitudes about Online Privacy*. AT&T Labs-Research Technical Report TR 99.4.3. April. http://www.research.att.com/library/trs/TRs/99/99.4/99.4/report.htm.

Culnan, Mary. 1999. *Georgetown Internet Privacy Policy Survey: Report to the Federal Trade Commission*. Washington, D.C.: Georgetown University. http://www.msb.edu/faculty/culnanm/gippshome.html.

Current, Richard N. 1995. "States' Rights." In *The Encyclopedia of the United States Congress.* Vol. 4., ed. Donald C. Bacon, Roger H. Davidson, and Morton Keller. New York: Simon and Schuster.

Curtis, Michael Kent. 1990. *No State Shall Abridge: The Fourteenth Amendment and the Bill of Rights.* Durham, N.C.: Duke University Press.

D'Amico, Francine. 2000. "Sexuality and Military Service." In *The Politics of Gay Rights,* ed. Craig A. Rimmerman, Kenneth D. Wald, and Clyde Wilcox. Chicago: University of Chicago Press.

Davidson, Roger H. 2001. "Senate Floor Deliberation: A Preliminary Inquiry." In *The Contentious Senate: Partisanship, Ideology, and the Myth of Cool Judgment,* ed. Colton C. Campbell and Nicol C. Rae. Lanham, Md.: Rowman & Littlefield.

Davidson, Scott. 1993. *Human Rights.* Bristol, Pa.: Open University Press.

Days, Drew S., III. 1989. "The Courts' Response to the Reagan Civil Rights Agenda." *Vanderbilt Law Review* 42(4): 1003–16.

de Araújo, António. 1997. *O Tribunal Constitucional (1989–1996).* Lisbon: Coimbra Editora.

Department of Health, Education and Welfare. 1973. *Records, Computers, and the Rights of Citizens.* Washington, D.C.: Government Printing Office.

DeRosa, Marshall L. 1991. *The Confederate Constitution of 1861: An Inquiry into American Constitutionalism.* Columbia: University of Missouri Press.

Dion, Douglas. 1997. *Turning the Legislative Thumbscrew: Minority Rights and Procedural Change in Legislative Politics.* Ann Arbor: University of Michigan Press.

Drake, Frederick, D., and Lynn R. Nelson, eds. 1999. *States' Rights and American Federalism.* Westport, Conn.: Greenwood.

Ducat, Craig R. 1995. *Constitutional Interpretation.* 6th ed. Minneapolis/St. Paul, Minn.: West.

Dworkin, Ronald. 1977. *Taking Rights Seriously.* Cambridge, Mass.: Harvard University Press.

Edelman, Martin. 1994. *Courts, Politics and Culture in Israel.* Charlottesville: University of Virginia Press.

Ehrenhalt, Alan. 1996. *The Lost City: The Forgotten Virtues of Community in America.* New York: HarperCollins.

Electronic Privacy Information Center (EPIC). 2001. *The Privacy Coalition Announces New Privacy Initiative: The Privacy Pledge Sets Standard for Privacy Proposals in Congress.* February. http://www.epic.org/privacycoalition/coalition_press_release.html.

Electronic Privacy Information Center and Junkbusters. 2000. *Network Advertising Initiative: Principles Not Privacy.* July. http://www.epic.org/privacy/internet/NAI_analysis.html.

Eskridge, William. 1994. *Dynamic Statutory Interpretation.* Cambridge, Mass.: Harvard University Press.

Etzioni, Amitai. 1994. *The Spirit of Community: The Reinvention of American Society.* New York: Simon and Schuster.

Evans, C. Lawrence, and Walter J. Oleszek. 2001. "Message Politics and Senate Procedure." In *The Contentious Senate: Partisanship, Ideology, and the Myth of Cool Judgment,* ed. Colton C. Campbell and Nicol C. Rae. Lanham, Md.: Rowman & Littlefield.

Federal Trade Commission. 2000. *Privacy Online: Fair Information Practices in the Electronic Marketplace.* Washington, D.C.: Federal Trade Commission, June. http://www.ftc.gov/privacy/index.html.

———. 1999. *Self-Regulation and Privacy Online: A Report to Congress.* Washington, D.C.: Federal Trade Commission. July. http://www.ftc.gov/os/1999/9907/privacy99.pdf.

———. 1998. *Privacy Online: A Report to Congress.* Washington, D.C.: Federal Trade Commission, June. http://www.ftc.gov/reports/privacy3/toc.htm.

Finer, S. E. 1997. *The History of Government.* New York: Oxford University Press.

Flaherty, David H. 1989. *Protecting Privacy in Surveillance Societies: The Federal Republic of Germany, Sweden, France, Canada, and the United States.* Chapel Hill: University of North Carolina Press.

Fletcher, William A. 2000. "The Eleventh Amendment: Unfinished Business." *Notre Dame Law Review* 75(3): 843–58.

Forrester Research, Inc. 1999. *Forester Technographics Finds Online Consumers Fearful of Privacy Violations.* October. http://www.forrester.com?ER/Press/Release/0,1769,177,FF.html.

Foster, James C., and Susan M. Leeson. 1998. *Constitutional Law: Cases in Context.* Vol. 1. Upper Saddle River, N.J.: Prentice-Hall.

Fox, Susannah. 2000. *Trust and Privacy Online: Why Americans Want to Rewrite the Rules.* The Pew Internet and American Life Project. August. http://www.pewinternet.org/reports/toc.asp?Report=19.

Fried, Charles. 1968. "Privacy." *Yale Law Journal* 77(3): 475–93.

Frühling, Hugo E. 1993. "Human Rights in Constitutional Order and in Political Practice in Latin America." In *Constitutionalism and Democracy,* ed. Douglas Greenberg, Stanley N. Katz, Melanie Beth Oliviero, and Steven C. Wheatley. New York: Oxford University Press.

Gerhardt, Michael. 1996. *The Federal Impeachment Process.* Princeton, N.J.: Princeton University Press.

Gibbons, John T. 1983. "The Eleventh Amendment and State Sovereign Immunity: A Reinterpretation." *Columbia Law Review* 83: 1889–2005.

Gillman, Howard. 1993. *The Constitution Besieged: The Rise and Demise of Lochner Era Police Powers Jurisprudence.* Durham, N.C.: Duke University Press.

Ginsberg, Benjamin, Walter R. Mebane, and Martin Shefter. 1995. "The Presidency and Interest Groups: Why Presidents Cannot Govern." In *The Presidency and the Political System,* 4th ed., ed. Michael Nelson. Washington, D.C.: CQ Press.

Glendon, Mary Ann. 1991. *Rights Talk: The Impoverishment of Political Discourse.* New York: Free Press.

Glennon, Michael J. 1998. "Who's the Client? Legislative Lawyering through the Rear-View Mirror." *Law and Contemporary Problems* 61: 21–30.

Graham, Hugh Davis. 1994. "Legislatures and Civil Rights." In *Encyclopedia of the American Legislative System.* Vol. 3, ed. Joel H. Silbey. New York: Charles Scribner's Sons.

———. 1990. *The Civil Rights Era: Origins and Development of National Policy.* New York: Oxford University Press.

Green, John C. 2000. "Antigay: Varieties of Opposition to Gay Rights." In *The Politics of Gay Rights,* ed. Craig A. Rimmerman, Kenneth D. Wald, and Clyde Wilcox. Chicago: University of Chicago Press.

Greenhouse, Linda. 1999. "High Court Faces Moment of Truth in Federalism Cases." *New York Times,* 28 March, 1999, 23.

Grofman, Bernard, ed. 2000. *Legacies of the 1964 Civil Rights Act.* Charlottesville: University Press of Virginia.

Gruenwald, Juliana. 1998. "Who's Minding Whose Business on the Internet?" *CQ Weekly Report* (July): 1986–90.

Gurak, Laura J. *Persuasion and Privacy in Cyberspace.* 1997. New Haven, Conn.: Yale University Press.

Hakim, Peter, and Abraham F. Lowenthal. 1993. "Latin America's Fragile Democracies." In *The Global Resurgence of Democracy,* ed. Larry Diamond and Marc F. Plattner. Baltimore, Md.: Johns Hopkins University Press.

Hall, Kermit, William Wiecek, and Paul Finkelman, eds. 1991. *American Legal History: Cases and Materials.* New York: Oxford University Press.

Halpern, Stephen C. 1995. *On the Limits of the Law: The Ironic Legacy of Title VI of the 1964 Civil Rights Act.* Baltimore, Md.: Johns Hopkins University Press.

Hamilton, Alexander, James Madison, and John Jay, ed., with introduction by Garry Wills. 1982. *The Federalist Papers.* Toronto: Bantam.

Harriger, Katy J. 1997. "The Federalism Debate in the Transformation of Federal Habeas Corpus Law." *Publius* 27: 1–22.

Harris, Louis, and Associates, and Alan Westin. 1998. *E-Commerce and Privacy: What Net Users Want.* Hackensack, N.J.: Privacy and American Business and Price Waterhouse, June.

Harris, Robert J. 1953. "States' Rights and Vested Interests." *Journal of Politics* 15(4): 457–71.

Harrison, Cynthia. 1988. *On Account of Sex: The Politics of Women's Issues, 1945–1968.* Berkeley: University of California Press.

Heclo, Hugh. 1978. "Issue Networks and the Executive Establishment." In *The New American Political System,* ed. Anthony King. Washington, D.C.: American Enterprise Institute.

Henkin, Louis. 1990. *The Age of Rights.* New York: Columbia University Press.

Henkin, Louis, Gerald L. Neuman, Diane F. Orentlicher, and David W. Leebron, eds. 1999. *Human Rights.* New York: Foundation.

Hill, Marvin, Jr., and Curtiss K. Behrens. 1981. "Love in the Office: A Guide for Dealing with Sexual Harassment under Title VII of the Civil Rights Act of 1964." *DePaul Law Review* 30: 581–622.

Horwitz, Morton J. 1992. *The Transformation of American Law, 1870–1960: The Crisis of Legal Orthodoxy.* New York: Oxford University Press.

Huntington, Samuel P. 1991. *The Third Wave: Democratization in the Late Twentieth Century.* Norman: University of Oklahoma Press.

Hurley, Patricia A., and Rick K. Wilson. 1989. "Partisan Voting Patterns in the U.S. Senate, 1877–1986." *Legislative Studies Quarterly* 14(2): 225–50.

Hutchful, Eboe. 1993. "Reconstructing Political Space: Militarism and Constitutionalism in Africa." In *Constitutionalism and Democracy,* ed. Douglas Greenberg, Stanley N. Katz, Melanie Beth Oliviero, and Steven C. Wheatley. New York: Oxford University Press.

Idelson, Holly. 1996a. "GOP Sets Pre-emptive Strike on Same-Sex Marriages." *Congressional Quarterly Weekly Report,* 18 May 1966, 1393.

———. 1996b. "Panel Gives Swift Approval to Gay Marriage Bill." *Congressional Quarterly Weekly Report,* 1 June 1996, 1539.

———. 1996c. "Panel OKs Bill to Undercut Same-Sex Marriages." *Congressional Quarterly Weekly Report,* 15 June 1996, 1682–83.

———. 1996d. "House Weighs in against Same-Sex Marriages." *Congressional Quarterly Weekly Report,* 13 July 1996, 1976.

Information Infrastructure Task Force. 1995. *Privacy and the National Information Infrastructure: Principles for Providing and Using Personal Information.* June. http://www. iitf.nist.gov/documents/committee/infopol/niiprivprin_final.html.

Interview. 2001. Salokar's interview with House General Counsel Geraldine R. Gennet, Deputy General Counsel Kerry W. Kircher, and Assistant Counsels Carolyn Betz and David Plotinsky. Washington, D.C. May 23.

Irons, Peter H. 1999. *A People's History of the Supreme Court.* New York: Viking.

Ivers, Gregg D. 2001. *American Constitutional Law: Power and Politics.* Vol. 1. Boston: Houghton Mifflin.

Jackson, Donald W. 1997. *The United Kingdom Confronts the European Convention on Human Rights.* Gainesville: University Press of Florida.

Jacobs, Clyde E. 1972. *The Eleventh Amendment and Sovereign Immunity.* Westport, Conn., Greenwood.

Johnson, Nevil. 1993. "Constitutionalism in Europe Since 1945: Reconstruction and Reappraisal." In *Constitutionalism and Democracy,* ed. Douglas Greenberg, Stanley N. Katz, Melanie Beth Oliviero, and Steven C. Wheatley. New York: Oxford University Press.

Jones, Peter. 1994. *Rights.* New York: St. Martin's Press.

Joseph, Richard. 1993. "Africa: The Rebirth of Political Freedom." In *The Global Resurgence of Democracy,* ed. Larry Diamond and Marc F. Plattner. Baltimore, Md.: Johns Hopkins University Press.

Jost, Kenneth. 2000. *1998–1999 Supreme Court Yearbook.* Washington, D.C.: CQ Press.

———. 1998. *1996–1997 Supreme Court Yearbook.* Washington, D.C.: CQ Press.

———. 1996. *1995–1996 Supreme Court Yearbook.* Washington, D.C.: CQ Press.

———. 1995. *1994–1995 Supreme Court Yearbook.* Washington, D.C.: CQ Press.

Katz, Stanley N. 1993. "Constitutionalism in East Central Europe: Some Negative Lessons from the American Experience." In *Constitutionalism and Politics,* ed. Irene Grudzinska Gross. Bratislava, Slovakia: Slovak Committee of the European Cultural Foundation.

Katzman, Robert A. 1997. *Courts & Congress.* Washington, D.C.: Brookings Institution.

Katzman, Robert A., ed. 1988. *Judges and Legislators: Toward Institutional Comity.* Washington, D.C.: Brookings Institution.

Kens, Paul. 1990. *Judicial Power and Reform Politics: The Anatomy of Lochner v. New York.* Lawrence: University Press of Kansas.

Killian, Linda. 1998. *The Freshmen: What Happened to the Republican Revolution?* Boulder, Colo.: Westview.

Lane, Charles. 2001. "Court Limits Scope of ADA." *Washington Post,* 22 February 2001, A8.

Lessig, Lawrence. 1999. *Code and Other Laws of Cyberspace.* New York: Basic.

Lev, Daniel S. 1993. "Social Movements, Constitutionalism, and Human Rights: Comments from the Malaysian and Indonesian Experiences." In *Constitutionalism and Democracy,* ed. Douglas Greenberg, Stanley N. Katz, Melanie Beth Oliviero, and Steven C. Wheatley. New York: Oxford University Press.

Levy, Leonard W. 1986. *American Constitutional History.* New York: Macmillan.

Lewis, Gregory B., and Jonathan L. Edelson. 2000. "DOMA and ENDA: Congress Votes on Gay Rights." In *The Politics of Gay Rights,* ed. Craig A. Rimmerman, Kenneth D. Wald, and Clyde Wilcox. Chicago: University of Chicago Press.

Lidsky, Lyrissa Barnett. 2000. "Silencing John Doe: Defamation and Discourse in Cyberspace." *Duke Law Journal* 49: 855–946.

Lienesch, Michael. 1989. "North Carolina: Preserving Rights." In *Ratifying the Constitution,* ed. Michael Allen Gillespie and Michael Lienesch. Lawrence: University Press of Kansas.

Linz, Juan. 1978. *The Breakdown of Democratic Regimes.* Baltimore, Md.: Johns Hopkins University Press.

Lipset, Seymour Martin. 1996. *American Exceptionalism: A Double-Edged Sword.* New York: W. W. Norton.

Lomasky, Loren E. 1987. *Persons, Rights, and the Moral Community.* New York: Oxford University Press.

Long, Carolyn N. 2001. "Congress, the Court, and Religious Liberty: The Case of *Employment Division of Oregon v. Smith.*" In *Congress Confronts the Court: The Struggle for Legitimacy and Authority in Lawmaking,* ed. Colton C. Campbell and John F. Stack, Jr. Lanham, Md.: Rowman & Littlefield.

Lowi, Theordore J., and Bemhamin Ginsberg. 2000. *American Government: Freedom and Power,* 6th ed. New York: W. W. Norton.

Machlowitz, David, and Marilyn Machlowitz. 1987. "Preventing Sexual Harassment." *ABA Journal* (October): 78–80.

MacKinnon, Catherine. 1979. *Sexual Harassment of Working Women.* New Haven, Conn.: Yale University Press.

Mair, Peter. 1996. "Comparative Politics: An Overview." In *A New Handbook of Political Science,* ed. Robert E. Goodin and Hans-Dieter Klingemann. New York: Oxford University Press.

Mamdani, Mahmood. 1993. "Social Movements and Constitutionalism: The African Context." In *Constitutionalism and Democracy,* ed. Douglas Greenberg, Stanley N. Katz, Melanie Beth Oliviero, and Steven C. Wheatley. New York: Oxford University Press.

Mandel, Michael. 1989. *The Charter of Rights and the Legalization of Politics in Canada.* Toronto: Wall & Thompson.

Mason, George. 1787 [1989]. "Objections to the Proposed Constitution," reprinted in Melvin I. Urofsky, *Documents of American Constitutional and Legal History.* New York: Alfred A. Knopf.

Maxwell, Kenneth. 1995. *The Making of Portuguese Democracy.* Cambridge: Cambridge University Press.

McDonald, Forrest. 1992. "Tenth Amendment." In *The Oxford Companion to the Supreme Court of the United States,* ed. Kermith L. Hall. New York: Oxford University Press.

Melnick, R. Shep. 1983. *Regulation and the Courts: The Case of the Clean Air Act.* Washington, D.C.: Brookings Institution.

Mény, Yves, and Andrew Knapp. 1998. *Government and Politics in Western Europe.* Oxford: Oxford University Press.

Mezey, Susan Gluck. 1992. *In Pursuit of Equality: Women, Public Policy, and the Federal Courts.* New York: St. Martin's Press.

Miller, Arthur R. 1971. *The Assault on Privacy: Computers, Data Banks and Dossiers.* Ann Arbor: University of Michigan Press.

Miller, Mark C. 1995. *The High Priests of American Politics: The Role of Lawyers in American Political Institutions.* Knoxville: University of Tennessee Press.

Morrison, Toni, ed. 1992. *Race-ing Justice, En-Gendering Power: Essays on Anita Hill, Clarence Thomas and the Construction of Social Reality.* New York: Pantheon.

Murphy, Walter. 1993. "Constitutions, Constitutionalism and Democracy." In *Constitutionalism and Democracy,* ed. David Greenberg, Stanley N. Katz, Melanie Beth Oliviero, and Steven C. Wheatley. New York: Oxford University Press.

National Information Infrastructure Advisory Council. 1995. *Common Ground: Fundamental Principles for the National Information Infrastructure.* Washington, D.C.: National Information Infrastructure Advisory Council.

National Telecommunications and Information Administration. 1998. *Elements of Effective Self-Regulation for the Protection of Privacy and Questions Related to Online Privacy.* http://www.ntia.doc.gov/ntiahome/privacy/6_5_98fedreg.htm.

Nelson, Michael. 1988. "The President and the Court: Reinterpreting the Court-packing Episode of 1937." *Political Science Quarterly* 103: 267–93.

Newton, Michael T. 1997. *Institutions of Modern Spain: A Political and Economic Guide.* Cambridge: Cambridge University Press.

Norton, Eleanor Holmes. 1988. "Equal Employment Law: Crisis in Interpretation—Survival against the Odds." *Tulane Law Review* 62(4): 681–715.

Nourse, Victoria F. 1996. "Where Violence, Relationship, and Equality Meet: The Violence against Women Act's Civil Rights Remedy." *Wisconsin Women's Law Journal* 11: 1–36.

Nowak, John E., and Ronald D. Rotunda. 2000. *Constitutional Law.* Minneapolis/St. Paul, Minn.: West.

Nye, Mary Alice. 1995. "Civil Rights" In *The Encyclopedia of the United States Congress,* ed. Donald C. Bacon, Roger H. Davidson, and Morton Keller. Vol. 1. New York: Simon and Schuster.

O'Brien, David M. 2000a. *Supreme Court Watch 1999.* New York: W. W. Norton.

———. 2000b. *Constitutional Law and Politics.* Vol. 1. *Struggles for Power and Governmental Accountability,* 4th ed. New York: W. W. Norton.

———. 2000c. *Constitutional Law and Politics.* Vol. 2. *Civil Rights and Civil Liberties,* 4th ed. New York: W. W. Norton.

———. 2000d. *Storm Center: The Supreme Court in American Politics,* 5th ed. New York: W. W. Norton.

———. 1996. *To Dream of Dreams: Religious Freedom and Constitutional Politics in Postwar Japan.* Honolulu: University of Hawaii Press.

O'Connor, John. 2000. "Taking TRIPS to the Eleventh Amendment: The Aftermath of the College Savings Case." *Hastings Law Journal* 51(5): 1003–45.

O'Connor, Karen, and Larry J. Sabato. 2000. *American Government: Continuity and Change.* New York: Longman.

O'Harrow, Robert, Jr. 2000. "Firm Tracking Consumers on Web for Drug Companies." *Washington Post,* 15 August 2000, E1, 4.

Oneglia, Stewart, and Susan French Cornelius. 1981. "Sexual Harassment in the Workplace: The Equal Employment Opportunity Commission's New Guidelines." *Saint Louis University Law Journal* 26(1): 39–61.

Opinion Research Corporation and Alan F. Westin. 1999. *"Freebies" and Privacy: What Net Users Think.* Hackensack, N.J.: Privacy and American Business.

Ornstein, Norman J., Robert L. Peabody, and David W. Rohde. 1997. "The U.S. Senate: Toward the 21st Century." In *Congress Reconsidered,* 6th ed., ed. Lawrence C. Dodd and Bruce I. Oppenheimer. Washington, D.C.: CQ Press.

Ota, Alan K. 2000. "Internet Privacy Issue Beginning to Click. *CQ Weekly Report* (March 25): 637–40.

Packard, Vance. 1964. *The Naked Society.* 1964. New York: D. McKay.

Patterson, Samuel C. 1995. "The Congressional Parties in the United States." Presented at the annual meeting of the American Political Science Association, Chicago.

Patterson, Samuel C., and Gregory A. Caldeira. 1987. "Party Voting in the United States Congress." *British Journal of Political Science* 18: 111–31.

Pennock, J. Roland, and John W. Chapman, eds. 1971. *Privacy*, Nomos Series 13, Yearbook of the American Society for Political and Legal Philosophy. New York: Atherton.

Powell, H. Jefferson, and Benjamin J. Priester. 2000. "Convenient Shorthand: The Supreme Court and the Language of State Sovereignty." *Colorado Law Review* 71: 1–29. Accessed on LEXIS-NEXIS, January 24, 2001.

Preuss, Ulrich K. 1993. "Democracy and Constitutionalism." In *Constitutionalism and Politics*, ed. Irena Grudzinska Gross. Bratislava, Slovakia: Slovak Committee of the European Cultural Foundation.

Prosser, William L. 1960. "Privacy." *California Law Review* 48(3): 383–423.

Putnam, Robert D. 2000. *Bowling Alone: The Collapse and Revival of American Community.* New York: Simon and Schuster.

Rae, Nicol C. 1998. *Conservative Reformers: The Republican Freshmen and the Lessons of the 104th Congress.* Armonk, N.Y.: M. E. Sharpe.

Rae, Nicol C., and Colton C. Campbell. 2001. "Party Politics and Ideology in the Contemporary Senate." In *The Contentious Senate: Partisanship, Ideology, and the Myth of Cool Judgment*, ed. Colton C. Campbell and Nicol C. Rae. Lanham, Md.: Rowman & Littlefield.

Regan, Priscilla M. 1995. *Legislating Privacy: Technology, Social Values, and Public Policy.* Chapel Hill: University of North Carolina Press.

Restatement [Second] of Torts. 1976. Philadelphia, Pa.: American Law Institute.

Rose, David. 1989. "Twenty-Five Years Later: Where Do We Stand on Equal Employment Opportunity Law Enforcement?" *Vanderbilt Law Review* 42(4): 1121–82.

Rouquié, Alain. 1991. "Demilitarization and the Institutionalization of Military-dominated Polities in Latin America." In *Transitions from Authoritarian Rule: Comparative Perspectives*, ed. Guillermo O'Donnell, Philippe C. Schmitter, and Laurence Whitehead. Baltimore, Md.: Johns Hopkins University Press.

Safran, William. 1995. *The French Polity.* White Plains, N.Y.: Longman.

Sajó, András, and Vera Losonci. 1993. "Rule by Law in East Central Europe." In *Constitutionalism and Democracy*, ed. Douglas Greenberg, Stanley N. Katz, Melanie Beth Oliviero, and Steven C. Wheatley. New York: Oxford University Press.

Salokar, Rebecca Mae. 1997. "Beyond Gay Rights Litigation: Using a Systematic Strategy to Effect Political Change in the United States." *GLQ: A Journal of Lesbian and Gay Studies* 3: 385–415.

———. 1993. "Legal Counsel for Congress: Protecting Institutional Interests." *Congress & the Presidency* 20: 131–55.

———. 1992. *The Solicitor General: The Politics of Law.* Philadelphia: Temple University Press.

Scalia, Antonin. 1997. *A Matter of Interpretation: Federal Courts and the Law.* Princeton: Princeton University Press.

Scheiber, Harry N., ed. 1992. *Federalism and the Judicial Mind: Essays on American Constitutional Law and Politics.* Berkeley, Calif.: Institute of Governmental Studies Press.

Schwartz, Bernard, ed. 1970. *Statutory History of the United States: Civil Rights.* Vol. 2. New York: Chelsea House.

Schwartz, John. 2001. "First Line of Defense: Chief Privacy Officers Forge Evolving Corporate Roles." *New York Times,* 12 February 2001, C1, 7.

Schwartz, Paul M. 2000. "Internet Privacy and the State." *Connecticut Law Review* 32(3): 815–59.

Sellers, Patrick J. 2000. "Promoting the Party Message in the U.S. Senate." Paper presented at the annual meeting of the Midwest Political Science Association, Chicago, April 15–17.

Senkbeil, Mary L. 2000. "Constitutional Law, Constitutional Trends: The New Majority Limits Congress' Power to Abrogate State Sovereign Immunity." *William Mitchell Law Review* 26: 1–34. Accessed on LEXIS-NEXIS, January 24, 2001.

Shamir, Ronen. 1995. *Managing Legal Uncertainty: Elite Lawyers in the New Deal.* Durham, N.C.: Duke University Press.

Sherry, Suzanna. 2000. "States are People Too." *Notre Dame Law Review* 75(3): 1121–31.

Sinclair, Barbara. 1995. *Legislators, Leaders, and Lawmaking: The US House of Representatives in the Post-Reform Era.* Baltimore, Md.: Johns Hopkins University Press.

Siskin, Alison. 2001. *Violence against Women Act: Reauthorization, Federal Funding and Recent Developments.* January 25. CRS Report No. RS20195. Congressional Research Service. Washington, D.C.

Smith, Richard M. 2000. *Web Bug FAQ and Find.* http://tiac.net/users/smiths/privacy/wbfind.htm.

Smith, Steven S. 1993. "Forces of Change in Senate Party Leadership and Organization." In *Congress Reconsidered,* 5th ed., ed. Lawrence C. Dodd and Bruce I Oppenheimer. Washington, D.C.: CQ Press.

Sorensen, Georg. 1993. *Democracy and Democratization.* Boulder, Colo.: Westview.

Stack, John F., Jr., and Colton C. Campbell. 2001. "The Least Dangerous Branch? The Supreme Court's New Judicial Activism." In *Congress Confronts the Court: The Struggle for Legitimacy and Authority in Lawmaking,* ed. Colton C. Campbell and John F. Stack, Jr. Lanham, Md.: Rowman & Littlefield.

Stone, Alec. 1992. *The Birth of Judicial Politics in France.* New York: Oxford University Press.

Sullivan, Andrew. 1995. *Virtually Normal: An Argument about Homosexuality.* New York: Knopf.

Thomas, Clarence. 1985. "The Equal Employment Opportunity Commission: Reflections on a New Philosophy." *Stetson Law Review* 15(1): 29–36.

Thurber, James A.. 1995. "Remaking Congress after the Electoral Earthquake of 1994." In *Remaking Congress: Change and Stability in the 1990s,* ed. James A. Thurber and Roger H. Davidson. Washington, D.C.: CQ Press.

———. 1991. "Dynamics of Policy Subsystems in American Politics." In *Interest Group Politics,* 3rd ed., ed. Allan J. Cigler and Burdett A. Loomis. Washington, D.C.: CQ Press.

Tiefer, Charles. 1998. "The Senate and House Counsel Offices: Dilemmas of Representing in Court the Institutional Congressional Client." *Law and Contemporary Problems* 61: 47–63.

U.S. Congress. House. 1966. Committee on Government Operations. Special Subcommittee on Invasion of Privacy. *The Computer and Invasion of Privacy: Hearings,* 89th Cong., 2d sess., 26–28 July.

U.S. Congress. Senate. 2000. Committee on Rules and Administration. Political Speech on the Internet. 106th Cong., 2d sess., 3 May.

———. Senate. 1976. *Representation of Congress and Congressional Interests in Court.* Subcommittee on Separation of Powers. Committee of the Judiciary." 94th Cong., 2d sess., 12 December 1975 and 19 February 1976.

———. Committee on Government Operations, Ad Hoc Subcommittee on Privacy and Information Systems, and Committee on the Judiciary, Subcommittee on Constitutional Rights. 1974. *Privacy: The Collection Use and Computerization of Personal Data.* Hearings, 93d Cong., 2d sess., 18, 19, 20 June.

U.S. Department of Health Education and Welfare. 1973. *Records, Computers and the Rights of Citizens.* Secretary's Advisory Committee on Automated Personal Data Systems. Washington, D.C.: Government Printing Office.

Uslaner, Eric. 1993. *The Decline of Comity in Congress.* Ann Arbor: University of Michigan Press.

Vaas, Francis J. 1966. "Title VII: Legislative History." *Boston College Industrial and Commercial Law Review* 7(3): 431–58.

Van Doren, Carl. 1948. *The Great Rehearsal: The Story of the Making and Ratifying of the Constitution of the United States.* New York: Viking.

Vento, Bruce. 1999. *Vento to Discuss Privacy in Washington Post on-Line Chat.* (accessed Nov. 9, 1999). http://www.house.gov/vento/postchat.html.

Volcansek, Mary L. 2001. "Separation of Powers and Judicial Impeachment." In *Congress Confronts the Court: The Struggle for Legitimacy and Authority in Lawmaking,* ed. Colton C. Campbell and John F. Stack, Jr. Lanham, Md.: Rowman & Littlefield.

———. 2000. *Constitutional Politics in Italy: The Constitutional Court.* Houndsmills, Basingstoke, Hampshire: Macmillan; New York: St. Martin's.

———. 1993. *Judicial Impeachment: None Called for Justice.* Urbana: University of Illinois Press.

Volokh, Eugene. 2000. "Freedom of Speech and Information Privacy: The Troubling Implications of a Right to Stop People from Speaking about You." *Stanford Law Review* 52: 1049–122.

Warren, Samuel, and Louis Brandeis. 1890. "The Right to Privacy." *Harvard Law Review* 4: 193–220.

Weisman, Jonathan. 1996. "Close Senate Vote on Jobs Bill Buoys Gay Rights Supporters." *Congressional Quarterly Weekly* Report, 14 September 1996, 2597–99.

Wellman, Carl. 1985. *A Theory of Rights: Persons under Laws, Institutions, and Morals.* Totowa, N.J.: Rowman & Allanheld.

Westin, Alan F. 1967. *Privacy and Freedom.* New York: Atheneum.

Whalen, Charles, and Barbara Whalen. 1985. *The Longest Debate: A Legislative History of the 1964 Civil Rights Act.* New York: Mentor.

Wheeler, Stanton. 1969. *On Record: Files and Dossiers in American Life.* New York: Russell Sage Foundation.

White, Alan R. 1984. *Rights.* Oxford: Clarendon.

Wilcox, Clyde, and Robin Wolpert. 2000. "Gay Rights in the Public Sphere: Public Opinion on Gay and Lesbian Equality." In *The Politics of Gay Rights,* ed. Craig A. Rimmerman, Kenneth D. Wald, Clyde Wilcox. Chicago: University of Chicago Press.

Yoo, John C. 1998. "Lawyers in Congress." *Law and Contemporary Problems* 61: 1–19.

JUDICIAL CASES

ACLU v. Miller. 1997. 977 F. Supp 1228 (N.D. Ga.).

Adams v. Clinton. 2000. 90 F. Supp. 2d 27 (D.D.C.).

Adams v. Richardson. 1994. 871 F. Supp. 43 (D.D.C.).

A.L.A. Schechter Poultry Corp. v. United States. 1935. 295 U.S. 495.

Albanese v. Federal Elections Commission. 1996. 78 F.3d 66 (2nd Cir.).

Albemarle Paper Company v. Moody. 1975. 422 U.S. 405.

Alden v. Maine. 1999. 119 S.Ct. 2240.

Anderson v. Dunn. 1821. 6 Wheat. (19 U.S.) 204.

Association of Community Organizations for Reform Now v. Miller. 1997. 129 F.3d 833 (6th Cir.).

Atascadero State Hospital v. Scanlon. 1985. 473 U.S. 926.

Atkins v. United States. 1977. 556 F.2d 1028 (Ct. of Claims).

Baehr v. Lewin. 1993. (No. 91-1394, Hawaii).

Banks v. United States. 1997. WL 1048133 (No. 96-C-1248, E.D. Wis.).

Barkley v. O'Neill. 1985. 624 F. Supp. 664 (S.D. Ind.).

Barnes v. Costle. 1977. 561 F.2d 983 (D.C. Cir.).

Barnes v. Train. 1974. 13 Fair Empl. Prac. Cas. 123 (D.D.C.).

Barry v. U.S. ex. rel. Cunningham. 1929. 279 U.S. 597.

Beverly Enterprises v. Trump. 1999. 182 F.3d 183 (3d Cir.).

Board of Trustees of the University of Alabama v. Garrett. 2001. 69 U.S.L.W. 4105.

Boehner v. Anderson. 1994. 30F.3d. 156 (D.C. Cir.).

Bowsher v. Synar. 1986. 478 U.S. 714.

Browning v. Clerk, U.S. House of Representatives. 1986. 789 F.2d 923 (D.C. Cir.).

Brzonkala v. Virginia Polytechnic Institute. 1997. 132 F. 3d 950 (3d Cir.).

Brzonkala v. Virginia Polytechnic Institute and State University. 1999. 169 F. 3d 820 (4th Cir.).

Bundy v. Jackson. 1981. 641 F.2d 934 (D.C. Cir.).

Bundy v. Jackson. 1979. 19 Fair Empl. Prac. Cas. 828 (D.D.C.).

Burlington Industries, Inc. v. Ellerth. 1998. 524 U.S. 742.

Bush v. Gore. 2000. 531 U.S. Slip Opinion.

Byrd v. Raines. 1997. 956 F. Supp. 25 (D.D.C.).

Cariddi v. Kansas City Chiefs Football Club. 1977. 568 F.2d 87 (8th Cir.).

Carter v. Carter Coal Co. 1936. 298 U.S. 238.

Chadha v. Immigration and Naturalization Service. 1980. 634 F.2d 408 (9th Cir.).

Champion v. Ames. 1903. 188 U.S. 321.

Chisholm v. Georgia. 1793. 2 Dall. 419.

City of Boerne v. Flores. 1997. 521 U.S. 507.

City of New York v. Clinton. 1998. 985 F.Supp. 168 (D.D.C.).

Civil Rights Cases. 1883. 109 U.S. 3.

Clinton v. City of New York. 1998. 118 S.Ct. 2091.

College Savings Bank v. Florida Prepaid Postsecondary Education Expense Board. 1999. 527 U.S. 666.

Compston v. Borden, Inc. 1976. 424 F. Supp. 157 (S.D. Ohio).

Corne v. Bausch and Lomb. 1975. 390 F. Supp. 161 (D. Ariz.).

Coxe v. McClenachan. 1798. 3 U.S. 478 (Sup. Ct. Pa.).

Dellmuth v. Muth. 1989. 491 U.S. 223.

Dickey v. CBS, Inc. 1975. 387 F. Supp. 1332 (E.D. Pa.).

Doe v. McMillan. 1973. 412 U.S. 306.

Dorman v. Sanchez. 1997. 978 F. Supp. 1315 (C.D. Ca.)

Dothard v. Rawlinson. 1977. 433 U.S. 321.

Dred Scott v. John F. A. Sanford. 1856. 60 U.S. 393.

Faragher v. City of Boca Raton. 1998. 524 U.S. 775.

Firefighters Institute for Racial Equality v. St. Louis. 1977. 549 F.2d 506 (8th Cir.).

Florida Prepaid Postsecondary Education Expense Board v. College Savings Bank. 1999. 119 S.Ct. 2199.

Franklin v. Gwinnett County Public Schools. 1992. 503 U.S. 60.

Fry v. United States. 1975. 421 U.S. 542.

Garcia v. San Antonio Metropolitan Transportation Authority. 1985. 469 U.S. 528.

Gebser v. Lago Vista Independent School District. 1998. 524 U.S. 274.

Gravel v. United States. 1972. 408 U.S. 606.

Gray v. Greyhound Lines, East. 1976. 545 F.2d 169 (D.C. Cir.).

Green v. Mansour. 1985. 474 U.S. 64.

Gregory v. Ashcroft. 1991. 501 U.S. 452.

Griggs v. Duke Power Company. 1971. 401 U.S. 424.

Hammer v. Dagenhart. 1918. 247 U.S. 251.

Harris v. Forklift Systems, Inc. 1993. 510 U.S. 17.

Hastings v. United States. 1992. 802 F. Supp. 490 (D.D.C.).

Hastings v. U.S. Senate. 1989. 716 F. Supp. 38 (D.D.C.).

Heart of Atlanta Motel, Inc. v. United States. 1964. 379 U.S. 241.

Hensen v. City of Dundee. 1982. 682 F.2d 897 (11th Cir.).

Hopwood v. Texas. 1996. 78 F.3d 932.

Humphrey v. Baker. 1988. 848 F.2d 211 (D.C. Cir.).

Hutchinson v. Proxmire. 1979. 443 U.S. 111.

Immigration and Naturalization Service v. Chadha. 1983. 462 U.S. 919.

In re Grand Jury Investigation of Ven-Fuel. 1977. 441 F. Supp. 1299 (M.D. Fla.).

In re Grand Jury Proceedings of Grand Jury No. 81-1. 1987. 669 F. Supp. 1072 (S.D. Fla.).

Interstate Commerce Commission v. Cincinnati, New Orleans, and Texas Pacific Railway Co. 1897. 167 U.S. 479.

Jacobson v. Massachusetts. 1905. 197 U.S. 11.

Katzenbach v. McClung. 1964. 379 U.S. 294.

Kennedy v. Sampson. 1974. 511 F.2d 430 (D.C.Cir.).

Kimel v. Florida Board of Regents. 2000. 120 S.Ct. 631.

Lochner v. New York. 1905. 198 U.S. 45.

Magee v. Hatch. 1998. 26 F. Supp. 2d 153 (D.D.C.).

Marbury v. Madison. 1803. 5 U.S. 137.

McClellan v. McSurely. 1976. 553 F.2d 1277 (D.C. Cir.).

McCray v. United States. 1904. 195 U.S. 27.

McCulloch v. Maryland. 1819, 4 Wheat. (17 U.S.) 316.

McDonnell Douglas v. Green. 1973. 411 U.S. 792.

McGrain v. Daugherty. 1927. 273 U.S. 135.

McIntyre v. Fallahay. 1985. 766 F.2d 1078 (7th Cir.).

McIntyre v. O'Neill. 1985. 603 F. Supp. 1053 (D.D.C.).

Meritor Savings Bank, FBD v. Vinson. 1986. 477 U.S. 57.

Michel v. Anderson. 1993. 14 F.3d 623 (D.C. Cir.).

Miller v. Bank of America. 1979. 600 F.2d 211 (9th Cir.).

Miller v. Bank of America. 1976. 418 F. Supp. 233 (N.D. Cal.).

Muller v. Oregon. 1908. 208 U.S. 412.

Myers v. United States. 1926. 272 U.S. 52.

National Labor Relations Board v. Jones and Laughlin Steel Corp. 1937. 301 U.S. 1.

National League of Cities v. Usery. 1976. 426 U.S. 833.

New York v. United States. 1992. 505 U.S. 144.

Nix v. Hoke. 1999. 62 F. Supp. 2d 110 (D.D.C.).

Nixon v. United States. 1993. 506 U.S. 224.

Office of the Sergeant at Arms v. Office of Senate Fair Employment Practices. 1996. 95 F.3d 1102 (Fed.Cir.).

Oncale v. Sundowner Offshore Services. 1998. 523 U.S. 75.

Page v. Shelby. 1998. 995 F. Supp. 23 (D.D.C.).

Parden v. Terminal R. Co. of Alabama Docks Dept. Pentagen Technologies International, Ltd. v. Committee on Appropriations of the U.S. House of Representatives. 1998. 20 F. Supp. 2d 41 (D.D.C.).

Parden v. Terminal Railway of the Alabama Docks Department. 1964. 377 U.S. 1010.

Pennsylvania v. Union Gas Co. 1989. 491 U.S. 1.

Pentagen Technologies International. Ltd. v. Committee on Appropriations of the United States House of Representatives. 1998. 20 F. Supp. 41 (D.D.C.).

Pittsburgh Press v. Pittsburgh Commission on Human Rights. 1973. 413 U.S. 376.

Popovic v. United States. 1998. 997 F. Supp. 672 (D.Md.).

Powell v. McCormack. 1969. 395 U.S. 486.

Pressler v. Simon. 1976. 428 F. Supp. 302 (D.D.C.).

Printz v. United States. 1997. 521 U.S. 898.

Printz v. United States and *Mack v. United States.* 1997. 117 S.C. 2365.

Raines v. Byrd. 1997. 521 U.S. 811.

Reno v. Condon. 2000. 528 U.S. 141. [Slip opinion No. 98-1464.].

Rogers v. EEOC. 1971. 454 F.2d 234 (5th Cir.).

Rosenberger v. Virginia. 1995. 515 U.S. 819.

Schaffer v. Clinton. 2001. 240 F.3d 878 (10th Cir.).

Schmelzer v. Office of Compliance. 1998. 155 F.3d 1364 (Fed. Cir.).

Schreibman v. Holmes. 1999. No. 98-5136; 1999 U.S. App. LEXIS 25159 (D.C. Cir.).

Seminole Tribe of Florida v. Florida. 1996. 517 U.S. 44.

Senate Select Committee v. Nixon. 1974. 498 F.2d 725 (D.C. Cir.).

Singer v. Office of the Senate Sergeant at Arms. 1999. 173 F.3d 837 (Fed. Cir.).

Skaggs v. Carle. 1997. 110 F.3d 831 (D.C.Cir.).

Skaggs v. Carle. 1995. 898 F. Supp. 1 (D.D.C.).

Slangal v. Cassel. 1997. 962 F. Supp. 1214 (D. Neb.).

Stone v. Mississippi. 1880. 101 U.S. 814.

Texas Department of Community Affairs v. Burdine. 1981. 450 U.S. 248.

Tomkins v. Public Service Electric and Gas. 1977. 568 F.2d 1044 (3d Cir.).

Tomkins v. Public Service Electric and Gas. 1976. 422 F.Supp. 553 (D. N.J.).

United States v. Brewster. 1972. 408 U.S. 501.

United States v. Butler. 1936. 297 U.S. 1.

United States v. Cooper. 1800. 4 U.S. 341.

United States v. Darby. 1941. 312 U.S. 100.

United States v. E. C. Knight Co. 1895. 153 U.S. 1.

United States v. Eichman. 1990. 496 U.S. 310.

United States v. Helstoski. 1979. 442 U.S. 477.

United States v. Johnson. 1966. 383 U.S. 169.

United States v. Lopez. 1995. 115 S.Ct. 1624.

United States v. Lopez. 1995. 514 U.S. 549.

United States v. McDade. 1995. 514 U.S. 1003 (cert. denied); 28 F.3d 283 (1994, 3d Cir.).

United States v. Morrison. 2000. 529 U.S. 598.

United States v. Oakar. 1996. 924 F. Supp. 232 (D.D.C.).

United States v. Peoples Temple of the Disciples of Christ. 1981. 515 F. Supp. 246 (D.D.C.).

United States v. Rostenkowski. 1995. 59 F.3d 1291 (D.C.Cir.).

United States Department of Commerce v. United States House of Representatives. 1999. 525 U.S. 316.

United States ex rel. Hollander v. Clay. 1976. 420 F.Supp. 853 (D.D.C.).

United States ex rel. Stillwell v. Hughes Helicopter, Inc. 1989. 714 F. Supp. 1084 (C.D. Ca.).

U.S. Term Limits, Inc. v. Thornton. 1995. 514 U.S. 779.

Vander Jagt v. O'Neill. 1982. 699 F.2d 1166 (D.C.Cir.).

Vinson v. Taylor. 1985. 753 F.2d 141 (D.C. Cir.).

Vinson v. Taylor. 1980. 23 Fair Empl. Prac. Cas. 37 (D.D.C.).

West Coast Hotel v. Parrish. 1937. 300 U.S. 379.

Whalen v. Roe. 1977. 429 U.S. 589.

Wickard v. Filburn. 1942. 317 U.S. 111.

Williams v. Bell. 1978. 587 F.2d 1240 (D.C. Cir.).

Williams v. Civiletti. 1980. 487 F.Supp. 1387 (D.D.C.).

Williams v. Saxbe. 1976. 413 F. Supp. 654 (D.D.C.).

Williamson v. United States. 1908. 207 U.S. 425.

Wisconsin v. Mitchell. 1990. 508 U.S. 476.

X-Men Security, Inc. v. Pataki. 1999. 196 F.3d 56 (2d Cir.).

X-Men Security, Inc. v. Pataki. 1997a. 983 F. Supp. 101 (E.D. N.Y.).

X-Men Security, Inc. v. Pataki. 1997b. 983 F. Supp. 101 (E.D. N.Y.).

LEGISLATION, STATUTES, AND OTHER GOVERNMENT WORKS

2 *U.S.C.* § 118. 2000. "Actions against Officers for Official Acts."

2 *U.S.C.* §130. 2000. "Officers and Employees of the Senate and House of Representatives."

2 *U.S.C.* §288. 2000. "Office of the Senate Legal Counsel."

2 *U.S.C.* §381. 1000. "Federal Contested Elections Act."

18 *U.S.C.* §6005. 2000. "Immunity of Witnesses, Congressional Proceedings."

Federal Rules of Civil Procedure.

H. R. Res. 49., 97th Cong., 1st Sess. (1981).

S. Res. 40., 97th Cong., 1st Sess. (1981).

U.S. Congress. 1993. 139 *Congressional Record* H 5. "Rules of the House."

U.S. Congress. 1978. *Ethics in Government Act* (originally proposed as Public Officials Integrity Act of 1977). Public Law 95-521, Title VII-Senate Legal Counsel, 92 *Stat.* §1875, October 26, 1978; 2 *U.S.C.* §288 (Office of Senate Legal Counsel).

U.S. Congress. 1977. *1998 Appropriations Act*. Public Law 105-119. (Authorizing the House to sue: § 209(6) 111 Stat., at 2481.)

U.S. Congress. House. 1993. H.Res.5. "A Resolution Adopting the Rules of the House for the One Hundred Second Congress."

U.S. Senate. 2000. "Standing Rules of the Senate."

U.S. Senate. 1977. "Report of the Committee on Governmental Affairs to Accompany S. 555, Public Officials Integrity Act of 1977." 95th Cong., 1st Sess. Report No. 95-170.

Index

183

About the Contributors

Colton C. Campbell is assistant professor of political science at Florida International University. He is the author of *Discharging Congress: Government by Commission.* He is also coeditor of three other Rowman & Littlefield titles: *New Majority or Old Minority? The Impact of Republicans on Congress, The Contentious Senate: Partisanship, Ideology and the Myth of Cool Judgment,* and *Congress Confronts the Court: The Struggle for Legitimacy and Authority in Lawmaking.* He served as an APSA congressional fellow in the office of U.S. Senator Bob Graham (D-Fla.).

Gregg Ivers is associate professor of government at American University. He is the author of the constitutional law casebook *American Constitutional Law: Constitutional Structure and Political Power* (Vol. 1) and *Civil Rights and Liberties* (Vol. 2) as well as *To Build a Wall: American Jews and the Separation of Church and State.* Ivers has published articles in *Polity, Law and Policy,* the *Journal of Church and State,* and *Publius,* as well as several chapters in edited books on American politics, constitutional law, and religion and politics.

David Kaib is a doctoral candidate in the Department of Government in the School of Public Affairs at American University.

David M. O'Brien holds the Leone Reaves and George W. Spicer chair at the University of Virginia. Among his publications are *Storm Center: The Supreme*

Court in American Politics, 5th ed., *Constitutional Law and Politics,* 2 Vols., 4th ed., and an annual *Supreme Court Watch.*

Nicol C. Rae is professor of political science at Florida International University. He is the author of *The Decline & Fall of the Liberal Republicans: From 1952 to the Present, Southern Democrats, Conservative Reformers: The Freshman Class of the 104th Congress,* and is coauthor of *Governing America.* He also is coeditor of two other Rowman & Littlefield titles: *New Majority or Old Minority? The Impact of Republicans on Congress,* and *The Contentious Senate: Partisanship, Ideology and the Myth of Cool Judgment.* He served as an APSA congressional fellow in the offices of U.S. Senator Thad Cochran (R-Miss.) and U.S. Representative George P. Radanovich (R-Calif.).

Priscilla M. Regan is associate professor of government and politics at George Mason University. She is the author of *Legislating Privacy: Technology, Social Values, and Public Policy.* She also has published over a dozen articles in academic journals on the formulation and implementation of public policies protecting individual privacy. She is on the advisory board of Privacy and American Business and the editorial board of the *Journal of Media Law and Practice.*

Rebecca Mae Salokar is associate professor of political science at Florida International University. She is the author of *The Solicitor General: The Politics of Law* and coeditor of *Women in Law: A Bio-Bibliographical Sourcebook.* She also has published articles and chapters on the General Counsel of the House of Representatives and Senate Legal Counsel, the Florida constitutional right to privacy, the Catholic Church's political activity with respect to abortion laws and litigation in Florida, the impact of Hurricane Andrew on South Florida courts, and gay and lesbian politics.

John F. Stack, Jr. is professor of political science at Florida International University and director of the Jack D. Gordon Institute for Public Policy and Citizenship. He is the author of *International Conflict in an International City: Boston's Irish, Italians, and Jews 1935–1944* and editor of *Ethnic Identities in a Transnational World, Policy Choices: Critical Issues in American Foreign Policy, The Primordial Challenge: Ethnicity in the Modern World.* He coedited *The Ethnic Entanglement, Congress Confronts the Court: The Struggle for Legitimacy and Authority in Lawmaking,* and *Congress and the Politics of Foreign Policy.*

Mary L. Volcansek is dean of the AddRan College of Humanities and Social Sciences at Texas Christian University. She is the author of *Constitutional Politics in Italy: The Constitutional Court, Judicial Misconduct: A Cross-National*

Comparison, Judicial Selection, Judicial Impeachment: None Called for Justice, and *Judicial Politics in Europe: An Impact Analysis.* She is also coeditor of *Law above Nations: Supranational Courts and the Legalization of Politics, Judicial Politics and Policy-Making in Western Europe,* and *Women in Law: A Bio-Bibliographical Sourcebook.*